# A
# POCKETFUL
# OF
# HISTORY

# A
# POCKETFUL
# OF
# HISTORY

★

*Four Hundred Years
of America—
One State Quarter
at a Time*

## JIM NOLES

DA CAPO PRESS
A MEMBER OF THE PERSEUS BOOKS GROUP

Quarter-dollar coin images from the United States Mint.

Designed by Linda Harper
Set in 11 point Caslon 540 by The Perseus Books Group

Library of Congress Cataloging-in-Publication Data
Noles, James L.
A pocketful of history : four hundred years of America—one state quarter at a time /
Jim Noles. — 1st ed.
   p. cm.
  Includes bibliographical references and index.
  ISBN 978-0-306-81578-2 (hardcover : alk. paper) 1. Quarter-dollar. 2. Coins,
  American. 3. Commemorative coins—United States. 4. Emblems, State—United
  States—Miscellanea. 5. U.S. states—History—Miscellanea. 6. United States—
  History—Miscellanea. 7. National characteristics, American—Miscellanea. I. Title.
CJ1840.S73N65 2008
737.4973—dc22

2007049433

Published by Da Capo Press
A Member of the Perseus Books Group
www.dacapopress.com

Da Capo Press books are available at special discounts for bulk purchases in the
U.S. by corporations, institutions, and other organizations. For more information,
please contact the Special Markets Department at the Perseus Books Group, 2300
Chestnut Street, Suite 200, Philadelphia, PA 19103, or call (800) 255-1514, or
e-mail special.markets@perseusbooks.com.

10 9 8 7 6 5 4 3 2 1

*For James and John*

# CONTENTS

FOREWORD *by Congressman Mike Castle*                          *xi*

PREFACE: A QUARTER FOR MY THOUGHTS . . .                       *xv*

THE PROGRAM                                                    *xix*


 1  Delaware: *Hail Caesar!*                                 1

 2  Pennsylvania: *The Key to the Keystone*                   7

 3  New Jersey: *The First Commute*                          13

 4  Georgia: *Peachy Keen*                                   19

 5  Connecticut: *An Oak Grows in Hartford*                  25

 6  Massachusetts: *Just a Minute*                           31

 7  Maryland: *The Oldest Line in the Book*                  37

 8  South Carolina: *Palmetto Proud*                         43

 9  New Hampshire: *Rock . . . and Roll*                     49

10  Virginia: *The Other Three Ships*                           55

11  New York: *"A Mighty Woman with a Torch"*            61

12  North Carolina: *"Damned if they ain't flew!"*        67

13  Rhode Island: *Relying on* Reliance                   73

14  Vermont: *Freedom, Unity, and Maple Syrup*            79

15  Kentucky: *A Quarter Horse? Hardly*                   85

16  Tennessee: *"Here's a Quarter . . . "*                91

17  Ohio: *The Illegal Astronaut*                         97

18  Louisiana: *The Pelican Brief*                       103

19  Indiana: *Gentlemen, Start Your Engines*             109

20  Mississippi: *Steel Magnolias*                       115

21  Illinois: *Lincoln's Hat Trick*                      121

22  Alabama: *The Other Helen Keller*                    127

23  Maine: *The Maine Attractions*                       133

24  Missouri: *Show Me (the Money)*                       139

25  Arkansas: *Diamonds Are a State's Best Friend*       145

26  Michigan: *Great Lakes, Great Drama, . . . and
     a So-So Quarter*                                     151

27  Florida: *The Costliest Quarter*                     157

28  Texas: *Texas Ties One On*                           163

29  Iowa: *An Education in Art*                           169

30  Wisconsin: *Got Milk? Got Cheese? Got Corn?*         175

31  California: *California Dreaming*                     181

32  Minnesota: *10,000 Lakes, 488 Million Quarters*      187

33  Oregon: *Hillman's Richest Find*                     193

34  Kansas: *Buffalo Soldier in the Heart of America*    199

35  West Virginia: *A Bridge Too Far*                    205

36  Nevada: *Horse Sense*                                211

37  Nebraska: *A Rock by Any Other Name . . .*           217

38  Colorado: *Secret(s) of the Mountains*              223

39  North Dakota: *Where the Buffalo (Still) Roam*       229

40  South Dakota: *"What Matter of Men They Were"*       235

41  Montana: *Where the Buffalo Roam (Again)*            241

42  Washington: *Profiles in Courage*                    247

43  Idaho: *"And Here We Have Idaho . . . "*                    253
44  Wyoming: *All Things Being Equal . . .*                      259
45  Utah: *Utah Makes a Good Point*                              265
46  Oklahoma: *Two for the Price of One*                         271
47  New Mexico: *The Circle of Life*                             277
48  Arizona: *The Grand Design*                                  283
49  Alaska: *Call of the Wild*                                   289
50  Hawaii: *All the King's Men*                                 295

*Acknowledgments*                                                301
*Selected Bibliography and Recommended Reading*                  303
*Index*                                                          317

# FOREWORD
## by Congressman Mike Castle

When traveling around my home state of Delaware to visit schools and civic groups, I often ask to see who collects the state quarters by a show of hands. Without fail, most of the people in the room raise their hand. What is it about this program that appeals to so many?

I have found that there is not just one answer to this question, which I believe speaks to the success of these coins. The government supports the program because it has raised more than six times the amount of revenue than was originally expected. Teachers adore this program because it supplies them with a new educational tool to engage their students in history. Children find excitement in the coins for their novelty and images. Authors like Jim Noles find such inspiration among the fifty varying designs that they put pen to paper and write a book such as this one. And readers like you are curious enough about the coins to pick up Jim's book and read it—at least so far.

None of us, however, could have foreseen such popularity or inspiration. In fact, the 50 State Quarters® Program has become a much greater success than I could have ever imagined. I must admit that when I was first approached with the idea of starting a program like this, I was skeptical. I saw the coins as nothing more than Monopoly money. Nevertheless, over time I was convinced of the positive effects of coin collection and the revenue that the program would bring to the government. But even when I eventually offered my support to the 50 State Quarters® Program, we still had difficulty convincing Secretary of the Treasury Robert Rubin and others of the program's value. Eventually, however, we all broke through the uncertainty and gave the coin program a try.

It was not until the unveiling of the Delaware quarter in Wilmington that I began to see and realize the type of excitement this program would generate. Almost instantaneously, there was an undeniably positive buzz surrounding these coins. I was impressed that the 50 State Quarters® Program was immediately embraced by teachers. By and large, teachers have found that children love the coins because the images make learning about the states fun. In turn, children began to collect the coins and companies began to print books that children could use to display their coins.

The success of the program really hit home when a group of students from Delaware visited my Washington, D.C., office about a year ago. One young lady noticed my coin collection that is displayed in my front office. She started to ask me questions about the coins and was especially curious why the Delaware coin displayed the image of a man on horseback. I briefly explained to her the story of Caesar Rodney's famous ride to Philadelphia and his significance with the formation of our country. Children often consider it a chore to learn about history, but in this instance, the girl was enthralled in the story. She and the other students continued to ask me questions about the other state's coins, and I began to see firsthand why these coins are so helpful to teachers. It was easy to see the excitement. All of the fears I had about the program drifted away as I realized that these coins would forever help to encourage the education of American children about the rich heritage each state holds.

For that very same reason, I was delighted to learn that Jim was pursuing a book of this nature. When I first spoke with him in the summer of 2007, I realized that he had also recognized that same fundamental value of the 50 State Quarters® Program—specifically, the program's ability to educate, excite, and, ultimately, inspire us all about the awesome width and breadth of our fifty states' history and culture.

And now that I've had a chance to read *A Pocketful of History*, I am even more pleased to see that Jim has succeeded. On the pages that follow, he takes the imagery and symbolism jangling in your pocket or purse today and, using words as his currency, parlays that spare change into a greater understanding of our nation, illustrates where it has been, and perhaps even reminds us of where it should be heading. It is intellectual venture capitalism at its finest, and I am sure you will enjoy this book as much as I did.

# PREFACE:
# A QUARTER FOR MY THOUGHTS . . .

I have a confession to make.

This is not the book that I set out to write.

When the United States Mint first announced its 50 State Quarters® Program ten years ago, I had a vision of fifty quarters spanning the scale and sweep of America's history. In my mind's eye—clouded, perhaps, with a bias for things historical—I could imagine a series of fifty quarters that, if lined up, would almost offer a national numismatic time line.

Surely, I thought, one could count on the fifty states—even if individually focusing on their own history and experience—to offer up designs that would, collectively, commemorate the great themes and epochs of American history. And what would we get?

A set of coins that, twenty-five cents at a time, would speak of discovery, exploration, colonization, revolution, evolution, immigration, emancipation, and migration. Of civil war, civil reconciliation, and civil rights. Of the fear of God and the rule of law. Of a great war, a Great Depression, and a great crusade. Of the breadbasket of the world, and the arsenal of democracy. Of an Industrial Age, a Gilded Age, a Jazz Age, a Space Age, and an Information Age.

Such were the historical themes that I hoped might emerge. And once cobbled together, those fifty quarters would paint a decipherable mosaic of American history, offering compelling opportunities to segue into some of the great individuals, episodes, and events in American culture and history.

It was wistful—and, in reality, hopelessly misplaced—thinking.

As I write these lines in the summer of 2007, only the first forty-four quarters have actually been issued. The quarters commemorating the final six states to enter the Union—ranging from Utah (January 4, 1896) to Hawaii (August 21, 1959)—have yet to be minted. But we now know, thanks to increasingly publicized design conceptualization and selection processes, what imagery will grace each state's quarter. We know that Alaska's quarter will feature a grizzly bear. Hawaii's will display King Kamehameha the Great.

In short, we now know that on the fifty state quarters, you won't find the ratification of the Constitution or John Marshall's court. There is no Battle of New Orleans, Battle of the Alamo, or Battle of Gettysburg. There is no *Amistad*, no Trail of Tears, no Dred Scott, no Wounded Knee, no Selma March. There is no *Merrimac*, or *Monitor*, or USS *Missouri*. There are no Rough Riders in Cuba, no doughboys going over the top at Chateau Thierry, no marines storming Iwo Jima, and no helicopters over Vietnam.

There are no Mississippi riverboats, Boeing 747s, or Apple computers. For that matter, neither does Edison's light bulb or Henry Ford's Model T make an appearance. There is no Panama Canal, no Brooklyn Bridge, no Hoover Dam, and no Los Alamos. Elvis does not enter or leave the building. Neither does Ed Sullivan, Edward R. Murrow, or Johnny Carson. Hollywood and Broadway are absent, and no one seems to want their MTV. And as far as abbreviations are concerned, the NFL, the NBA, and MLB are all MIA.

Rather, Alaska's and Hawaii's quarters, once issued, will follow coins that depict revolutionaries and race cars, peaches and palmettos, astronauts and activists, flowers and fishermen, bridges and buffalo (and more buffalo), sailing ships and syrup.

In other words, my original idea lies in complete shambles.

But, at the same time, the fifty state quarters offer more than I ever anticipated. Look closely at them—on many, state mottoes and phrases resonate: "Live Free or Die"; "Virtue, Liberty, Independence"; "Crossroads of the Revolution"; "Wisdom, Justice, Moderation"; "First Flight"; "Gateway to Freedom"; "Crossroads of America"; "Land of Lincoln"; "Birthplace of Aviation Pioneers"; "Spirit of Courage"; "Foundation in Education"; "Forward"; "Big Sky Country"; "Crossroads of the West"; "Land of Enchantment"; and "The Great Land."

In short, these quarters are not so much about who we are or what we are but are instead a polyglot reflection on how we think of ourselves. They identify what we cherish and value. Although many of the coins offer a look back, just as many others point the way forward.

So perhaps it is not surprising that as each of our individual states put forth its design, we saw that it was choosing—sometimes directly, sometimes less directly—to celebrate patriots such as Caesar Rodney, who chose to put a vote for freedom above his own failing health, or King Kamehameha, who likewise saw strength in unity.

They chose to celebrate pelicans, and buffalo, and peregrine falcons, battling back from extinction.

They showed their admiration for American pioneers—of settlement, of discovery, of flight, and of space.

They elected to praise nature's wonders—soaring mountains, scenic gorges, spectacular flowers, and idyllic coasts.

They honored the competitive thrill of sport, whether on the racetrack at Indianapolis, off a bridge in West Virginia, or in the waters off Rhode Island.

They singled out admirable individuals: a blind girl from Alabama who dared to make the world a better place, an immigrant from Scotland who dared to argue that parts of it could not get any better.

They celebrated music, and education, and cowboys and farmers working from dawn to dusk to feed a hungry nation and a hungrier world.

In summary, the individual states chose to celebrate endeavor as much as accomplishment, effort as much as success, opportunity as much as exploits.

Simply put, that new spare change jangling in our pockets thanks to the 50 State Quarters® Program celebrates change and the history of change. Change in the way we govern ourselves, and in the way we live our lives. Change in the way we earn our livings. Change in where we live, where we go, and how we get there. And change in what we think of preserving and protecting.

Of course, perhaps not all of that change was always for the better. Nevertheless, it is hard to argue that such change, whatever it might have been, was not made with the hope for a better tomorrow. As one looks at America—and all fifty of its states—it is difficult to find a more defining trait over the course of our history than such hopefulness.

To quote Idaho's quarter, "Esta Perpetua": May it be forever.

# THE PROGRAM

If you are a cynic, then to hear that a loonie inspired congressional legislation may not surprise you at all. But beware of jumping to conclusions. The story is slightly more complicated than you might think.

In 1991, the Canadian Mint decided to mark Canada's 125th anniversary the following year with an ambitious new coin program. One aspect of the program, called "Canada 125," solicited a new design for Canada's $1 coin—irreverently called the "loonie," thanks to the loon depicted on its reverse.

An equally important part of Canada 125, however, was the minting of a sequence of twelve commemorative Canadian quarters, with a new quarter design to be issued at a rate of one per month. Each quarter would represent one of the twelve Canadian provinces in existence at the time (Canada's thirteenth province, Nunavut, did not become a province until 1999) and would be based on designs submitted from any and all of Canada's 27 million citizens.

The response was enormous. Figures differ, but somewhere between 9,277 and 11,003 individual designs were received for both the loonie and the individual quarters. The volume of submissions easily eclipsed the 939 entries received in 1973 to 1974 by the U.S. Mint when a similar competition was held to redesign the Washington quarter, Kennedy half dollar, and Eisenhower dollar to mark the 1976 Bicentennial. And once the coins and quarters were minted, the popularity of the idea became even more apparent. Within a year, most had disappeared from circulation, hoarded by collectors across Canada and the world.

The idea of replicating Canada 125 in the United States, however, remained in circulation. Numismatists (coin collectors) in the United States cited the success of Canada 125—often referred to in conversational shorthand as simply "the loonie"—as they pressed for a similar program to honor America's fifty states.

Those numismatists found a sympathetic ear on Capitol Hill in 1995 and 1996, when representatives of America's coin collectors testified before the House Banking Committee's Domestic and International Monetary Policy Subcommittee. At the time, the subcommittee was chaired by Representative Mike Castle, a Republican representing Delaware.

"Groups representing the coin collectors of America approached my staff about the idea of a fifty-state quarter program based on Canada's success with the loonie," Castle explained to me in a telephone interview. "My staff then sold the idea to me—I'm a little slower than they are," he added self-deprecatingly.

Castle and his staffers, including their colleagues on the House Subcommittee on Domestic and International Monetary Policy, were key ingredients—catalysts, even—for the program that eventually transpired, but credit for the state quarters rests on several shoulders. The private sector, led by such enthusiasts as New Jersey attorney, writer, and numismatists David Ganz, originally pushed for the idea of a fifty-state series as early as 1993. Meanwhile, U.S. Mint officials, led by Director Philip Diehl, were increasingly receptive to a program that would replicate the success of the earlier Bicentennial coins. They further warmed to the idea when a second die shop boosted the Mint's production capacity. But it was certainly Castle who got the proverbial ball—or coin, as the case may be—rolling.

In July 1996, Castle and eight co-sponsors introduced HR 3793, a House bill to legislate what he called the "50 States Commemorative Coin Program Act." Castle's legislation passed in the House but stalled that year in the Senate.

Undeterred, Castle took up the cause once again the following September, when he introduced HR 2414 to again enact the "50 States Commemorative Coin Program Act." The bill again passed the House overwhelmingly and was forwarded to the Senate. In the Senate, John H. Chafee, a Republican representing Rhode Island, added Castle's legislation to S.1228, a larger bill that also encompassed the "United States $1 Coin Act of 1997" and authorized the minting of a collection of coins to commemorate the Wright brothers' first flight at Kitty Hawk. Twenty-seven senators joined Chafee in co-sponsoring the bill.

Meanwhile, on October 31, 1997, the Congressional Budget Office drafted a cost estimate that examined the fiscal repercussions of the pending legislation. The office's conclusion was a positive one:

> In addition to the bill's effects on direct spending, by increasing the public's holding of quarters, S.1228 also would result in the government acquiring additional resources for financing the federal deficit. Based on the previous experience of both the United States, with the bicentennial quarter in 1975 and 1976, and Canada, with its series of quarters commemorating its 12 provinces and territories in 1992, CBO expects that enacting the bill would lead to a greater production of quarters. The

seigniorage, or profit, from placing the additional coins in circulation would reduce the amount of government borrowing from the public. Such profits are likely to be very significant—the Mint estimates that the seigniorage from making a quarter is 20.2 cents, so for each additional $100 million worth of quarters put into circulation each year for 10 years, the amount of seigniorage earned by the federal government would increase by about $808 million over the ten-year period. (Congressional Budget Office 1997, 5)

Buoyed by such forecasts, the Senate voted unanimously to pass the bill on November 9, 1997. Four days later, the House passed the amended bill as well, and on December 1, 1997, President William J. Clinton signed it into law as Public Law 105-124.

The Congressional finding that prefaces the new act speaks for itself:

The Congress finds that it is appropriate and timely to honor the unique Federal republic of 50 States that comprise the United States; and to promote the diffusion of knowledge among the youth of the United States about the individual States, their history and geography, and the rich diversity of the national heritage; the circulating coinage of the United States has not been modernized during the 25-year period preceding the date of enactment of this Act; a circulating commemorative 25-cent coin program could produce earnings of $110,000,000 from the sale of silver proof coins and sets over the 10-year period of issuance, and would produce indirect earnings of an estimated $2,600,000,000 to $5,100,000,000 to the United States Treasury, money that will replace borrowing to fund the national debt to at least that extent; and it is appropriate to launch a commemorative circulating coin program that encourages young people and their families to collect memorable tokens of all the States for the face value of the coins. (Public Law 105-124, Section 2)

The specifics of the program would be as follows: beginning in 1999, and continuing for the next decade, the U.S. Mint would issue five new quarters per year, each commemorating a new state in the order that the states joined the Union. Castle's home state of Delaware, admitted to the Union on December 7, 1787, would lead the charge, followed at ten-week intervals for the remainder of 1999 by quarters for Pennsylvania, New Jersey, Georgia, and Connecticut, respectively. After ten years, the program would end, forty-five quarters later, in 2008, with the issuance of quarters for Oklahoma, New Mexico, Arizona, Alaska, and Hawaii. The order of issuance is reflected in the order of chapters in this book—starting with Delaware and ending with Hawaii.

Over the course of the program, the U.S. Mint's presses in Denver and Philadelphia would mint particular state designs in quantities reflective of the national economy's need for quarters (and thus reflective of the relative vibrancy of America's economy as a whole—the more economic activity projected, the greater the need for coinage). In other words, there was no guarantee that California (the most populated state) would see any more quarters than Wyoming (the least populated state). For the record, as of the typing of these words, Virginia can claim to have had the most quarters minted (with over one and a half billion of them minted in 2000). Ironically, Maine, whose quarter is widely recognized as among the most aesthetic of the group, trails the rest of the Union with a mere 448.8 million quarters minted in 2003.

In a program of such magnitude, Castle and his fellow members of Congress knew that the selection of fifty acceptable designs would be particularly challenging. To that end, their legislation mandated a particular process. Specifically, each of the fifty designs would be selected by the secretary of the Treasury, but only after consultation with the governor of the state being commemorated and the federal Commission of Fine Arts, and review by the Citizens Commemorative Coin Advisory Committee (a federal committee later abolished in 2003 and replaced by the Citizens Coinage Advisory Committee).

The act also established certain standards for would-be designs, noting that as "it is important that the Nation's coinage and currency bear dignified designs of which the citizens of the United States can be proud, the Secretary shall not select any frivolous or inappropriate design for any quarter dollar minted under this subsection." The act also added that "no head and shoulders portrait or bust of any person, living or dead, and no portrait of a living person may be included in the design of any quarter dollar under this subsection."

To that list of prohibitions and admonitions, the Mint offered further guidance. Quoting directly from the U.S. Mint's Web site, the following became the relevant design criteria:

- Designs shall have broad appeal to the citizens of the state and avoid controversial subjects or symbols that are likely to offend.
- Suitable subject matter for designs includes state landmarks (natural and man-made), landscapes, historically significant buildings, symbols of state resources or industries, official state flora and fauna, state icons (e.g., Texas Lone Star, Wyoming bronco, etc.), and outlines of the state.
- State flags and state seals are not considered suitable for designs.
- Consistent with the authorizing legislation, the states are encouraged to submit designs that promote the diffusion of knowledge among the youth of the United States about the state, its history and geography, and the rich diversity of our national heritage.
- Priority consideration will be given to designs that are enduring representations of the state.

- Inappropriate design concepts include, but are not limited to, logos or depictions of specific commercial, private, educational, civic, religious, sports, or other organizations whose membership or ownership is not universal.

With the act signed into law at the end of 1997, and the first coins due to be released in 1999, states such as Delaware and Pennsylvania had little time to waste and little precedent to employ. But rising to the challenge, the U.S. Mint issued Delaware's quarter on January 1, 1999, and in doing so, inaugurated the program with a coin that generally gets high marks both from historians and for its aesthetics.

As the years passed, however, and as more and more quarters were issued, time proved that, to play a little with George Orwell, some quarters are more equal than others. Some quarters would go on to earn high marks for their originality and artistry; others, to put it simply, would not. Meanwhile, a handful of highly publicized controversies regarding the ultimate implementation and engraving of selected designs on certain quarters—notably Missouri's and California's—arose as well. Adequate recognition of winning designers at the state level also raised recurring questions.

One could certainly argue that the level of attention and angst being generated provided proof positive that the 50 State Quarters® Program was a success. Nevertheless, to help address the various artistic concerns the program faced in the state quarter program (and others), the U.S. Mint instituted its Artistic Infusion Program (AIP) in 2003. Following a nationwide call for artists, the Mint inducted a total of twenty-four artists in its initial AIP class. Their assignments included work on designs for the 2006 state quarters—those of Nevada, Nebraska, Colorado, North Dakota, and South Dakota. Meanwhile, in 2005, the U.S. Mint changed its design solicitation and acceptance policy. Rather than accepting drawings from the states of their preferred designs, the Mint began requiring that design concepts or themes simply be submitted in narrative form.

Regardless of such issues, Congressman Castle could not have been happier with the result of the modest piece of legislation he introduced back in 1997.

"The country has really gotten into it. It's been an absolute success—in every way possible," Castle said. "First, some estimates are that it has generated $6 billion in seigniorage, so it's made that money for the government. How many government programs can say that?

"Second, people are excited about it," he added. "People who never collected coins before are collecting the quarters and are anticipating when the next designs will be out. People are receiving change and immediately looking at it to see what quarter they have.

"Finally, it's educational, and that's important for the kids," he concluded. "The program provides a vehicle for them to learn about our country's history, and culture, and geography."

In the end, the program may prove to be even more successful than Castle ever envisioned. Proving that imitation is the sincerest form of flattery, Representative José E. Serrano (D-NY) successfully introduced an amendment to the Consolidated Appropriations Act of 2008 that required the U.S. Mint to issue six new quarters in 2009—honoring Washington, D.C., American Samoa, Guam, Puerto Rico, the Virgin Islands, and the Commonwealth of the Northern Mariana Islands.

But for now, fifty quarters—and the fifty chapters that follow—will have to suffice.

# 1

# DELAWARE
## *Hail, Caesar!*

When Delaware first solicited prospective designs for the 50 State Quarters® Program's inaugural quarter, high school arts and drama teacher Eddy Seger did not even have to look beyond his own campus for inspiration. Seger teaches at Caesar Rodney High School in Camden, Delaware, and as he well knew, his school's namesake held a special place in the hearts of Delaware's citizens.

"In my Art II classes, we do bas-reliefs," Seger explained, "and that spring, I had my students sculpt designs to submit for Delaware's quarter. As an example, I did a relief of Caesar Rodney on his famous ride."

Outside of Delaware, however, Rodney's ride is far from famous, and nationally, his is hardly a household name. But in 1776, Rodney stood foremost among America's patriots—for his dedication to the cause of an independent United States, if not necessarily for his looks.

"The oddest looking man in the world," John Adams described him. "[S]lender as a reed—pale—his face is not bigger than a large apple. But there is sense and fire, spirit, wit, and humor in his countenance."

Caesar Rodney was born in 1728, on a Kent County, Delaware, plantation called Byfield. Orphaned at seventeen, Rodney was left to help run Byfield and raise his seven siblings. In 1755, already a captain in Delaware's militia, he emerged on Delaware's political scene as high sheriff of Kent County. From the outset, Rodney seemed a natural statesman, with "a great fund of wit and humor of the pleasing kind, so that his conversation was always bright and strong and conducted by wisdom."

Once engaged in politics, Rodney occupied a series of colonial offices, ranging from register of wills to justice on the Delaware Supreme Court. In 1761, his fellow colonists elected him to Delaware's House of Assembly, where he eventually served four terms as its Speaker. Today, Rodney is recognized as having held more public offices than any other citizen of Delaware.

But even as Rodney's political career flourished, his personal fortunes waned. A cancerous sore appeared on his nose and soon spread to the left side of his face. Although doctors in Philadelphia managed to halt the cancer's spread, the results were repellent. Rodney eventually took to wearing a green silk veil to cover his scarred face and its unsightly sores. Bouts of asthma, pleurisy, and gout also plagued him, even as he represented Delaware in the First Continental Congress in 1775.

In that Congress, and in the one that followed, Rodney preserved a reputation as a moderate—one of the "cool, considerate men," as such statesmen were later called when the Second Continental Congress convened in Philadelphia on May 10, 1776. A month later, when delegates introduced a resolution calling for independence, cool consideration was needed more than ever.

By June 28, a draft declaration lay before the Congress and required a vote. Even though the thirteen colonies' delegation sizes varied, each colony possessed only one vote in the matter of independence. Unanimity was the ultimate goal. A unanimous vote would send a strong message through the colonies and to London. Indecision would have the opposite effect.

But when the first vote on the resolution came on Monday, July 1, only nine colonies voted in favor. Both Pennsylvania and South Carolina voted against it. New York's delegation, still hoping for reconciliation rather than revolution, elected to abstain. For its part, the Delaware delegation did not vote when two members of its three-man delegation—Thomas McKean and George Read—deadlocked.

At the time, Rodney, the delegation's third member, was home in Delaware, some eighty miles away. While the Continental Congress debated, Delaware's population had become increasingly polarized. Opposed to rebellion, loyalist Tories had gathered a force several hundred strong in Sussex County, and Rodney, in his role as a militia brigadier general, had returned to Delaware to deal with them. His efforts, coupled with a show of force by the Delaware militia, bore fruit. The counterrevolutionaries either vowed no further mischief or escaped offshore to British ships. Relieved, Rodney repaired to Byfield to recuperate.

Meanwhile, in Philadelphia, McKean was well aware of Rodney's yeoman service against the Loyalists. He also knew of his friend's precarious health. At the same time, however, McKean refused to allow Delaware's deadlock to stand. He scribbled a note to Rodney, warning him that the critical vote loomed, and dispatched an express rider to summon him.

The rider, galloping through a driving rainstorm, reached Rodney's distant plantation shortly before midnight. As soon as he read the note, Rodney rushed to leave for Philadelphia. But how he actually undertook the ensuing journey remains one of the unsolved mysteries of American history. Some people point to a subsequent comment by his younger brother that refers to Rodney "call[ing] for his carriage." Indeed, that would have been the likely manner in which most country gentlemen—and certainly an ailing middle-aged asthmatic—would have traveled.

Popular legend, however, offers a different story. According to that version, the sickly Rodney pulled himself onto his best horse and, ignoring the pelting rain, galloped north to Philadelphia. Throughout the night, his horse's hooves thudded and splashed along the King's Highway. Stretches of the rutted road, poorly drained, became muddy quagmires that sucked at both steed and rider. Branches and limbs cracked and broke in the tempestuous wind, littering the dark road with dangerous obstacles. Once-gentle streams swelled into raging torrents, buffeting wooden bridges and turning fords into treacherous cataracts. The ride would have been grueling for a man half Rodney's age in the best of health. For him, it must have been torturous.

Nevertheless, Rodney forged ahead. Reaching Philadelphia on the afternoon of July 2, he met his old friend McKean at the door to the Pennsylvania State House where Congress had convened. Taking the muddy, gangling apparition by the arm, McKean led Rodney into the brick building.

No sooner had they taken their seats than the clerk began calling for votes on the declaration. When Delaware's turn came, Rodney spoke in a tired but clear voice.

"As I believe the voice of my constituents and of all sensible and honest men is in favor of independence, and my own judgment concurs," Rodney exclaimed, "I vote for independence!"

With independence declared, Rodney focused his immediate efforts on raising levies for the Continental Army. Later, Delaware appointed him as a delegate to the Continental Congress and, in short order, elevated him to the governor's office in 1778. But by 1781, Rodney's cancer returned—"that horrid and most obstinate disorder," as he called it. Although selected to represent Delaware in the United States Congress, his illness forced him to decline the honor. Within three years, he was dead.

Today, a statue depicting Rodney's ride graces Wilmington's Rodney Square. Another statue of him stands in the U.S. Capitol's Statuary Hall. But when Eddy Seger decided to honor Delaware's favorite son, he kept in mind that Rodney, ashamed of his cancerous face, never sat for a portrait. Certainly, Seger reasoned, he would not have wanted the left side of his face shown. Accordingly, Seger's suggested design depicted Rodney on a horse galloping from right to left—so that only Rodney's right side was visible.

Eventually, three designs emerged as finalists for the state quarter—Seger's, another design depicting a piece of parchment and a quill (intended to symbolize Delaware's historic ratification of the U.S. Constitution), and an allegorical image of Lady Liberty holding a baby Delaware. With regard to the latter, Seger minced no words.

"It looked terrible," he said. "I'll be honest with you—she looked like a slut showing up with a surprise at a family reunion. It was a mess."

At that point, however, Seger was not particularly happy with his design, either. In the final mock-up, which was out of his hands, Rodney's direction of travel had been reversed: He was galloping from left to right. In real life, such a perspective would have exposed the cancerous left side of his face, though it was shown as unscarred.

"Rodney would have never allowed himself to be portrayed that way," Seger said sorrowfully.

Nevertheless, despite Seger's misgivings, a telephone and e-mail poll convinced Delaware's leadership to select what is generally recognized as Seger's design for final submission to the U.S. Mint for engraving. On December 7, 1998, the U.S. Mint struck the first quarter bearing Delaware's design. When the first coins were shipped to the Federal Reserve on January 4, 1999, the 50 State Quarters® Program became a reality for the American public.

So did the program's first—but not last—controversy. Although the U.S. Mint originally identified Seger as the designer of the quarter, Delaware officials reportedly disagreed, subsequently maintaining that Seger's was only one of several designs submitted that featured Rodney's ride.

Regardless of the state's disavowal, Seger remains unruffled. This is not a surprising reaction from a man who once, about to embark upon a solo canoe trip down the Mississippi River, realized that he had lost all his cash. Undeterred, he cast off on the two-month-long voyage anyway, financing his way downstream by drawing and selling artwork along the way.

"Now, I give out the quarter when I travel overseas and tell people that I designed it," he said. "It's a great way to start a conversation."

# PENNSYLVANIA
## *The Key to the Keystone*

Although Pennsylvania and Delaware were originally part of the same colony, the two states took distinctly different artistic paths when it came to the imagery on the reverse of their state quarters. Whereas Delaware relied on a literal image—the iconic ride of Caesar Rodney—to represent and reflect its identity, Pennsylvania opted for a more symbolic approach.

Pennsylvania's design centers on a well-proportioned, toga-clad woman, unabashedly showing a flash of her left thigh as she looks coyly over her right shoulder. Framed by an outline of Pennsylvania's borders, she grasps a ribbon mace in her left hand, while her right arm extends down, palm open, and slightly to the side. The mace symbolizes justice; the outstretched hand, kindness. The woman's name is Commonwealth, and she resides atop Pennsylvania's state capitol in Harrisburg, at 250 feet above the street.

In reality, Commonwealth is a three-ton statue of gilded bronze, thirteen and a half feet tall. Although designed by Joseph Miller Huston, the architect responsible for the capitol while it was being constructed from 1902 to 1906, Commonwealth was sculpted by Roland Hinton Perry. Educated in Paris, Perry earned acclaim for his bas-reliefs at the Library of Congress, followed by his sculpting of the library's *Fountain of Neptune.*

Working from Huston's design, Perry sculpted the working model for Commonwealth in 1905. His later works can be found across the nation, ranging from the sentrylike lions on the Taft Bridge in Washington, D.C., to the Soldiers and Sailors Monument in Middleton, Ohio, to the Elk Statue in Portland, Oregon. What Commonwealth would be worth today is anyone's guess—a mere figurative inkwell sculpted by Perry sold for $4,200 in 2006.

Nearly a century after Perry created the original work, Commonwealth found a second home on Pennsylvania's state quarter. The words "Virtue, Liberty, Independence" are inscribed on her left. A keystone, emblematic of Pennsylvania's nickname, the Keystone State, is engraved on her right. And therein is a mystery. Why is Pennsylvania called the Keystone State?

Theories abound. The simplest may be that Pennsylvania, given its central location, was the geographic keystone to the original thirteen colonies. A question posed to the Pennsylvania Archives, however, yielded a more sophisticated explanation.

According to Louis Waddell, a historian with the state of Pennsylvania, the state's nickname can be traced to editorials in the *Aurora,* an early Philadelphia newspaper. Edited by William Duane, the *Aurora* was an unabashed opponent of President John Adams and the Federalists at the turn of the eighteenth century. In fact, Duane was twice indicted—although never convicted—under the Alien and Sedition Acts. The partisan attacks of papers such as the *Aurora* helped to turn the presidential election of 1800 into what Adams biographer David McCullough described as "a contest of personal vilification surpassing any presidential election in American history."

That election pitted the incumbent Adams and his anointed vice presidential candidate, Charles Cotesworth Pinckney, against Vice President Thomas Jefferson and his running mate, Aaron Burr. At the time, debate regarding the proper relationship of the federal government and the Republic's individual states was more than merely academic, while a "quasi-war" with France enflamed the ongoing argument further. For the first time in American history, partisan party politics dominated the race, with Adams's Federalists on one side and the Jeffersonian Republicans on the other.

The race for the White House—a new residence into which Adams had just moved—climaxed with an unprecedented political crisis. Under the Constitution of the day, the states' electors voted for two men. The one with the highest number of votes would become the president; the second-highest, the vice president. In short, to avoid a tie and to successfully put his slate into office in this new era of party politics, at least one of the electors had to take care not to cast his votes for the same two men for whom his fellow party members were voting.

In 1800, however, the system broke down in dramatic fashion. Failing to properly coordinate their efforts, all of the Republican electors faithfully cast one vote for Jefferson and one vote for Burr. The final result produced totals of seventy-three electoral votes each for both Jefferson and Burr, sixty-five votes for Adams, sixty-four votes for Pinckney, and one token vote for Federalist John Jay. For their part, Pennsylvania's electors narrowly sided with the Republicans by an 8–7 margin.

In the end, because of the Republicans' miscalculations, Jefferson and Burr were tied for the highest office in the land. According to the Constitution, the House of Representatives would have to vote to break the tie. However, the Federalists still held a majority there that would presumably prefer a political stalemate rather than an affirmative vote to elect Jefferson.

Burr could have defused the issue by conceding to Jefferson; but, consumed by unrestrained presidential ambitions, he refused to do so. Accordingly, the contest shifted to the House. There, in February 1801, the Federalists cobbled together enough diehards to steadfastly vote for Burr through thirty-five ballots and thus preserve the impasse. With the scheduled inauguration day approaching, the House holding the election hostage, and Republican states warning ominously of a shattered Union, the nation slipped perilously close to political chaos.

Eventually, however, calmer heads prevailed. On February 17, 1801, James A. Bayard, a Federalist from Delaware and the state's sole member of the House of Representatives, cast a blank ballot rather than continuing to vote for Burr. His blank ballot enabled a majority vote for Jefferson. Delighted, the *Aurora* carped that God had cast Adams out of the White House like "polluted water out at the back door." "May he return in safety to Braintree [his home in Massachusetts]," the paper added, "that Mrs. Adams may wash his befuddled brains clear."

The *Aurora*'s writers were still gleeful a year later, when they described a Pennsylvania gubernatorial victory dinner for the Republicans' Thomas McKean on October 16, 1802, at the Hamburgh House on the Schuylkill River. Reporting on the event, the paper described a dinner in which a "mammoth turtle" was consumed, along with sixteen toasts of Madeira and claret. The ninth of those toasts, according to the *Aurora*, reflected on the previous year's victory and prayed "may the Republicans of Pennsylvania never forget that their commonwealth is the keystone of the federal union." Exaggeration or not, this toast, according to historian Waddell's careful research, marked the first time Pennsylvania was referred to as a "keystone."

Waddell admits, however, that other theories continue to challenge the *Aurora*'s claim. One theory traces its roots to Pierre Charles L'Enfant, the French architect assigned to design Washington, D.C. In 1792, he spanned the city's Rock Creek with a bridge of arch stones engraved with each of the original thirteen states' names. In the middle of that arch, the stone labeled "Pennsylvania" forms the arch's keystone. Pennsylvania is, therefore, literally the "keystone state."

Another legend has John Morton, one of Pennsylvania's delegates to the Second Continental Congress, declaring Pennsylvania to be the "keystone state" when he voted for independence. At the time, Pennsylvania's delegation of nine men was almost evenly divided on the issue of declaring independence from Great Britain. Morton's vote within the delegation, therefore, was indeed key.

Pennsylvania faced another key decision twenty-two decades later, when, in 1998, it came time to select a design for its state quarter. Recognizing that his state was making numismatic history, Governor Tom Ridge formed the diverse fourteen-member Commemorative Quarter Committee to determine what image would represent the Keystone State. Lucy Gnazzo, a senior member of his staff, served as the governor's liaison to the committee.

"It was a really exciting project," said Gnazzo. "Governor Ridge wanted to open up the selection process to the public and invited the public to submit designs. He wanted a quarter that would educate, highlight the state's history, and market Pennsylvania to the country."

Prospective designs—5,300 of them—poured into Harrisburg.

"It was an amazing process," said Gnazzo. "We'd open up those envelopes and things would pour out—photos, drawings, and even actual coin design mock-ups. The level of interest was just incredible."

Proposed designs included one that offered a more prominently displayed keystone and another that displayed the ruffed grouse, the official state bird. In the end, five final concepts were selected and forwarded to Washington, D.C., where four of them survived review by the Citizens Commemorative Coin Advisory Committee and the Fine Arts Commission and won approval by the secretary of the Treasury. Left with those four options, Governor Ridge chose the current design. The U.S. Mint issued the first Pennsylvania state quarter on March 8, 1999; in total, 707.332 million were eventually minted.

"The final design was a fabulous way to commemorate our state," Gnazzo said. "If you've ever driven across the Susquehanna River into Harrisburg and seen Commonwealth reflecting the sun and peering through the city's skyline, you know what I mean."

# 3

# NEW JERSEY
## *The First Commute*

For its state quarter, New Jersey selected one of the most iconic images of American history—the scene depicted in Emanuel Leutze's painting *Washington Crossing the Delaware*. Leutze's masterpiece portrays a stalwart George Washington, standing steadily in a crowded boat of Continental soldiers, as he navigates the ice-choked Delaware River to attack Trenton. "Crossroads of the Revolution," the quarter declares, referring to dozens of skirmishes and battles fought in New Jersey during the American Revolution. Of all of those battles, none is seared into America's subconscious more deeply than Washington's strike against Great Britain's Hessian mercenaries on December 26, 1776. A year and a half earlier, Washington had taken command of a collection of state militiamen and new recruits that was grandly labeled the Continental Army. It was, in Washington's words, "a mixed multitude of people . . . under little discipline, order or government." Nevertheless, at its head, he managed to masterfully maneuver the British out of Boston.

Washington's decision to confront the enemy in New York, however, nearly proved fatal. British redcoats and their Hessian mercenaries sent the Continentals reeling southward in a strategic retreat. The withdrawal did not pause until the battered core of Washington's soldiers managed to slip across the Delaware River into Pennsylvania. Meanwhile, their pursuers settled comfortably into their winter quarters.

At that point in the Revolution, the mere fact that Washington's army was still intact represented a significant moral victory. But the need for real victories grew ever more pressing. The enlistment contracts for many of Washington's soldiers expired on December 31, 1776, and without a victory in the field to restore spirits, much of the Continental Army would likely melt away at the end of the year. Accordingly, as Christmas approached, Washington gathered his staff and regimental commanders and hatched a plan to deliver such a victory.

On a map of New Jersey and Pennsylvania, Washington drew out a bold scheme of maneuver. Dividing his army into three strike forces, he decided to lead one group of 2,400 across the Delaware River at McKonkey's Ferry, Pennsylvania, ten miles upstream of Trenton, on Christmas night. Once on the New Jersey side of the river, he would divide his troops into two columns and march them south under the cover of darkness to Trenton. There, he would launch a dawn attack, hoping to surprise the brigade of 1,500 Hessian mercenaries garrisoning the town.

In the meantime, a smaller force of 700 Pennsylvania militia under Brigadier General James Ewing would attack Trenton by crossing the river directly across from Trenton in order to block the Hessians' escape route across Assunpink Creek. A third force, commanded by Colonel John Cadwalader and consisting of 1,000 Pennsylvania militia and 500 veteran Rhode Island troops, would row across the river and strike the enemy garrison at Bordentown, further south. The three forces would then consolidate and, capitalizing on their success, strike against British garrisons in Princeton and New Brunswick.

To support his plan, Washington ordered Colonel John Glover, who commanded a regiment of fishermen-turned-soldiers from Marblehead, Massachusetts, to gather as many boats as he could. Fortune smiled on Glover's efforts, and his men soon located two dozen so-called Durham boats—sixty-foot-long, flat-bottomed boats used locally for hauling pig iron along the river but also capable of carrying up to forty men at a time. In short, they seemed well-suited for ferrying a large number of troops in an amphibious assault.

Washington unleashed his raid immediately after the Continental Army's afternoon parade on Christmas Day. Carrying three days' worth of rations and sixty rounds of ammunition each, the Continentals marched resolutely toward the river and into the teeth of a ferocious winter storm. Pursuant to Washington's orders, "Victory or Death" was the agreed-upon password for the operation.

Despite such a ringing sentiment, Ewing's force did not even attempt to cross the icy Delaware River in the face of deteriorating weather conditions. Cadwalader's infantry were more successful, but when he was unable to ferry his artillery pieces across, he withdrew his men to the Pennsylvania side of the river.

Washington, however, was not so easily discouraged. Urging his men forward, and capitalizing on the experience of Glover's seamen-soldiers, he managed to get his men to the east bank of the Delaware, albeit several hours behind schedule. Dividing his force into two columns, he began to advance on Trenton at approximately 3:00 AM, though he was slowed by snow, sleet, and frigid temperatures. At least two of the Continentals froze to death at some point that evening.

"For God's sake, keep with your officers," Washington urged his men as they slogged silently through the swirling snow and bitter cold. When a messenger arrived from one of his commanders that warned the men's muskets were too wet to fire, Washington responded simply: "Tell the General to use the bayonet," he said.

Advancing on Trenton, Washington's columns rolled up surprised groups of Hessian pickets before slamming into the sleepy town at 8:00 AM. They found, in the words of historian David McCullough, a village that, in addition to a large two-story stone barracks dating back to the French and Indian Wars, consisted of "perhaps a hundred houses, an Episcopal church, a marketplace, and two or three mills and iron furnaces." It was "a busy but plain little place of no particular consequence."

In Trenton, the German commander, Colonel Johann Rall, quickly regretted his decision not to construct a redoubt at the intersection of Trenton's two main streets. The Continentals seized the critical juncture and occupied it with artillery pieces. Then, they capitalized on their fields of fire as the Hessians came boiling out of the town's homes and their tents, preventing them from forming up for an effective defense. The retreating Hessians slipped out of town as best they could, where Rall formed his regiments for a counterattack.

By then, the Continentals had occupied the town's stone buildings. With withering volleys of musket fire, they broke the Hessians' assault and mortally wounded Rall. The Germans withdrew into a nearby orchard where, once surrounded, they surrendered en masse. In all, the battle cost Britain's German mercenaries over 100 casualties, with some 900 captured. For his part, Washington suffered only a handful of wounded. The small number of wounded, however, included a young officer named James Monroe, who was destined to survive his wound and become the fifth president of the United States. Future secretary of the Treasury Alexander Hamilton also participated in the battle, as did future Supreme Court chief justice John Marshall.

Washington's strike against Trenton, followed by another successful raid on Princeton a week later, restored both his own prestige and his men's confidence in themselves. It is not too much of an overstatement to say that, but for Trenton, the Continental Army might have melted away at the end of the year, taking with it any hope of an independent United States.

It is no wonder, then, that when Emanuel Leutze began work on a piece of art that he hoped would capture the revolutionary fever sweeping Europe in 1848, he selected Washington crossing the Delaware as his inspiration. And even as Europe's revolutions sputtered out, Leutze painted on, allowing his work to celebrate revolutionary struggle as much as revolutionary victory. Although a fire damaged the original painting, he completed a copy in 1851 and sent it to America for display, where it eventually found a home in New York's Metropolitan Museum of Art.

Leutze's painting provides careful detail. Immediately behind Washington, holding the Stars and Stripes, stands Lieutenant James Monroe. One of the boat's occupants wears the red-trimmed blue coat of a soldier assigned to Haslet's Delaware Regiment. Another, sheltering under an oiled hat and boat cloak, reveals enough of the uniform beneath to indicate he is with Smallwood's aristocratic Maryland Regiment. Others, in blanket coats and broad-brimmed hats, seem to be simply militiamen from Pennsylvania or New Jersey, as may be the case with the Scottish immigrant still wearing his Balmoral bonnet. One of their comrades, wearing the garb of a New England seaman, is an African American. Another might be female. Frontier riflemen man the bow and stern of the boat, clad in hunting shirts and deerskin leggings.

That is not to say, however, that *Washington Crossing the Delaware* is not without its historical gaffes. The boat depicted is not a Durham boat, the Stars and Stripes carried by Lieutenant Monroe was not adopted until the following year, and the jagged icebergs in the painting bear little resemblance to the sheet ice that would have actually formed in the river. Furthermore, as the river crossing actually occurred in the dead of night, Leutze took considerable artistic license in illuminating his scene.

Despite such historical incongruities, Leutze's painting so in-delibly stamped America's folk memory that it is hard to fault New Jersey's fifteen-member Commemorative Coin Design Committee for unanimously co-opting it for its state quarter. In response, the U.S. Mint issued the first of 662.228 million New Jersey state quarters on May 17, 1999.

# 4

# GEORGIA
## *Peachy Keen*

If you don't recognize the large orb in the middle of Georgia's state quarter, then take a summer drive along U.S. Highway 341. The branches in the orchards lining the highway will be heavy with succulent spheres by then, and if you are still confused, your arrival in Fort Valley should dispel any remaining uncertainty. There, each June the county seat of Peach County hosts the annual Georgia Peach Festival, bakes the world's largest peach cobbler, and crowns Miss Georgia Peach.

According to U.S. Census data from 2002, there are 304 peach farms in Georgia, with 13,242 acres of peach trees. That number was down from 446 farms reported five years earlier, 582 in 1992, and 688 in 1987. In fact, today California and South Carolina both produce more peaches than the Peach State. And as far as agricultural commodities are concerned, Georgia instead leads the nation in the production of broilers (young chickens), peanuts, and pecans.

Such facts failed to dissuade the Georgia General Assembly from declaring the peach Georgia's "'official fruit'—recognized for their wonderful flavor, texture, and appearance"—in 1995. Nor has it ever sparked the survivors of Lynyrd Skynyrd to rethink the band's lyrical declaration in 1974's "Call Me the Breeze": "I dig you Georgia peaches—makes me feel right at home."

Despite its third-place national ranking, the value of Georgia's peach crop nevertheless topped $48 million in 2003. Relatively speaking, that sum paled in comparison to the Georgia figures for such agricultural commodities as tomatoes ($122 million) and was actually more in line with the values of Georgia's cabbage and squash crops. But the "Cabbage State" lacks a certain ring to it, and it is likewise difficult to imagine calling a Southern belle a "Georgia squash." And so, economic statistics aside, a Georgia peach will always be a Georgia peach, Georgia will always be the Peach State, and Lynyrd Skynyrd will still dig Georgia peaches—of one form or the other.

Georgia's history with the peach, a fruit that dates back to China in the 5th Century BC, began in approximately 1571, when Franciscan monks introduced the fruit, in addition to artichokes, citrus, figs, olives, and onions, at Spain's coastal missions running through St. Simon's and Cumberland Islands. Thanks in large part to the Cherokee and Creek Indians, the peach tree worked its way west into the state's interior, a fact noted by the famed naturalist William Bartram in the course of his travels across the Southeast at the time of the American Revolution. In fact, the land across which modern-day Atlanta sprawls was once referred to by the Indians as

Standing Peach Tree, after a lone tree atop a hill overlooking the Chattahoochee River.

Although American and European settlers followed the Indians' lead and began raising peaches in their own orchards, cotton remained king among Georgia's crops. It was not until 1851 that men like Raphael Moses, a lawyer and planter in Columbus, envisioned a commercial market for Georgia's peaches. Shortly thereafter, Macon nurseryman Robert Nelson shipped a box of Georgia peaches to New York in 1854, where the fruit sold for 50 cents a peach.

The promise of Northern markets, coupled with the realization—credited by many to Moses—that growers could successfully preserve the flavor of peaches by packing them in champagne baskets instead of in pulverized charcoal, spurred further exports. In the summer of 1858, a steamship departed Charleston stocked with thirty-four railroad cars' worth of Georgia and South Carolina–grown peaches. Upon arrival in New York, the peaches sold for between $3 and $15 a bushel.

The Civil War, however, deflated the booming peach industry, and, for his part, peach promoter Raphael Moses turned his attention to the Confederate cause. Although already fifty years old, he served as General James Longstreet's chief commissary officer and earned praise as "the best commissary officer of like rank in the Confederate service." When Moses' own death came on a business trip to Brussels, Belgium, in 1893, he was still carrying business cards that read, "Major Raphael J. Moses, CSA."

By then, Georgia's peach industry had recovered its antebellum promise, due in no small part to Samuel H. Rumph. In 1870, the Marshallville peach grower discovered a new, tastier, yellow-fleshed peach variety. Rumph named the new variety Elberta, after his wife. Devising cleverly partitioned packing crates and refrigerated railcars to keep his peaches fresh, Rumph helped ensure that his peaches would find hungry mouths outside of the state. Prosper J. A. Berckmans, a nurseryman who headed the Georgia State Horticultural Society, lent the society's efforts to the cause. Berckmans Nursery is now the site of the Augusta National Golf Club.

The efforts of men such as Rumph, Berckmans, and their progeny paralleled socioeconomic shifts in Georgia's agriculture that became more pronounced with each new generation. Cotton had long dominated the state as its premier cash crop. Cotton, however, not only placed harsh demands on Georgia's soil and its rural labor force but was also susceptible to the infamous boll weevil.

The profitable peach, on the other hand, with its high yields on relatively small parcels of land, seemed to offer a promising alternative. Soon, sprawling orchards sprouted in Crawford, Peach, Taylor, and Macon Counties. Those counties lie far enough north to receive sufficient winter chilling for the trees to go seasonally dormant, but they are far enough south to avoid late frosts and guarantee early harvest dates.

Over the years, as its peach industry grew, Georgia's inherent advantages in the production and marketing of the fruit became apparent. Proximity to the lucrative Northeastern and Midwestern markets was one. Favorable prices because of early harvests and high-quality fruit production was another. Buoyed by such factors, peach production in Georgia reached an all-time high of almost 8 million bushels by 1928.

The stock market crash of 1929, however, dealt Georgia's peach industry a blow from which it never fully recovered. By 1935, the state was no longer the nation's top peach producer. Today, the state's peach production is slightly over one-third of the 1928 numbers, although it encompasses over forty varieties of the fruit—one of which found its way onto Georgia's state quarter in 1999.

On that coin, the peach in question is centered within an outline of the state. A pair of live oak branches (the official state tree) frames the image, which is further adorned with a banner that proclaims the state's motto: "Wisdom, Justice, Moderation."

In at least one sense, though, too much moderation proved a bad thing. Rather than depict the whole of Georgia, the quarter's outline inexplicably cut out Dade County, in the far northwestern corner of the state. The omission was only the latest in a long series of slights suffered by Dade County over the years; for example, the mountainous county did not even have a reliable state highway connecting it to the rest of Georgia until 1948.

"The first I was ever aware that it looked that way was when an elderly gentleman showed [the quarter] to me," said Deborah Tinker, the director of Dade County's Chamber of Commerce. "He laughingly said he supposed Dade County was truly the "Independent State of Dade"—a reference to the county's long-standing nickname.

Such issues of cartography aside, the quarter's design evolved from five concepts developed by the Georgia Council on the Arts. Although Governor Zell Miller had the honor of selecting the final design in 1998, the unveiling of the quarter the following year fell to his gubernatorial successor, Governor Roy Barnes. "It perfectly depicts the grace and beauty of our state," Barnes declared at the quarter's launch ceremony in Atlanta on July 19, 1999. Whether or not Dade County's citizens agreed that it was a "perfect depict[ion]" is unrecorded. Nearly 940 million Georgia state quarters later, the question is probably moot anyway.

For her part, the current Miss Georgia Peach finds no fault with the quarter's design. She is Catheryn Shaw, originally of Perry, Georgia, and now a senior at Columbus State University. Crowned at the annual Peach Festival in Fort Valley, Shaw is, understandably, a staunch supporter of the quarter's prominent peach.

"I've lived in Georgia all my life," Shaw told me, "and peaches are such a big part of our state. After all, we're the Peach State, even if California and South Carolina produce more peaches. It's not a cliché. It's a proud tradition and it fits us perfectly."

All the same, today Georgia earns more than twice as much income from onions as it does from peaches. When I reminded her of that fact, Shaw simply laughed.

"I have a friend who is Miss Onion Capital," she reflected, referring to a pageant based in Vidalia, Georgia. "But I don't think I could ever bring myself to do that! I know onions are important, but it's just not the same as Miss Georgia Peach."

# 5

# CONNECTICUT
## *An Oak Grows in Hartford*

Connecticut's state quarter offers an elegantly simple design. The coin's reverse depicts a robust oak tree, its branches filling the quarter. "The Charter Oak," the coin offers by way of explanation. But unlike the iconic image of Washington crossing the Delaware displayed on the quarters of New Jersey, the lone tree requires more explanation.

The genesis of the image derives, more or less, from 1639. At the time, English settlement in the wide fertile valley that the local Pequot Indians called "Quinnehtukqut" consisted merely of three small, rival towns: Windsor, Wetherford, and Hartford. The travails of the bloody Pequot War, however, encouraged mutual defense and stoked further amity.

In 1639, their cooperation evolved into formal union as a single colonial endeavor, governed by the dictates of a document known as the Fundamental Orders of Connecticut. Under these Fundamental Orders, the colonists established qualifications for voting (which, despite the colony's Puritan ties to Massachusetts, did not expressly require church membership as a condition of suffrage) and elected their own governor and magistrates.

Buttressed by such democratic assurances, Connecticut's settlers turned confidently to the task of carving a vibrant colony out of the American wilderness. Their numbers included Samuel Wyllys, who established a large estate near Hartford and wasted little time in clear-cutting his newly claimed land. At the behest of local Indians, however, he spared a majestic white oak, revered by them as a symbol of an ancient peace treaty forged by their ancestors. In those early days of Connecticut's democracy, Wyllys could not imagine the role his oak—or his decision to spare it—would play in perpetuating that same democracy.

A generation later, in 1662, the bulwarks of Connecticut's self-government grew even stronger. King Charles II granted the colony an unusual royal charter. Rather than establishing firm British control over the colony, as was the case with so many of the other colonial charters, this one affirmed the colonists' ongoing political freedom and system of self-government as established by the Fundamental Orders. Not surprisingly, Connecticut's settlers cherished their charter, and to a large extent, it stoked the feisty streak of independence that characterized the colony's collection of small towns and settlements.

That same streak of independence ran headlong into the forces of history two decades later. King James II, seeking to consolidate his control over his North American colonies, merged Massachusetts, Rhode Island, New Hampshire, and Maine into a single province in

1686 under the rule of governor Sir Edmund Andros. This was the so-called Dominion of New England.

The fifty-year-old Andros was a stern, dictatorial, and short-tempered autocrat determined to oversee the dominion with an iron fist. As governor of New York several years earlier, he had failed in an attempt to expand his colony east into Connecticut when confronted with a defiant fort at Saybrook. Now, he thought, he had a golden opportunity to avenge his earlier humiliation as he archly ordered Connecticut's governor, Robert Treat, to surrender his colony's charter and send it to him in Boston.

Treat, however, had no such intention and firmly declined. In angry response, Andros mounted his steel-gray horse in late October 1687 and led a column of seventy scarlet-clad soldiers, armed to the teeth with muskets and pikes, to Hartford to seize the charter himself.

Andros's chagrin only increased when his militant arrival failed to produce the immediate surrender of the charter. Confronted with the colonists' intransigence but hesitant to resort to open violence, Andros fell into a heated debate at Moses Butler's tavern with Governor Treat and an assorted collection of assemblymen and magistrates. Even as the daylight faded and temperatures cooled outside, the argument inside grew ever more heated as Andros threatened to totally dismember Connecticut, with all of the colony's lands east of the Connecticut River to be annexed to Massachusetts and the western remainder to become part of New York. Resigned to enduring a lengthy debate, the tavern keeper lit a pair of candelabra to illuminate the scene.

Meanwhile, the subject of debate—the charter itself, which was housed in a box—was brought into the tavern. At that point, history merges, somewhat fuzzily, into legend—but the story, if one accepts the legend, becomes even more dramatic.

Upon the charter's arrival in the tavern, Andrew Leete, of Guilford, rose to his feet and, gesticulating angrily, warned that "measures obtained by force do not endure." Then, either by prearranged signal or purely by accident, Leete knocked over both candelabra, suddenly plunging the room into thick darkness. By the time they were lighted once more, the table was bare. Someone—some say Nathaniel Stanley, others John Talcott—had snatched the charter from under Andros's very nose and, according to legend, passed it out the window to Captain Joseph Wadsworth.

Wadsworth, a middle-aged officer in the local militia and a first-generation American, was a resolute, practical man, well respected within the local colonial community but with scant patience for outside interference or officious arrogance. If there was a man capable of seizing the moment by seizing the charter, it was certainly Wadsworth.

As chaos erupted inside the tavern, Wadsworth darted across town, picking his way through the darkness to the Wyllys estate, where the charter had originally been stored. Clearly, however, Andros would search the Wyllys's home. A better hiding place had to be picked, and soon.

Fortunately, Ruth Wyllys offered a clever suggestion—to hide it in the ancient oak tree down the hill from the main house. Taking her advice, Wadsworth stuffed the charter, wrapped in his coat, into a crevice at the base of the tree. In doing so, he secured not only the charter but his own place in Connecticut's historical lore. Some historians call his and his accomplices' larceny the first act of civil disobedience in Britain's North American colonies.

Despite Wadsworth's good intentions, his seizure of the charter was little more than a symbolic gesture. Ignoring Hartford's defiance, Andros proceeded to absorb Connecticut into the Dominion of New England's autocratic fold. Nevertheless, Andros's rule lasted little more than a year. When the Glorious Revolution deposed James II in England, Andros's own days were numbered. A coup d'état toppled his regime shortly after James lost the throne, and in 1689, Connecticut's charter was restored. After a brief intermission in England, Andros returned to North America to govern the colonies of Virginia and Maryland, albeit with scarcely more success.

Meanwhile, as the years passed, the charter's erstwhile hiding place became known as the "Charter Oak." Already ancient in Wadsworth's time, it stood for another 150 years before being toppled by a ferocious storm on August 21, 1856. That same day, Hartford draped an American flag over the splintered trunk and placed an honor guard around the tree's shattered remains. Colt's Band of Hartford performed a solemn funeral dirge and, as the day drew to an end, all of the city's church bells chimed in mourning.

Such sentiment soon gave way to souvenir hunting. Before long, wood from the oak was being used to fashion a variety of keepsakes, including the chair used by the Speaker of the House in Connecticut's General Assembly. Confronted with the multitude of such relics when he came to live in Hartford fifteen years later, Mark Twain declared that there were so many of them that they could all be lumped together and used as supports for the city's Charter Oak Bridge over the Connecticut River.

Twain's cynicism aside, the oak remained firmly rooted in the hearts and minds of Connecticut's population as a living symbol of their rights as free citizens. The development of a design for Connecticut's state quarter provided ample proof of the felled oak's staying power. Of 112 design concepts submitted in 1998 in response to a statewide contest, nineteen featured renditions of the Charter Oak. The Connecticut Commission on the Arts selected five of those submissions and forwarded them to the U.S. Mint. The Mint returned three designs to Governor John Rowland for the state's ultimate consideration.

In response, the Connecticut Commemorative Coin Design Competition Review Committee, with the governor's approval, unanimously selected the final design, conceived by W. Andy Jones, currently an art professor at Eastern Connecticut State University.

Because of Jones's work, and that of U.S. Mint engraver Jim Ferrell, on October 7, 1999, the Charter Oak grew once more—this time on the state's quarter as the first Connecticut quarter was struck. Over 1.3 billion would follow.

Ironically, that massive quantity stands in marked contrast to Captain Wadsworth's financial remuneration for his good deed. In 1715, Connecticut's General Court awarded the daring Captain Wadsworth the sum of twenty shillings "upon consideration of faithful and good service . . . especially in securing the . . . charter, in a very troublesome season, when our constitution was struck at." Converted into modern U.S. currency, that amount would be approximately $225—or 900 Connecticut state quarters.

# 6

# MASSACHUSETTS
## *Just a Minute*

In 1837, Ralph Waldo Emerson penned "The Concord Hymn." To commemorate the Revolutionary War battles at Lexington and Concord on April 19, 1775, Emerson wrote of "embattled farmers" firing "the shot heard 'round the world" and sacrificing their lives to "leave their children free." Two hundred and twenty-four years later, a pair of Massachusetts schoolchildren recognized that same birthright when they submitted the winning design concept for Massachusetts' state quarter. Their design focused on Concord's famed Minuteman Statue, which stands by the village's North Bridge.

The bronze Minuteman Statue should not be confused with Lexington's statue, which some historical purists stress is not really a statue of a "minuteman" at all, because it represents a member of a force that insisted on calling itself militia. Concord's statue, however, does indeed depict a minuteman, with a plow at his feet to remind the viewer of his livelihood and a musket in his hand to demonstrate his martial defiance.

Daniel Chester French, who, like Emerson, called Concord home, sculpted the statue. Until he was commissioned to create the work in 1873, the talented twenty-two-year-old had never sculpted a bronze statue, much less a life-size one. Nevertheless, French set about sculpting a likeness of Captain Isaac Davis, one of the minutemen killed on the North Bridge. In French's eyes, Davis was the logical choice to symbolize the approximately fifty colonists who lost their lives in the fighting at Lexington and Concord.

Somewhat ironically, however, Davis was not from Concord. Rather, he commanded a company of minutemen from nearby Acton. Nor was he an "embattled farmer." Instead, Davis was a gunsmith by trade, a fortunate choice of profession that contributed significantly to his ability to outfit his company of minutemen with well-crafted muskets.

The existence of such minutemen and their stores of armaments were, by the spring of 1775, increasingly disconcerting to Great Britain. By April, King George III and his ministers had had enough. They ordered the royal governor of Massachusetts, Major General Sir Thomas Gage, to seize the colonists' growing caches of weapons and ammunition.

Gage wasted little time in acting. On the evening of April 18, 1775, a force of between 700 and 800 British troops—infantry, grenadiers, and marines—mustered on Boston Common. Under the command of Lieutenant Colonel Francis Smith, their mission was to destroy the collection of military stores gathered in Concord, twenty miles west of Boston. By 10:00 PM, the redcoats were boarding boats to be ferried across the Charles River to begin what they hoped would be a surprise raid.

Surprise, however, proved impossible to achieve. The colonists, forewarned by unusual British mounted patrols outside of Boston and perhaps even by Gage's American-born wife, Margaret, had already surmised that military action was imminent. But it was the "midnight ride" of Paul Revere, William Dawes, and, later, Samuel Prescott, that helped spread immediate word of the coming excursion into the surrounding countryside.

Meanwhile, the redcoats disembarked in waist-deep water, waded ashore at Cambridge, and regrouped in the unfriendly darkness. Then, burdened with heavy packs and sodden boots, they began their march at 2:00 AM. Sensing trouble with his slow-moving column, Smith pushed forward a force of ten light companies under the command of John Pitcairn, a major in the Royal Marines.

On the village green at Lexington, Pitcairn's vanguard found a company of seventy-five militiamen, under the command of John Parker, assembled to meet their force's advance. Parker, a veteran of the French and Indian War, was battling the tuberculosis that would claim his life a few months later. Nevertheless, he arrayed his small militia company in a single file across the village green. Parker did not actually block the redcoats' advance, but his collection of armed militiamen presented a clear threat to the British line of communications.

"Stand your ground," Parker exhorted his men as the first British companies marched into Lexington. "Don't fire unless fired upon, but if they mean to have a war, let it begin here." His words may be apocryphal, but they became legendary nevertheless.

"Disperse, you rebels; damn you, throw down your arms and disperse!" Pitcairn shouted in reply. From there, the tense confrontation unfolded with tragic effect. Someone—his identity, Briton or colonist, has never been ascertained—fired his weapon, even as Parker's company began to slowly disperse. Responding instinctively, the redcoats unleashed a ferocious volley and then charged with the bayonet. As the smoke cleared from the small battlefield, it revealed that eight dead and ten wounded Americans lay on the ground.

Undeterred, the British pressed on for Concord. Local companies of minutemen and militia, loosely under the command of James Barrett, gathered initially at Concord, but in the face of the advancing columns of redcoats, they ceded the village to the British. The Americans' numbers included Davis's company from Acton, and for a time, they simply observed the British occupy Concord from afar. For their part, the British began searching the village, burning gun carriages, and dispatching smaller raiding parties into the surrounding countryside.

As the morning wore on, the colonial militia and minutemen spotted smoke curling into the sky above Concord. Spurred to action, Barrett ordered his 500 troops forward. Arrayed in a pair of files, they advanced toward the Old North Bridge and the Concord River. Two outnumbered companies of redcoats withdrew in good order, retreated over the Old North Bridge, and fell in with their comrades to hold the crossing.

The Americans, however, moved ever closer. Pressing forward toward the bridge, they were met with a crashing volley of musket fire. Captain Isaac Davis fell dead, his company's wounded fifer falling alongside him. Undeterred, Davis's comrades continued their advance to within fifty yards of the British position and, firing over the bridge's span, unleashed an even deadlier volley. Their gunfire killed four of the British officers; the demoralized redcoats beat a hasty retreat from the charging colonists.

Worried, Smith consolidated his dispersed force and moved back into Concord; by noon, they began the long march back to Boston. At this point, an estimated 1,000 militia had taken the field and, for the redcoats who had already marched twenty miles that morning, the road home was a much harder one to travel. Mile by mile, they battled through one skirmish and ambush after another. Even Smith fell wounded, shot in the thigh. At this point, the British situation was becoming increasingly precarious and, at times, threatened to deteriorate into a rout. And as if the defiant militia companies were not bad enough, individual snipers began to take their toll on the redcoats as well.

By 2:30 that afternoon, Smith's troops—exhausted, thirsty, and running low on ammunition—were approaching not only Lexington but also the end of their physical and emotional endurance. Even the officer in the vanguard of the retreat was considering surrender when, to his front, he heard cheering. A thousand British soldiers and marines, supported by artillery, had marched out to rescue Smith's raid. Leaving Boston, their musicians had mockingly played "Yankee Doodle" to taunt their opponents. Now, their long-range cannon fire dispersed Smith's pursuers and allowed the British to reorganize their battered ranks.

Even then, however, the beleaguered British were still a long way from the safety of Boston. Several more hard hours of fighting followed before the exhausted redcoats limped into Charlestown under the covering guns of the Royal Navy's ships. For the British, it was an inauspicious beginning to six years of conflict that would, in turn, lead to the loss of its American colonies and the creation of an independent United States. In the more immediate term, the raid on Concord had netted Gage little more than 273 casualties, including seventy-three killed. In turn, approximately fifty colonists lost their lives.

For his part, Daniel French enjoyed a far happier experience with Concord. The success of "The Minuteman" propelled him to a long and successful career. He studied abroad in Italy, opened a studio in Washington, D.C., and again returned to Europe. More ambitious projects followed, including a statue of Ohioan Lewis Cass for the U.S. Capitol's National Statuary Hall. By the turn of the century, French was one of America's foremost sculptors, and in 1922, he completed perhaps his most memorable work—the statue of Abraham Lincoln seated in the Lincoln Memorial. French died in 1931 and, fittingly, is buried in Concord.

French's legacy, however—and that of Captain Isaac Davis and his fellow minutemen—survives in more than bronze statuary or Emerson's prose. Rather, it can be found on the almost 1.164 billion quarters that commemorate the Bay State, largely because of the efforts of a seventh-grader from Belmont Day School and a sixth-grader from St. Bernard's Elementary. The pair were just two of over 100 elementary students who entered a statewide contest, submitting design concepts to Governor Paul Cellucci and a ten-person advisory council. Besting the competition, the pair's design graced the coins released into circulation on January 3, 2000—the first state quarters of the new millennium.

## 7

# MARYLAND

## *The Oldest Line in the Book*

Maryland's design for its state quarter easily claims the title of the most symmetrical of the state quarters. On the quarter's reverse, the distinctive narrow cupola of Maryland's state capitol juts sharply upward, bisecting the coin, while neatly flanked by a pair of white oak branches, Maryland's state tree.

"In our view, the statehouse best favors Maryland's rich history, and the unique role the state has played in our nation's history," explained Governor Parris Glendening, speaking of the design submitted by Bill Krawczewicz. The seventeen-member Maryland Commemorative Coin Committee had evaluated design submissions submitted from across the state that included such iconic images as Fort McHenry and the pair of ships—the *Ark* and the *Dove*—that brought Maryland's first colonists to its shores. The committee narrowed Glendening's options down to five selections, and in the end, the statehouse design prevailed.

Seemingly in keeping with the geometric theme, the quarter proclaims Maryland as "The Old Line State." Although the cupola is readily identifiable, the origin of the nickname "The Old Line State" is less obvious. Nor was its path to the quarter particularly clear.

Krawczewicz's original vision for the quarter relied simply on the image of the state capitol. But the winning concept was too stark for Tom Rogers, an engraver with the U.S. Mint tasked with implementing the chosen design. Accordingly, he added the clusters of white oak and the words "The Old Line State."

Later, when questioned by the *Washington Post* regarding the origin of the phrase, Rogers reportedly explained that he "pulled it out of a book or off the Internet someplace . . . I know I got it somewhere official." But when the U.S. Mint unveiled the new quarter in Annapolis in the very same building depicted on its reverse, many a Marylander wanted a more definite answer.

"It's one of the oldest monikers we've ever had," Maryland state archivist Edward C. Papenfuse told the *Post.* He proceeded to trace it to the Revolutionary War, when the steadfast performance of Maryland's troops earned the sobriquet "the old line" from none other than General George Washington. The American commander, Papenfuse explained, could always count on his reliable men from Maryland. The earning of that nickname, however, came at a stiff price.

In the early days of the American Revolution, the cities of Baltimore and Annapolis raised and outfitted an infantry battalion of militia. Reflecting on the volunteers he commanded, Mordecai Gist described his company as "composed of gentlemen of honor, family, and fortune and, though of different countries, animated by a zeal and reverence for the rights of humanity." Gist's gentlemen rankers poetically committed themselves to the revolutionary cause with "sacred ties of honor and love and justice."

The so-called Maryland Battalion's nine well-equipped companies quickly earned a well-deserved reputation as one of the best-trained, best-disciplined units fielded by any of the colonies. Bedecked in gold-buttoned scarlet coats trimmed in buff, and armed to the teeth with muskets, cutlasses, and braces of pistols, the battalion contrasted handsomely with the levies of enthusiastic but unorganized volunteers that so many of the other colonies were providing the Continental Army.

On July 17, 1776, the battalion, 1,000 strong and under the command of William Smallwood, marched to join what Washington was already calling the "American continental army." As they arrived in Philadelphia, they were, according to one observer, "distinguished by the most fashionably cut coat[s], the most macaroni cocked hat[s], and the hottest blood in the union."

The well-heeled Marylanders, however, were more than simply elegant parade-ground soldiers, and Washington wasted little time in dispatching them to join the Continental Army's defense of New York City. That defense relied on a partially fortified cordon that stretched across Long Island's rugged and thickly wooded Brooklyn Heights. Washington assigned his newly arrived Marylanders to William Stirling's brigade. They filed into position on the Continental Army's right flank on the Gowanus Road. Intent on the deadly business at hand, they traded their handsome scarlet coats for hunting shirts and prepared for battle.

That battle was not long in coming. After landing on Long Island on August 22, the British and their Hessian allies moved against the Continental forces five days later. At 3:00 AM on August 27, British redcoats pushed their way into the Gowanus Pass, driving panicked militiamen before them.

Rallying, the militiamen forced the advancing British column to deploy into a battle line. In doing so, they gave Stirling the precious opportunity to bring his brigade, including the Maryland Battalion and equally disciplined soldiers from Delaware, into position to square off against the British regulars. With Smallwood on court-martial duty in New York City, the Marylanders were under Gist's command.

Lined up in neat rows 200 yards apart, the Continentals and the British coolly traded vicious volleys. Outnumbered, Stirling's men withdrew in good order for a few hundred yards until reinforced by the stiffening presence of a battalion of Pennsylvania troops. Then, for the next hour, the American troops held their ground, twice beating back the charges of the enemy infantry. For a time, it seemed that the Continental Army was holding its own against the vaunted British opponents.

Tragically, that success was deceptive. A stealthy night march by the British slipped through the undefended Jamaica Pass on Washington's far left flank. By midmorning, the hard-marching British were behind the American lines, threatening to cut off their retreat back into the city. As soon as the Americans realized their predicament, their defenses along the Brooklyn Heights crumbled like a house of cards. Panicked soldiers fled pell-mell, desperate to reach the comparative safety of Brooklyn's fortified defenses.

Nevertheless, on the far right flank, the Maryland Battalion and their stalwart comrades from Pennsylvania, Connecticut, and Delaware stood their ground. Outnumbered by nearly six to one, they fought on until 11:00 AM, when another British frontal assault coincided with a charge of Hessians sweeping in from the right. The unexpected appearance of the Hessians convinced Stirling that the day was lost. Nevertheless, he had bought hundreds of his fellow Continentals the time to beat a safe retreat.

Disengaging his brigade from the fight, Stirling retreated down the Gowanus Road. He soon realized, however, that a British division under Lord Cornwallis blocked his escape route to Brooklyn. Now, the only escape route was along the coast, through a tidal marsh and a muddy creek, and the British were moving forward to cut off that route as well.

Determined to buy the men time to negotiate the marsh, Stirling, Gist, and a band of 250 Marylanders hurled themselves repeatedly at Cornwallis's superior force. Five times, a blaze of musket fire drove them back. But each time, Stirling and Gist rallied their troops and struck again and again, fighting with a remarkable fury.

"Good God, what brave fellows I must this day lose," Washington exclaimed as he watched the Maryland Battalion's ferocious charges. Later, looking back on the battalion's stubborn delaying action, he described it as an "hour more precious to American liberty than any other." Few of the Marylanders survived to learn of such praise. By one account, only Gist and nine others managed to make it back to the American lines the next day.

As 1776 passed into 1777, Washington's staff reorganized the battle-scarred remnants of the Maryland Battalion, complemented by new recruits, into what became known as the First Maryland Regiment. In Washington's mind, though, the unit that had saved his army on Long Island was "the old line"—in the military jargon of the day, regiments were often referred to as "lines." The American commander often referred to it as such throughout his correspondence with the Maryland General Assembly, General William Smallwood, Governor Thomas Johnson, and others. He also complimented Maryland for providing more than the state's quota of soldiers for the Continental Army.

By 1780, another reorganization occurred, and the "old Maryland line" became the First and Second Maryland Regiments. It also became the backbone of Nathaniel Greene's southern army operating in the Carolinas. At the Battle of Cowpens, the Second Maryland once again held the line—this time in furtherance of an American victory rather than a desperate retreat. In all, the Old Line saw hard fighting at such battles as Trenton, Princeton, White Plains,

Brandywine, Germantown, Monmouth, Camden, and Guilford Courthouse.

After the war, the young republic entered an uneasy adolescence, threatened by partisan politics and divisive growing pains. Looking hopefully for unifying images of a triumphant past, Americans found one in the form of the "Old Line." And even as the revolutionary generation and veterans of the Old Line passed from the scene, all Marylanders could declare themselves to be citizens of the Old Line State—as Maryland's state quarter reminded them all once again on March 13, 2000, when the first of the almost 1.235 billion coins was issued.

<br>

## SOUTH CAROLINA
### *Palmetto Proud*

South Carolina is another state that, like Pennsylvania, relied on an amalgamation of symbols for its quarter design—and created a difficult task for an author left to craft a chapter about a bird, a flower, and a palm tree. Fortunately, however, one can, with a little bit of research, find an amazing story behind that simple palm.

The tree in question is a palmetto palm (also known as the common palmetto, the Carolina palmetto, or, scientifically, *Sabal palmetto*). Another name is cabbage palm, called that because of its edible bud, which reportedly tastes somewhat like cabbage whether eaten raw or cooked. These palms are the most northerly and abundant of America's native palm trees. They are widespread across Florida (where it is the state tree) but can also be found along the coasts of Georgia and the Carolinas—particularly on such coastal islands as Sullivan's Island.

For its part, Sullivan's Island, named for its late-seventeenth-century lighthouse keeper, Captain Florence O'Sullivan, stands at the entrance of Charleston Harbor. Accordingly, the navigational relevance of that island goes hand in hand with its military significance. Control Sullivan's Island and you controlled the way into—and out of—Charleston. Defend Sullivan's Island, and you defended Charleston.

In 1776, defending Charleston was of no small import. Not only was it America's fourth-largest city, but it was also the gateway to South Carolina, the British Crown's richest North American possession. Not surprisingly, in the wake of their rude ejection from Boston early that spring, Great Britain's military leaders turned their attention south.

On June 2, 1776, British warships gathered off Sullivan's Island. From on board his flagship HMS *Bristol*, Sir Peter Parker commanded a flotilla of twenty warships and troop transports. Nearly 3,000 redcoats and Royal Marines accompanied the expedition under the command of Sir Henry Clinton. In all, it was a formidable expeditionary force, defied only by a half-completed fort on Sullivan's Island commanded by Colonel William Moultrie.

Moultrie was a forty-six-year-old native of Charleston. He served ably in the colony's 1761 expedition against the Cherokees, earning military experience that served him well in the coming years. Although a moderate, he supported revolution and was elected to the First Continental Congress in 1774. Later, in 1775, he was commissioned as a colonel in the Second South Carolina Regiment and, at the outbreak of the Revolution, was the second-in-command of Charleston's defenses. Fortifying Sullivan's Island was Moultrie's responsibility.

Moultrie's assignment proved a formidable task. Constructing a fort was the first logical defensive step. The stone necessary for a fort, however, was a scarce commodity on Sullivan's Island. Undeterred, the resourceful Moultrie made do with the resources on hand—namely, palmetto trees and sand. Using palmetto logs, he built two parallel walls sixteen feet apart and filled the gap with sand. By the time the British fleet appeared, only the south and east walls were complete, leaving what was christened Fort Sullivan little more than an L-shaped fortification with a paltry twenty-six cannons.

Two days later, Major General Charles Lee, appointed by George Washington to command the Continental Army's Southern Department, arrived on the scene. Surveying the British warships gathered offshore and the incomplete status of the fort, Lee ordered Fort Sullivan abandoned. But South Carolina's governor, John Rutledge, was determined to defend Charleston. He overruled Lee and ordered Moultrie to stand by his post.

Moultrie needed little further encouragement, and now committed to the defense of the island, the 425 men under his command redoubled their efforts. With pick and shovel, they labored under the watchful eye of such officers as Francis Marion, who would later gain renown as the fabled "Swamp Fox," and Thomas Sumter, who, for his part, would later lend his name to another famous fort. Another group, under the command of William Thomson, threw up makeshift fortifications on the northeastern side of the island to face the narrow strait of water that separated it from nearby Long Island.

Undeterred, Clinton landed his redcoats on Long Island, whence they hoped to ford the strait between the two islands and flank the colonists' defenses from the northeast. In the meantime, Sir Parker dispatched three of his warships, including the twenty-eight-gun HMS *Acteon*, on a flanking run around Sullivan Island's western side. Once behind the island, the ships could fire into the unprotected rear of the fort.

There is an old military proverb, however, that declares that few military plans survive their first contact with the enemy. That axiom certainly proved true when the British launched their attack on June 28. *Acteon* and the other British ships ran aground in the treacherous shallow water when they attempted to slip around to Fort Sullivan's rear. Two of His Majesty's ships managed to free themselves and escape to open water; *Acteon*, however, was abandoned and partially scuttled by its embarrassed skipper.

As the Royal Navy's attack floundered, the British assault from Long Island failed as well. Foiled by shoulder-deep water, treacherous tides, and Thomson's steady marksmen behind their own makeshift fortifications, the redcoats beat a waterlogged retreat. The pair of repulses left Parker with little choice but to slug it out directly with Moutrie's gunners inside Fort Sullivan.

For ten hours, the Royal Navy's guns barked and flashed, hurling shell after shell over the white-capped surf to smash into Moultrie's fort. The fort's palmetto-log walls, however, proved remarkably resilient. In fact, some cannonballs simply bounced off the spongy palmetto logs. Even when hit more forcefully, the logs simply absorbed the impact without shattering into deadly splinters.

Nevertheless, the British gunfire took its toll. At one point, a shell knocked down the garrison's flagpole. The colony's flag—a blue banner sporting a white crescent—fluttered ignominiously to the ground. In Charleston, where the city's citizens watched the battle through telescopes and spyglasses, a collective groan met the sight. Groans soon turned to cheers, however, when Sergeant William Jasper sprang into action.

"Colonel, don't let us fight without our flag!" Jasper reportedly shouted. Clambering to the fort's rude ramparts, he jumped outside the fort's walls and, under heavy British fire, cut the flag from its fallen pole. He then climbed back inside the fort, fastened the banner to an artillerist's sponge-staff, and planted the makeshift flagpole defiantly back atop the fort.

Suitably inspired, Moultrie's outnumbered gunners continued to trade shots with the ships offshore. As the afternoon wore on, their gunfire began to take its toll on the fort's attackers. An American cannonball crashed into *Bristol*, wounding Lord William Campbell, the colony's ousted royal governor, with a jagged splinter in his side from which he never recovered. Another splinter slashed across the back of Parker's breeches, exposing his backside to an amused crew.

By 9:30 that evening, the wounded Parker had had enough. Leaning on a pair of sailors for support, he ordered his crews to cease firing and, shortly before midnight, slipped away into the Atlantic darkness. Behind him, he left Charleston safe and *Acteon* ablaze, abandoned to the victorious colonists. British military historian Sir John Fortescue admitted ruefully that the defense of Charleston was an accomplishment on which the rebels "might justly plume themselves on their success."

Observing the scene from Charleston, the more poetic of the colonial observers claimed that the smoke rising from the burning *Acteon* looked like a giant palmetto palm. Such symbolism soon worked its way onto South Carolina's flag, where a palmetto tree joined the white crescent to represent the Carolinians' defiance.

Unfortunately, Charleston did not fare as well four years later when the British returned. After a two-month siege, the city, along with Fort Moultrie, fell to British control, under which it remained until the end of the Revolution. The fall of Charleston in 1780 gave all the more reason to remember the happier outcome of its earlier fight for freedom.

The brave Sergeant Jasper fared equally poorly. In 1779, his regiment joined a combined band of Continental, French, and free Haitian forces that tried unsuccessfully to recapture Savannah from the British. In one of the final assaults on the fortified defenses, Jasper went to the aid of his regiment's fallen banner. That time, however, he paid for his heroism with his life.

Generations later, an outpouring of design suggestions for South Carolina's state quarter reflected the love that later generations of South Carolinians shared with Jasper for their native state. Winnowing the slate of suggestions to five, South Carolina submitted the semifi-nalists to the Citizens Commemorative Coin Advisory Committee and the Fine Arts Commission. The committee and commission, in turn, narrowed these five semifinalist design concepts down to three choices for Governor Jim Hodges's consideration.

In the end, Governor Hodges selected the design that graces the quarters today. At its launch ceremony on May 26, 2000, he declared, "These state emblems symbolize what is best about South Carolina. The Palmetto tree represents our strength. The song of the Carolina wren symbolizes the hospitality of our people. And the Yellow Jes-samine flower is part of the vast natural beauty of our state."

# 9

# NEW HAMPSHIRE
## *Rock . . . and Roll*

In the whole of the 50 State Quarters® Program, it is difficult to find a more bitter piece of irony than New Hampshire's decision to depict the fabled Old Man of the Mountain on the reverse of its state quarter. Within three years of the Granite State's commemoration of the distinctive rock formation on its coin in 2000, the Old Man was little more than a pile of granite rubble.

Its ultimate fate aside, it is difficult to fault New Hampshire's choice for its state quarter. A surveying crew, working the mountainous region of Franconia Notch, discovered what was soon christened the "Old Man of the Mountain" on Mount Cannon in 1805. In doing so, they became the first—other than the region's Native Americans, of course—to marvel at its craggy visage.

Upon scaling Mount Cannon, the surveyors were able to inspect the formation even more closely. They determined that it consisted of five separate ledges of Conway red granite, approximately forty feet high and twenty feet wide, formed in such a way to create the appearance of a man's face if viewed from the side. Geographers would later surmise that the layers of granite were formed by the melting and subsequent movement of an ice sheet that covered the Franconia Mountains at the end of its last glacial period, a time they dated as 2,000 to 10,000 years earlier.

Famed New Hampshire son Daniel Webster offered a more poetic and philosophical explanation of the remarkable rock formation. Reflecting on the Old Man of the Mountain, Webster offered a signature piece of prose. "Men," he said, "hang out their signs indicative of their respective trades; shoemakers hang out a gigantic shoe; jewelers a monster watch, and the dentist hangs out a gold tooth; but in the mountains of New Hampshire, God Almighty has hung out a sign to show that there He makes men."

In 1905, 100 years after the rock formation's discovery, a sharp-eyed clergyman named Guy Roberts recognized that trouble loomed for the Old Man. The Old Man's forehead, it seemed, was slipping down and toward the valley below. After several years of puzzling over the problem, a series of turnbuckles—large cable devices used in quarries to secure rocks—were installed in 1916 to stabilize the formation. Initially, the tactic proved very successful, and years passed without any measurable movement being detected.

Meanwhile, New Hampshire established Franconia Notch as a state park in 1928 and, in 1945, elected to make the Old Man of the Mountain the official state emblem. Within a decade, however, the state realized that its emblem was deteriorating and that, in particular, a crack at the top of the head was widening. In 1958, repair work and preventative maintenance on the Old Man included the installation of four new turnbuckles, the waterproofing of the crack, and the digging of a drainage ditch to divert water away from the top of the formation.

In 1960, not only did annual inspections of the Old Man of the Mountain begin, but Niels F. F. Nielsen, Jr., an employee of the state's highway department, became the Old Man's official caretaker. In later years his son, David, assumed that role, and between the two of them, they maintained a careful watch on the Old Man's rocky profile, repairing and securing it as necessary, often going over the edge of the formation in carefully rigged boatswain's chairs. The elder Nielsen paid his last visit to the Old Man in 1989; he passed away in 2001. Quite appropriately, Nielsen's son, David, and his wife, Deborah, managed to bury some of Nielsen's ashes in the Old Man's left eye.

By then, no doubt to Nielsen's satisfaction, the Old Man to whom he had devoted so many years of work was already gracing the reverse of roughly 1.169 billion quarters around the country. New Hampshire's Commemorative Quarter Committee—convened by Governor Jeanne Shaheen and consisting of representatives of the state's Department of Cultural Affairs, art educators, numismatists, historical society members, politicians, and private citizens—had selected a design concept for the state quarter following a statewide contest for the same.

The winning quarter design provided a left profile of the Old Man; the state motto, "Live Free or Die"; and a collection of nine stars, signifying that New Hampshire was the ninth state to ratify the U.S. Constitution. It trumped such other iconic images of New Hampshire as a colonial-era meeting house and a covered bridge.

"The New Hampshire quarter is a fitting tribute to our state's beauty and history," Governor Shaheen said at the quarter's launch ceremony on August 7, 2000. "The Old Man of the Mountain is one of New Hampshire's most recognized and beloved images. Our state motto, 'Live Free or Die,' epitomizes our state's proud tradition of freedom and independence. The New Hampshire quarter will give the rest of the nation a sense of New Hampshire's natural beauty, its rich history, and the character of our people."

Less than three years later, however, disaster struck. On the morning of May 3, 2003, a pair of state park employees looked up to misty Mount Cannon and realized that the iconic rock formation had collapsed.

"The Old Man of the Mountain, the enduring symbol of the state of New Hampshire, is no more," said the New Hampshire Division of Parks and Recreation. "The weather has been extremely harsh in Franconia Notch over the last few days. High winds, fog, and heavy rain, along with freezing temperatures overnight, may all have contributed to the collapse, although no official cause can be determined until a full inspection of the site takes place."

In the end, therefore, the motto "Live Free or Die" may prove to be more enduring than the massive chunk of granite that formed the Old Man. For that phrase, the residents of New Hampshire can thank General John Stark, a native son and one of Washington's most capable officers. Stark fought at such early battles as Bunker Hill and Trenton. Later, in 1777, he led the successful defense of Bennington, Vermont, an important engagement that denied the British much-needed supplies and helped contribute to their defeat at Saratoga latter that summer.

Stark survived the Revolution to become one of the Continental Army's last surviving generals. In 1809, approaching the age of seventy-nine and too old to travel, he sent a stirring toast to his old comrades gathering to celebrate the anniversary of the Battle of Bennington: "Live free or die," Stark declared. "Death is not the worst of evils."

Stark's words became part of New Hampshire's historic lore, and in 1945, New Hampshire adopted them as the state motto. In 1969, the state emblazoned the motto on its license plates. But even such noble rhetoric can prove vulnerable—as an ensuing legal battle demonstrated.

In the winter of 1974 to 1975, a Jehovah's Witness, George Maynard, was arrested three times—and even jailed—for repeatedly concealing the phrase on his own license plate. "I refuse to be coerced by the State into advertising a slogan which I find morally, ethically, religiously and politically abhorrent," he stated.

Appealing to the local federal district court, Maynard argued that, ironically, New Hampshire was violating his First Amendment right to free speech. The district court agreed, which sparked New Hampshire to appeal his case to the U.S. Supreme Court.

In Washington, D.C., a six-justice majority of the Court agreed, holding that New Hampshire could not constitutionally require an individual such as Maynard to participate in the dissemination of an ideological message by displaying it on his private property. "The First Amendment protects the right of individuals to hold a point of view different from the majority and to refuse to foster, in the way New Hampshire commands, an idea they find morally objection-able," the majority wrote.

And so, in the end, New Hampshire's state quarter leaves us with a simple moral: Even granite rock can be rolled by the weather, and even a Revolutionary War hero can be foiled by a majority of the Supreme Court.

# 10

# VIRGINIA
## *The Other Three Ships*

In the pantheon of historic sailing ships, the *Nina, Pinta,* and *Santa Maria* roll readily off the tongues of American school children. Three other ships—specifically, the *Discovery, Susan Constant,* and *Godspeed*—deserve similar respect, but they will have to settle for being featured on the reverse of Virginia's state quarter. That coin honors them for delivering the first colonists to Jamestown, a colonial settlement whose quadricentennial Virginia celebrated in 2007.

It is entirely fitting to commemorate Jamestown on currency. At its heart, the colony was simply a calculated commercial endeavor. As historian David Price noted pithily in his book *Love and Hate in Jamestown:*

*John Smith, Pocahontas, and the Heart of a New Nation,* "English America was a corporation before it was a country." In 1606, the British Crown granted letters of patent to The Society of Adventurers to establish a pair of settlements in North America. The society formed two joint stock companies—the Virginia Company of Plymouth and the Virginia Company of London—and sold shares in their companies at approximately $2,750 per share at modern exchange rates. The Society of Adventurers was, in short, venture capitalism in the truest sense of the phrase.

Eager to recoup such investments, the Virginia Company of London cobbled together an expedition of 105 settlers. According to a contemporary account, some of those men seemed to be the stuff of a successful colony. The group included a mason, several laborers, carpenters, bricklayers, a fisherman, a pair of surgeons, a preacher, a barber, and even a drummer. Several soldiers joined them as well, among them Captain John Smith, a lowly farmer's son who had carved out hard-won experience fighting in the Netherlands against the Spanish and later as a mercenary battling the Turks in Hungary. Smith was a competent and energetic officer, well-equipped because of his experiences on Europe's distant battlefields for the challenges and rigors of a new frontier.

Far too many of the colonists, however, simply listed their occupation as "gentleman." They were idle dandies who, in the words of one contemporary chronicler, "daily vexed their fathers' hearts at home." Shockingly unprepared for life on a distant frontier and hostile shore, their hearts burned with the delusional hope of discovering gold for the easy taking on North America's shores. For leadership, these men looked initially to Edward-Maria Wingfield, a well-born lawyer, military officer, and charter member of the Virginia Company, for leadership. Despite that pedigree, Wingfield lasted less than a year in the New World. Nevertheless, he would count himself as among the fortunate ones. He lived to see England once again. The vast majority of the men who sailed with him would not.

For the dangerous transatlantic voyage to Virginia, the expedition could count on the leadership of the famed privateer Christopher Newport, commander of a modest fleet that consisted of the ships *Susan Constant, Godspeed,* and *Discovery*. At 116 feet in length, the *Susan Constant* was the largest and carried seventy-one sailors and colonists. The *Godspeed*, crewed by thirteen sailors and carrying thirty-nine colonists, was a smaller ship, at only sixty-eight feet in length. The brigantine's usable deck space was really only fifteen feet wide and fifty-four feet long. The pinnace *Discovery*, crowded with twenty-one men, was even tinier.

Newport's three ships left London on December 20, 1606. Five months later, they reached Virginia. For his new settlement, Wingfield picked a site on a marshy peninsula along the James River. The colonists—minus an unfortunate comrade (one of the expedition's "gentlemen") who had died of dehydration on a hunting expedition on a Caribbean island—disembarked on May 14, 1607, and on a modest spot so unassuming that even the local Indians scorned it, they founded Jamestown.

Although Jamestown was destined to become the first successful English settlement in North America, such success seemed far from certain. Two weeks after the colonists landed, an Indian attack nearly overwhelmed the nascent settlement and encouraged the hasty construction of a rough triangular fort while Newport sailed back to England for more supplies. As the summer wore on, over half of the colonists succumbed to disease and malnutrition. Meanwhile, a second expedition, financed by the Virginia Company of Plymouth and led by George Popham, managed to establish a colony on Maine's Monhegan Island. Beset by a brutal winter, it lasted barely a year, which perhaps explains why Maine's state quarter depicts the Pemaquid Point Lighthouse and not George Popham.

Newport returned to Jamestown in January 1608, bringing sixty more colonists, including one man who accidentally burned down most of the settlement with a careless fire. John Smith suffered his share of misfortune as well. Stung by a stingray, he became the first celebrity adventurer in history to suffer that particular fate. Later, burned by an accidental explosion of gunpowder in his canoe, he reluctantly quitted the colony for good in the fall of 1609.

Smith's departure coincided with the arrival of several hundred more settlers. Bereft of Smith's sturdy leadership, Jamestown degenerated into a winter known to history as "the starving time." After gnawing their way through the colony's horses, dogs, and cats, Jamestown's inhabitants devoured shoe leather and the starch once intended for the ruffs of their Elizabethan collars. Some sank even lower, resorting to murder and cannibalism. By the spring of 1610, only sixty of Jamestown's 500 inhabitants were still alive.

Reinforced the following spring, the colony lurched along for another four years, although the Virginia Company never lived up to its investors' hopes. "Only the name of God," Price reported, "was more frequently profaned in the streets and market places of London than was the name of Virginia." The company eventually resorted to holding lotteries to finance its colony and assuage its investors, while in Jamestown, relations with the local Indians deteriorated even further.

Despite such troubles, tobacco offered some hope of the quick riches that had eluded the earlier gold-seeking colonists. In 1614, John Rolfe exported Virginia's first shipment of tobacco in four barrels. Tobacco exports quickly climbed to nearly 50,000 pounds within four years, although opposition came from an unexpected quarter. Disgusted by his pipe-smoking countrymen but appreciative of the imports' customs revenues, King James II tried to encourage colonists to plant vineyards and raise silkworms instead. It was an exercise in futility, as a veritable "tobacco rush" took hold in Virginia.

Stoked by such hopes, Jamestown grew to be home to 1,240 settlers by 1622. That spring, however, a massive Indian attack claimed one-third of the colonists. The massacre not only cost the Virginia Company its royal charter—causing Jamestown to revert to being a royal colony—but also launched a decade-long war between the settlers and the Indians. By the time a peace treaty was signed, the English had carved out a formidable foothold in Virginia. Even a second surprise attack in 1644 that killed approximately 450 Englishmen could not dislodge the colony. Instead, it simply sparked a war of reprisal that effectively erased what remained of an Indian nation in eastern Virginia.

Jamestown remained the capital of colonial Virginia for another fifty-five years, until 1699, when the colony moved the capital inland to Williamsburg. Within a generation, the settlement was under private ownership, remaining so for another two centuries before Jamestown became part of a national historic park in 1934. By then, the *Susan Constant, Godspeed,* and *Discovery* were surely little more than barnacle-encrusted fragments of wood resting on an anonymous patch of riverbank or seabed.

Regardless of the ignominy of their final resting places, Newport's modest fleet sailed once more on October 16, 2000, across the reverse of Virginia's state quarter. Perhaps the ghost of the old privateer, still appreciative of a good haul of booty, might take some satisfaction in knowing that almost 1.595 billion of those state quarters were minted, thus making it the largest minting of a state's quarters to date.

That minting represented the culmination of a selection process that began with Governor James Gilmore III's solicitation of ideas from colleges, universities, museums, and state agencies. He garnered an overwhelming public response that numbered in the thousands and included such suggestions as Mount Vernon and the colonial capital of Williamsburg. Assisted by representatives from the Library of Virginia, the Department of Historic Resources, the Virginia Tourism Corporation, and the Department of General Services, Virginia's governor selected a collection of final design concepts and forwarded his final recommendation—the Jamestown Quadricentennial—to the U.S. Mint.

Fittingly, the quarter's launch ceremony took place at Jamestown, heralded by the boom of ten cannons firing a historic salute. "These coins will circulate throughout the nation for years to come," Governor Gilmore declared, "and will stand as a symbol to all Americans that the courage and perseverance of our forefathers began here in Jamestown."

# 11

# NEW YORK
## *"A Mighty Woman with a Torch"*

When the U.S. Mint unveiled the first state quarter of 2001, it became apparent that New York had joined the ranks of Pennsylvania and Massachusetts in looking to an iconic statue to do double duty for the state. One might be forgiven for not immediately recognizing Pennsylvania's Commonwealth or even Concord's Minuteman. But hardly a soul in the nation—if not the world—would fail to immediately place the Statue of Liberty in New York.

Technically, however, New York was not the statue's place of birth. Like so many of the immigrants welcomed to America's shores in the nineteenth and twentieth centuries, the Statue of Liberty—to be precise, the "Statue of Liberty Enlightening the World"—was a child of the Old World, transplanted to the New.

Eager to celebrate the impending centennial of the United States in 1876, patrons in both the United States and France commissioned sculptor Frederic-Auguste Bartholdi to design a statue to commemorate 100 years of U.S. independence and Franco-American friendship. Conceiving the project as a joint venture, the American patrons committed to build the pedestal, at an approximate cost of $334,000; the French would craft the statue itself and assemble it in the United States, which would cost $250,000.

Fund-raising was easier said than done, and it quickly became apparent that there would be no statue in time for the centennial. In the United States, fund-raising efforts ranged from prizefights and auctions to benefit theatrical events and art exhibitions. On the other side of the Atlantic, fund-raising included, among other tools, a lottery. Embarrassingly, American fund-raising lagged behind even the flagging French efforts.

Responding to the trickle of donations, Joseph Pulitzer used the editorial pages of his newspaper, the *World*, to fan the dying embers of support for the project. In blistering prose, Pulitzer and his writers not only criticized the rich who had failed to finance the pedestal construction but also the middle class, which seemed content to rely upon the wealthy to provide the funds. Stung into action, America responded with open wallets and purses. The fund-raising crisis had been averted.

Meanwhile, another crisis loomed in France. It became apparent that Bartholdi's copper colossus would be so massive that a number of structural engineering issues had to be addressed. Accordingly, Alexandre-Gustave Eiffel, who had also designed the Eiffel Tower, was commissioned to design a massive iron pylon and secondary skeletal framework for Bartholdi's copper-skinned statue. Thanks to Eiffel's work, the statue's plates of copper would be able to move independently yet remain upright.

Bartholdi and Eiffel completed their work in France in July 1884. For the shipment to America, they reduced their creation to 350 individual pieces—including 300 copper plates—packed in 214 crates. The French frigate *Isere* transported the disassembled statue to New York the following summer, battling heroically through rough seas that nearly sank the vessel. The shipment arrived safely in New York on June 17, 1885.

By then, fund-raising for the granite pedestal was in its final stages. With financing complete that August, pedestal construction commenced on what was then called Bedloe's Island, within the star-shaped walls of the War of 1812–era fort known as Fort Wood. By the following April, the pedestal was finished and the assembly of the French statue could commence. In less than a year, the statue was completed.

On October 28, 1886, at a ceremony attended by President Grover Cleveland and thousands of spectators, Bartholdi's creation was unveiled to an eager public. The very magnitude of the project was nothing short of awe-inspiring. At 122 feet, it was the tallest structure in New York at the time. In total, the statue's steel skeleton weighs 125 tons; its copper sheets add another thirty-one tons to the total. Those same sheets are $\frac{3}{32}$ of an inch thick (the thickness of two pennies put together). Because of Eiffel's flexible design, the statue is able to sway in high winds without danger to the superstructure. Winds of fifty miles per hour cause the statue to sway three inches and its torch five inches.

Elements other than engineering intrigued the crowd, however. Titillating rumors claimed that although Bartholdi had modeled the face of the statue on that of his mother, he had based the statue's body on that of his mistress. And although the veracity of such rumors remains open to question, the symbolism incorporated throughout the Statue of Liberty is more straightforward.

A set of chains and a broken shackle lie at the statue's feet, unseen from below but symbolic of the statue being free from oppression and servitude. The seven spikes in its crown stand for the seven continents and seven seas; the twenty-five windows in that crown represent gemstones found on the earth and the heaven's rays shining over the world. The tablet that the statue holds in her left hand reads (in Roman numerals), "July 4th, 1776."

For the first fifteen years of its existence, the Statue of Liberty was the responsibility of the United States Lighthouse Board. Then, in 1902, the War Department took charge of the island and the statue. A year later, an important addition to the statue came with the addition of a bronze plaque on the pedestal's base. On that plaque, visitors can read the famous sonnet "The New Colossus," composed by New York poet Emma Lazarus. Although its last lines are well known, the poem in its entirety is well worth reading:

*Not like the brazen giant of Greek fame,*
*With conquering limbs astride from land to land;*
*Here at our sea-washed sunset gates shall stand*
*A mighty woman with a torch, whose flame*
*Is the imprisoned lightening, and her name*
*Mother of Exiles. From her beacon-hand*
*Glows world-wide welcome; her mild eyes command*
*The air-bridged harbor that twin cities frame.*
*"Keep ancient lands, your storied pomp!: cries she*
*With silent lips. "Give me your tired, your poor,*
*Your huddled masses yearning to breathe free,*
*The wretched refuse of your teeming shore.*
*Send these, the homeless, tempest-tost to me,*
*I lift my lamp beside the golden door."* (Lazarus 2005, 58)

Lazarus penned "The New Colossus" in 1883 in support of one of the pedestal's fund-raising art auctions. Tragically, she suffered an early death at the age of thirty-eight from Hodgkin's disease and never saw her poem placed with the statue it commemorated and helped to finance.

Lazarus's poem was a welcome addition to the statue; a decidedly unwelcome addition came on the night of July 29, 1916, while World War I raged in Europe. Bold German saboteurs detonated an ammunition barge, full of munitions bound for England, moored at nearby Black Tom Island. The resulting explosion peppered the Statue of Liberty with shrapnel, shattered thousands of windows in lower Manhattan, and was reportedly felt twenty-five miles away.

After the Black Tom attack, the torch was permanently closed to visitors. Eight years later, in 1924, a presidential proclamation declared Fort Wood (and the Statue of Liberty within it) a national monument and, in 1933, its care and administration was transferred to the National Park Service.

As the statue's own centennial approached, it became apparent that a major restoration would be required. In May 1982, President Ronald Reagan turned to Lee Iacocca, CEO of Chrysler Corporation, to head up a private-sector effort to do so. Iacocca proved remarkably successful, raising $86 million for what was, in 1984, designated by the United Nations as a World Heritage Site. The newly restored statue opened to the public on July 5, 1986.

After its restoration, annual park visitation climbed steadily to eventually reach over 5 million. Although the tragedy of September 11, 2001, initially sparked the closure of Liberty Island, it reopened after 100 days. The statue, however, remained closed for almost another two years. Today, visitors have access to the statue's pedestal observation deck, promenade, museum, and areas of Fort Wood. Access to the crown of the Statue of Liberty and the copper structure itself remains closed.

Because of the 50 State Quarters® Program, however, the Statue of Liberty is as close to a citizen as his or her own pocket, after beating out other semifinalist designs that included a depiction of Henry

Hudson and his ship, the *Half Moon;* a rendering of the historic painting, *Battle of Saratoga;* and the New York Federal Building.

Governor George Pataki turned to his fellow New Yorkers for input on the final selection. With the Statue of Liberty capturing 76 percent of the vote, he selected it to adorn the reverse of the New York quarter, along with an outline of the state and the phrase "Gateway to Freedom." The final design was the handiwork of Daniel Carr, a 3-D computer modeler—sometimes called a "virtual sculptor"—from Colorado. At Pataki's request, however, the U.S. Mint ensured that the Hudson River and the Erie Canal were etched into the coin's state outline in order to reflect the key role that those waterways played—and continued to play—in the Empire State's development.

# 12

# NORTH CAROLINA
### *"Damned if they ain't flew!"*

North Carolina's state quarter offers an image that transcends state, and even national, history. By depicting the Wright brothers' historic first flight, the Tar Heel State proudly serves notice that one of mankind's greatest technological leaps took place on North Carolina soil. The selection of this historic venue belongs in large part to Outer Banks native William J. "Bill" Tate.

In August 1900, Tate was not only an officer in the United States Lighthouse Service but also a respected notary, a Currituck County commissioner, and a former and future postmaster of Kitty Hawk. Perhaps it was not surprising, therefore, that when a peculiar letter arrived from Dayton, Ohio, addressed to Kitty Hawk's U.S. Weather Bureau office, the office's sole employee shared it with Tate.

The letter in question was penned by Wilbur Wright and inquired about local weather conditions with an eye toward testing the Wright brothers' gliders. For several months, Wilbur and his brother, Orville, had been corresponding with the U.S. Weather Bureau, searching for a location where they could "get dependable winds of 15 mph without rain or too inclement weather, suspecting they are rare. A sandy area is needed."

Initial responses from the Weather Bureau and the brothers' mentor, Octave Chanute, had identified likely areas near San Diego, California, or St. James City, Florida, as having "steady sea breeze but no sand hills." Chanute offered that "perhaps even better locations can be found on the Atlantic coasts of South Carolina or Georgia." It was likely that Chanute's suggestion, along with further data collected from the Weather Bureau, led Wilbur to write his letter to Kitty Hawk.

Fortunately for North Carolina's place in aviation history, Wilbur Wright's letter found in Tate a man of unusual intellectual curiosity. "As it happened," Tate remembered years later, "I had read only a few months before an article in a magazine about gliders and the attempts which then were being made by men to fly. I could tell by the tone of the letter that I was dealing with honest-to-goodness flying machine men."

Joining in with the Weather Bureau employee's response, Tate wrote to Wilbur, assuring him, "I will take pleasure in doing all I can for your convenience & success & pleasure & I assure you [that] you will find a hospitable people when you come among us." Tate accompanied his letter with vivid descriptions of Kitty Hawk, including a number of sketches.

Convinced by Tate to give his hometown a try, Wilbur set out to reconnoiter Kitty Hawk the following month. From Dayton, he took a train to Elizabeth City, North Carolina, where he hired a local trapper to take him by boat and foot the rest of the way. Fifty-five hours later, an exhausted and hungry Wilbur Wright arrived at Tate's doorstep. Without skipping a beat, Tate and his wife, Addie, offered Wright a bed in their home of five children.

Later that month, Orville arrived to join his brother, and for several weeks, they tested their gliders at Kitty Hawk, relying on the soft sands and steady winds to provide them with a natural wind tunnel. Through trial and error, they engineered a flying machine over the course of the next three years during a series of lengthy visits. A comment by Darrel Collins, of the U.S. Park Service at the Kitty Hawk National Historical Park, summed up the brothers' progress as they nibbled away at the mystery of powered flight. "Before the Wright brothers, no one in aviation did anything fundamentally right," Collins said. "Since the Wright brothers, no one has done anything fundamentally different."

In the fall of 1903, the brothers returned once again to Kitty Hawk. Bad weather hampered their efforts, but by November 5, they were able to ground test a powered version of their earlier gliders. The test revealed problems with their propeller shafts, which necessitated Orville's return to their Ohio workshop to rework them. So did a cracked propeller blade. But by December 12, 1903, their aircraft was ready for its first flight—should the weather cooperate.

An initial effort at powered flight came two days later. It began with a promising run down the sloping track built down Kill Devil Hill and ended within seconds with an ignominious stall. After the necessary repairs were completed, the brothers' next opportunity for flight came on December 17, the morning after a fierce nor'easter had left puddles of ice between the sand dunes. The wind, gusting in from the ocean at speeds of up to thirty miles an hour, created a wind chill factor of 4°F. It was not a particularly comfortable day on which to make history, and when a coin toss dictated that Orville would be the day's pilot on the brutally exposed lower wing, it was not clear whether he had won or lost the toss.

Defying the weather, the two brothers, with the help of five men from the local lifesaving station, dragged their 600-pound flying machine through the biting wind and prepared it for takeoff. Then, at approximately 10:35 that morning, Orville rode what had been christened the Flyer down the launch rail and into the air. Later, Orville described the moment in his diary as follows:

On slipping the rope the machine started off increasing in speed to probably 7 or 8 miles. The machine lifted from the truck just as it was entering on the fourth rail. [John] Daniels [one of the local lifesaving crew] took a picture just as it left the trucks [sic]. I found the control of the front rudder quite difficult on account of its being balanced too near the center and thus had a tendency to turn itself when started so that the rudder was turned too far on one side and then too far on the other. As a result the machine would rise suddenly to about 10 ft. and then as suddenly, on turning the rudder, dart for the ground. A sudden dart when out about 100 feet from the end of the tracks ended the flight. (Kelly 2002, 114–115)

Daniels's photo captured the image found today on North Carolina's state quarter. Controlled, powered flight had been achieved for the first time, and it had been accomplished in the skies of North Carolina—for a grand total of 120 feet and twelve seconds.

Next came Wilbur's try. He logged a flight of 175 feet, bested by Orville in a third flight of 200 feet. Wilbur was at the controls again for the fourth and final flight of the day. This time, Wilbur covered 852 feet in 59 seconds. A snapped elevator support ended the day's flying; a sudden gust of wind that flipped and mangled the Flyer ensured that its fourth flight was its last.

But by then history had been made, announced to Kitty Hawk by lifesaver Johnny Moore, who ran back into the village yelling, "They done it! They done it! Damned if they ain't flew!"

Nearly a century later, it became apparent that Moore's fellow North Carolinians were still equally impressed with the Wright brothers' accomplishment. Invited to provide the U.S. Mint with a design concept for his state's quarter, Governor James B. Hunt appointed the North Carolina Department of Cultural Resources as the leader in the state's design concept process. The department, in turn, established the North Carolina Commemorative Coin Committee, which consisted of members from the State Department of Cultural Resources, the Division of Archives and History, and coin collectors, and it solicited design ideas from the residents of North Carolina.

The committee was soon awash in ideas. Alternate design concepts suggested the Wright brothers' Flyer superimposed over an outline of the state, the Hatteras Lighthouse superimposed over an outline of the state, and the Hatteras Lighthouse shown with a dune and seagulls. In the end, however, the committee and Governor Hunt selected the "First Flight" theme for the official design. It fell to Hunt's successor, Governor Michael F. Easley, to mark the release of North Carolina's quarter on March 12, 2001, in a minting that would eventually total more than 1.055 billion.

"On behalf of the State of North Carolina I want to commend the U.S. Mint for the commemorative quarters program," Easley declared. "It is an opportunity to share a bit of North Carolina history with the rest of the nation."

It is hard to imagine William Tate—the man whose warm hospitality helped ensure that such aviation history would be North Carolina history—disagreeing with the governor one bit.

# 13

# RHODE ISLAND
## *Relying on* Reliance

Rhode Island's state quarter offers an elegant design—a vintage schooner tacking across Narragansett Bay, with the Claiborne Pell Bridge in the background. The phrase "Ocean State" completes the image, paying homage to Rhode Island's 400 miles of coastline and a nautical heritage that dates back to 1524, when Giovanni da Verrazzano first sailed into the bay. But the identity of the schooner on the quarter, and its remarkably brief history, may well be the most impressive fact associated with the Ocean State's commemorative coin.

The schooner in question is the *Reliance*, a massive yacht built in 1903 for one single, overriding purpose—to stave off increasingly strident foreign challenges and keep yacht racing's prestigious America's Cup in American hands. In short, America was relying on *Reliance*.

To fully appreciate the importance of *Reliance* on Rhode Island's— and the sporting world's—history, an understanding of racing for the America's Cup is essential. The race traces its origin to 1851, when Great Britain's Royal Yacht Squadron hosted its Annual Regatta in conjunction with that year's Great Exhibition. Inviting the world's yachtsmen to test their skills against Britannia's legendary rule of the seas, the Royal Yacht Squadron's challenge sparked the competitive fire of the New York Yacht Club. A syndicate of five members of the club built a ninety-foot schooner they proudly christened *America*. *America* cost the syndicate $45,000, a mere pittance compared to the $200-million price tag that accompanies serious America's Cup challenges today.

Launched in June 1851, *America* sprinted across the Atlantic, making the crossing in a record-breaking twenty days. Once in England, the yacht made equally short work of the fifteen competitors fielded by the Royal Yacht Club in the waters around the Isle of Wight and returned home triumphantly with the race's trophy, a silver-plated bottomless ewer crafted by Garrards of London. According to legend, Queen Victoria, when learning of America's victory, asked whose yacht had placed second. "There is no second, Your Majesty," she received in reply.

Back in the United States, the syndicate donated its prize to the New York Yacht Club as an international trophy for friendly yachting competition. The British, rather formally, had called the trophy the "Royal Yacht Squadron Cup" or the "RYS Cup for One Hundred Sovereigns." Rather irreverently, the syndicate simply called it the "One Hundred Guineas Cup." In time, the trophy became known as the America's Cup in honor of the yacht that claimed it, although yachting insiders are known to refer to it as "the Auld Mug."

Several years passed before a challenge to the cup arose. It finally came in 1870 in the form of James Ashbury and his yacht *Cambria*. Forced to race against the New York Yacht Club's entire fleet, Ashbury's foray failed. Another effort—this time against a single champion representing the New Yorkers—failed the following year and engendered so much bad blood that another fourteen years passed before a British challenger tried again.

In the interim, Alexander Cuthbert, a Canadian boatbuilder, stepped into the gap. Cuthbert's dreams exceeded his means, however, and he failed so spectacularly in his quest to claim the cup that the New York Yacht Club declined to allow any further challenges from the Canadian Great Lakes.

The British returned to the scene in 1885 and 1886 with the yachts *Genesta* and *Galatea*. Again the British failed, although the *Galatea*'s challenge earned that yacht a special place in the history books as the first challenger to have a woman on board as one of the contestants. The Scottish made a singular, and unsuccessful, challenge in 1887, followed by further British efforts in 1893 and 1895 by the yachts *Valkyrie II* and *Valkyrie III*.

Sir Thomas Lipton (of Lipton Tea fame) and the Royal Ulster Yacht Club brought the next five challenges in *Shamrock* through *Shamrock V* from 1899 to 1930. Lipton was a self-made man, a descendant of Ulster Scots, and a friend of the Prince of Wales, who encouraged Lipton to try to reclaim the cup for Great Britain. Lipton's persistence, fueled in further part by his desire to publicize his tea company, made it clear that the New York Yacht Club could not take the cup's continued sojourn in the United States for granted.

Fortunately, to help it fight off Lipton's stubborn assaults, the Americans—financed by such legendary financiers as J. P. Morgan and John Rockefeller—could rely on legendary yacht designer Nathanael Greene Herreshoff. Herreshoff, a native of Bristol, Rhode Island, and a graduate of the Massachusetts Institute of Technology, was a naval architect-engineer of such excellence that he earned the sobriquet "the Wizard of Bristol." He also lent his name to the so-called Herreshoff period of yacht racing that lasted from 1893 to 1920.

For the 1903 race, Herreshoff turned his considerable genius to designing a massive yacht. In those days, the America's Cup competitors were limited to a waterline length of ninety feet. The Wizard of Bristol, however, craftily designed a boat—*Reliance*—that, while measuring ninety feet in the waterline, possessed overhangs at the bow and stern of such length that the overall waterline length of the yacht increased by some two-thirds when it heeled over. This increase in waterline enabled a corresponding increase in speed as well.

*Reliance* was unique in other areas as well. Designed purely as a racing yacht, it was completely unfinished below deck, where winches (a Herreshoff innovation below deck) supplemented the manpower of its sixty-four crewmen. This beauty possessed an enormous area of sail, namely, 16,200 square feet of canvas, which was close to 12 percent more than its Irish competitor. The steel welded mast, with a telescopic topmast, soared 199 feet above the water, almost the height of a twenty-story building. Other innovations were less visible but equally impressive, including a hollow rudder that could be filled or emptied of water depending on the point of sail.

To handle this behemoth, the New York Yacht Club turned to Charlie Barr, an equally legendary yachtsman who had successfully skippered the *Columbia* in the 1899 and 1901 matches against the *Shamrock* and *Shamrock II*. In the late summer of 1903, in the coastal waters off New York, Barr and *Reliance* met *Shamrock III* in head-to-head competition. Herreshoff's design and Barr's seamanship dominated the set of races, including a dramatic final match that concluded with *Reliance* emerging dramatically from a fog bank to claim the victory.

Faced with his third defeat in four years, Lipton remarked despairingly: "They tell me I have a beautiful boat. I don't want a beautiful boat. What I want is a boat to lift the Cup—a *Reliance*. Give me a homely boat, the homeliest boat that was ever designed, if she is as fast as *Reliance*."

*Reliance*'s racing days, however, were already over. Immediately after the victory over *Shamrock III*, the owners laid *Reliance* up in dry dock. Ten years later, in the wake of rule changes that rendered *Reliance* competitively obsolete, they scrapped the yacht—an ignoble ending for a noble ship.

For his part, Lipton tried twice more to claim the America's Cup, culminating in a final effort in 1930 against the *Enterprise*. This time, the race was held in the waters off Newport, Rhode Island, which was to become the race's home for the next fifty-three years. Once again, however, Lipton went down to defeat. He died the following year, disappointed but heralded nevertheless as "the best of the losers" and ultimately successful in his quest to make his tea company an international household name.

The coveted cup remained in the United States until 1983, when a yacht whose innovations rivaled those of Herreshoff's arrived in the form of the *Australia II*. The Australians captured the cup that year, bringing a renewed sense of international vigor to the competition. Subsequent competitions—and, unfortunately, a variety of acrimonious legal challenges—saw the cup rotate through the hands of U.S. and New Zealand racers.

In 2000, when it came time for Rhode Island to select a design for its state quarter, the cup was held by the New Zealanders. That fact failed to deter 57 percent of the 34,566 voters in a statewide poll from honoring the role that *Reliance*, Herreshoff, and Rhode Island played in the America's Cup history. After a statewide vote, a majority selected the image designed by Daniel Carr (the designer of New York's quarter). Carr's design bested competitors such as a design depicting the arrival of colonial forefather and religious dissident Roger Williams from the less congenial Massachusetts Bay Colony.

Released on May 21, 2001, the U.S. Mint eventually minted over 870 million of Rhode Island's state quarters—an impressive haul for the smallest state in the Union. And although the America's Cup currently resides in Switzerland, Rhode Islanders and yachtsmen alike can take solace in the fact that the U.S. Mint estimates that the average life of a Rhode Island state quarter will be thirty years—in other words, plenty of time to return the America's Cup home to America.

# 14

# VERMONT
## *Freedom, Unity, and Maple Syrup*

When the U.S. Mint tasked Vermont with selecting a design for the fourteenth state quarter, Governor Howard Dean and the Vermont Arts Council embarked upon an eighteen-month quest to choose the design that most ably represented the Green Mountain State. The council narrowed the proposed designs to three, giving the governor the final vote in choosing the winner.

"Last summer, as I traveled around talking to Vermonters," Dean said, "the maple sugaring scene [featuring two maple trees, a view of Vermont's Camel's Hump Mountain, and the inscription "Freedom and Unity"] was everyone's favorite design throughout the state. I'm happy and proud that it was chosen so clearly by the people of Vermont because it reflects our rural heritage and highlights our beautiful landscape. I'm sure this coin, like our state, will be valued by everyone for a long time."

If anyone in Vermont disagreed with Governor Dean's assessment, it certainly wasn't Rick Marsh, the president of the Vermont Maple Sugar Makers' Association.

"I was very happy to see a sugaring scene incorporated into the design of Vermont's new state quarter," Marsh said. "In many ways the Vermont maple industry depicts what our state is all about, a tradition known for being pure and natural. This scene represents our state very well; it shows how we take pride in preserving a beautiful working landscape with the maple industry in the forefront and the high mountains in the background."

Today, Vermont's maple syrup production is valued at approximately $13 to 14 million annually. In 2006, it produced 460,000 gallons, making it the national leader in maple syrup production well ahead of Maine, New York, and Ohio, the other leading syrup-producing states.

Although Vermont is the leading producer of maple syrup in the United States, the top honor in terms of productivity in North America today belongs to the Canadian province of Quebec. With fierce cross-border competition, it is not surprising that, for years, Vermont's sugar makers have relied on Marsh's organization. Founded in 1893 to "safeguard the tradition of maple sugaring while maintaining the highest standards possible in the production of pure maple products," the association ranks as one of the oldest known agricultural organizations in the nation.

And when one speaks of the maple syrup industry in Vermont, to call it "tradition" is not merely a cliché. Whether at a state-of-the-art high-tech facility or a historic wooden "sugarhouse," each of the state's approximately 2,500 "sugar makers" share a historic process tied inescapably to Vermont's forest of sugar maple trees *(Acer saccharum).*

That historic process, known as "sugaring" in the local parlance, takes place during Vermont's "sugaring season." The season lasts from four to six weeks, sometimes starting as early as February in southern Vermont and lasting into late April in northern Vermont. Timing to catch the first run of the season is important because, in the spring, maple sap contains a small quantity of the sugar sucrose (ranging from 1 to 4 percent)—the basic building block of what will become maple syrup.

But first, a sugar maker must obtain the maple tree's sap. To do that, sugar makers drill one or more holes, called "tap holes," into the trunk of a maple tree. The holes are less than two inches deep, barely ⁵⁄₁₆ of an inch in diameter, and drilled sparingly into the precious maple trees. Sugar makers know that a maple tree ten to eighteen inches in diameter takes forty years to reach that size; accordingly, they will only put one tap hole in such a tree. Larger trees warrant two or three tap holes. The entire collection of the sugar maker's trees, whether 100 or 40,000, is known as the "sugarbush."

After drilling the tap hole, the sugar maker fits his tap hole with a plastic or metal spout in order to prevent the sap from simply running down the side of the tree. Now, nature again plays a key factor in sugaring. In order for the sap to drip from the tap hole, the right weather conditions are required. A freeze will pull water into the maple tree's roots from the surrounding soil, thereby creating a small suction effect in the tree's wood. Later, as the wood thaws, the tree's sap is placed under enough pressure to ooze out of the tap hole.

At this point in the process, modern technology and historic tradition diverge. Modern facilities collect the sap from their sugarbush through plastic pipes that run from the tap hole spouts and through an intricate network of tubing to a main pipe—the main line—and on to the sugarhouse. Some rely on mere gravity to conduct the slow flow of sap; many others, however, use vacuum pumps to facilitate the sap flow.

At a traditional sugaring operation, however, the collection of sap is a far different process—and the one depicted on Vermont's state quarter. At those operations, the sugar makers simply hang a bucket on the spout that has been placed in the tap hole and then the tree's sap will drip into the bucket. Each day that the sap flows, these buckets need to be emptied into a gathering tank placed on the back of a tractor-drawn wagon or, in increasingly rare instances, a horse-drawn sleigh, which then transports the collected sap to the sugarhouse.

"When people think of maple sugaring they automatically think of buckets hanging on trees and folks gathering the sap with pails," Marsh said, "but the Vermont maple industry has definitely changed over the years. Most sugar makers now use a pipeline system to collect sap, but some of our sugar makers still do use this method to collect sap."

Once at the sugarhouse, whether traditionally rustic or efficiently high-tech, the process is, on paper, a deceptively simple one—although modern techniques, such as reverse osmosis or steam recovery, are finding increasing favor. At any rate, in the sugarhouse, the goal is to boil the newly arrived sap as soon as possible to separate the sap's water from its sucrose. Otherwise, as the sap warms, it will begin to break down, leaving the sugar maker with dark, stronger tasting syrup or possibly even spoiled sap.

To boil the sap, the sugarhouse utilizes an evaporator; this is a collection of large rectangular pans atop an arch, which suspends the pans over the heat source—traditionally fueled by wood, but today usually fueled by oil. Inside the evaporator pans, a winding series of channels, or flues, first directs the sap through the back of the superheated device, known as the "flue pan." There, as the sap is heated, its excess water is boiled away.

After its journey through the flue pan is complete, the sap enters the front of the evaporator, moving into what is called the "syrup pan." That pan is divided into two or more compartments. As the sap moves through these compartments and toward the front of the evaporator, it continues to lose water to evaporation. By the time the end of the pathway is reached, the sap is 7.1°F above the boiling point of water, has a density of 66.9 percent sugar, and, at that point, is no longer really sap. It is now, for all practical purposes, pure maple syrup, and the sugar maker opens a valve in the compartment and draws off a batch from the pan before it gets too dense and begins to burn.

At that point, however, several steps in the process still remain. First, sugar makers check the new batch with a special instrument, called a hydrometer, to ensure proper density (i.e., sugar content). Second, they run the syrup through a wool cone filter or a filter press in order to remove a natural but gritty substance known as "niter," or "sugar sand," from the syrup.

Finally, the syrup—by now clear and golden—is taste-tasted and color-graded to determine which of the Vermont maple grades will be placed upon its label. Vermont maple syrup typically falls into one of the four table grades: Fancy, Medium Amber, Dark Amber, or Grade B. If the maple syrup is too dark or too strong in flavor, then it is labeled for commercial use. In the end, it typically takes about forty gallons of sap to make one gallon of pure maple syrup.

In 2005, the Vermont maple crop, despite the use of 2.1 million tap holes, was down 18 percent from the previous year, a decrease that reflected unfavorable weather conditions across New England that season. Some blame global warming; others fault cyclical patterns in the weather, harkening back to the 1950s, when similar warm spells plagued the maple syrup industry. Regardless of the long-term prognosis for sugaring seasons in Vermont, it will, fortunately, always have a home on Vermont's state quarter.

# KENTUCKY

## *A Quarter Horse? Hardly*

When you look at Kentucky's state quarter, beware of jumping to conclusions. First, it is probably a misnomer to call it a "state quarter." Actually, Kentucky, like Massachusetts, Pennsylvania, and Virginia; is a commonwealth—which makes it a commonwealth quarter, right?

Second, although the coin expressly celebrates "My Old Kentucky Home," as composed by Stephen C. Foster, it would be a mistake to assume that Foster ever called Kentucky home. Foster, born and bred in Pittsburgh, Pennsylvania, scarcely visited Kentucky and certainly never lived there.

And finally, even though the quarter features a horse, the equine in question is anything but a quarter horse—no offense to the American Quarter Horse. In contrast to the Thoroughbred, the American Quarter Horse is a smaller, heavily muscled steed, ideal for running quarter-mile races or even shorter sprints. And although the Quarter Horse is a proud breed, Kentucky's coin understandably depicts a Thoroughbred—a breed that can indeed lay claim to an "old Kentucky home."

In truth, the Thoroughbred actually traces its history to England and three foundation sires—the Darley Arabian, the Godolphin Arabian, and the Byerly Turk—named for the Englishmen who brought the Middle Eastern stallions to England in the seventeenth century to breed to native horses. Their efforts were rewarded with a horse capable of carrying weight at sustained speed over extended distances, in short, a perfect racing machine.

The Thoroughbred arrived in America around 1730 when an English colonist imported his first Thoroughbred stallion. Within the next 100 years, 300 more would follow to form the foundation of American Thoroughbred racing. From that modest beginning, the breed grew to its present success. Today, the Jockey Club, which serves as the breed registry for all Thoroughbreds in North America, registers approximately 37,000 foals annually.

In Kentucky—named, according to some, for the Cherokee word for "land of meadows"—there are 500 Thoroughbred farms in and around Lexington alone. In total, according to 2003 numbers, the state births approximately 10,000 foals a year, which in turn give life to roughly 40,000 jobs—for trainers, jockeys, blacksmiths, veterinarians, handicappers, and even painters. A typical 300-acre horse farm in the heart of the Bluegrass can count on budgeting $20,000 annually to keep its traditional white wooden fences gleaming with fresh paint.

Raising and training Thoroughbreds is a serious business in Kentucky, a reality underscored every year at Lexington's Keeneland

Race Course, where horses are auctioned off for as much, in one case, as $13 million for a yearling. Of the eleven horses to have claimed the Triple Crown, eight of them were foaled at Kentucky horse farms, beginning with Sir Barton in 1919 and ending, most recently, with Seattle Slew in 1977. And for each of those horses, their first step toward claiming the first jewel in that crown came at the Kentucky Derby, held at Louisville's historic Churchill Downs.

At the time of Churchill Downs's first race in 1875, Thoroughbred racing in Kentucky had already enjoyed nearly nine decades of history in Kentucky—a legacy that predated the commonwealth's entry into the Union in 1792. The U.S. Mint was founded that same year, a coincidence that perhaps explains Kentucky's legendary affinity for the mint julep. Or perhaps not.

At any rate, in Louisville itself, reports of horse races can be found as early as 1783 that detail racing being held on Market Street in the downtown area. Market Street was, however, a busy thoroughfare—and thus, ironically, no place for Thoroughbreds—and by 1805, a racecourse had been constructed on Shippingport Island. As the years passed, one could find other racecourses at the Elm Tree Gardens, the Hope Distillery Course, Peter Funk's Beargrass Track, the Oakland Race Course, and the Woodlawn Course.

In 1873, however, M. Lewis Clark returned from a tour of Europe infused with the idea of building a racetrack capable of showcasing Kentucky's then-struggling Thoroughbred breeding industry. To fund his track, Clark raised $32,000 by selling 320 membership subscriptions to the track at $100 each. He then leased eighty acres of land, approximately three miles south of Louisville's downtown, from his uncles, John and Henry Churchill. The Churchills, in turn, eventually lent their name to Clark's racecourse, which Clark opened for its first race on May 17, 1875.

On that day, Clark's new racecourse hosted four races. A Thoroughbred named Bonaventure won Churchill Downs's first race, although a three-year-old chestnut colt named Aristides soon overshadowed Bonaventure's feat in the day's featured race—a race christened by Clark as the "Kentucky Derby" and patterned after England's Epsom Derby. In a nearly forgotten piece of American cultural history, Aristides was trained by and ridden by two African Americans, Ansel Williamson and Oliver Lewis, respectively.

In the years to come, Clark's Kentucky Derby shifted to being run on the first Saturday in May. As it did, it earned an enviable reputation in America's racing set as "the first race in which the best horses from one crop of foals meet at the accepted classic distance of a mile and a quarter" carrying 126 pounds. It was the alliterative pen of writer Bill Corum that dubbed the race "the run for the roses," in homage to the derby's official flower and the traditional garland of roses draped over the winning horse's withers.

Despite such promise, Churchill Downs's financial fortunes ebbed and flowed both metaphorically and literally—such as in 1937, when the course was inundated by that year's great flood of the Ohio River. Nevertheless, its triumphs, and that of the Kentucky Derby, have outweighed the travails. In 1894 to 1895, new owners constructed a new grandstand that incorporated two spires atop the roof, thus creating the simple but enduring symbol of both Churchill Downs and the Kentucky Derby. The race was nationally televised for the first time on May 3, 1952, and, in 1974, when the derby celebrated its 100th running, a record 163,628 spectators were on hand. Meanwhile, combined Kentucky Derby Day wagering, on-track and nationally, snowballed from $26,805,205 in 1985 to $123,215,302 in 2002.

Therefore, the appearance of a Thoroughbred on Kentucky's quarter likely surprised no one. Nevertheless, its inclusion was not a foregone conclusion. In order to develop and select an appropriate design, Kentucky's first lady, Judi Patton, chaired the Kentucky Quarter Project Committee. Patton's committee received 1,800

design suggestions, narrowed the submissions down to twelve finalists, and, from June 15 to 17, 1999, displayed the design finalists in
the front lobby of the capitol and over the Internet.

The dozen finalists illustrated the panoply of Kentucky's history.
Successful concepts included a portrayal of the mansion Federal
Hill, an antebellum plantation house in Bardstown, Kentucky, where
Stephen Foster reportedly visited his cousin John Rowan long
enough to pen "My Old Kentucky Home."

Other design concepts did not fare as well. One unsuccessful design sought to commemorate Daniel Boone, the famed "long
hunter" who helped blaze the so-called Wilderness Road through
the Appalachian Mountains' Cumberland Gap and into Kentucky
shortly before the American Revolution. Unable to legally validate
his land claims in Kentucky, Boone eventually settled in Missouri.
Nonetheless, his settlement of Boonesborough, and his reputation
as a mythic frontiersman, remained firmly in Kentucky.

Another unsuccessful design featured Abraham Lincoln, claimed
by Illinois—the self-proclaimed "Land of Lincoln"—but born near
Hodgenville, Kentucky, in 1809, where he spent the first seven years
of his childhood before moving to first Indiana and then Illinois.
Lincoln's wartime rival, Confederate president Jefferson Davis, had
been born a few miles away in present-day Todd County a year earlier. Suffice it to say that Davis did not join Lincoln in the ranks of
design finalists for Kentucky's quarter.

Offered such options, over 50,000 residents of Kentucky cast
votes for their favorite concepts. Finalists underwent review by
the Citizens Commemorative Coin Advisory Committee and the
Commission of Fine Arts. In the end, Governor Paul E. Patton selected the final design that features an iconic Thoroughbred, the
phrase "My Old Kentucky Home," and Federal Hill—where the
U.S. Mint unveiled the commonwealth's quarter on October 18,
2001.

But one final word of caution with respect to Kentucky's state quarter: The next time you purchase a Thoroughbred, do not let the spare change jangling in your pocket inspire you to name your steed "My Old Kentucky Home." The Jockey Club limits horses' names to eighteen characters—punctuation marks and spaces included. "Federal Hill," on the other hand, would seem to work just fine.

# 16

# TENNESSEE
## *"Here's a Quarter . . . "*

Tennessee is blessed with a remarkable musical heritage—one that stretches across the state's 432 miles, running from Bristol, in the east, past the site of the legendary *Grand Ole Opry* show in Nashville, and westward onto the streets of Memphis, where the blues were born.

Nevertheless, Tennessee's history and culture includes more than simply music, and when Governor Don Sundquist launched a statewide contest on March 27, 2000, to select a design for the Volunteer State's quarter, nearly 1,000 suggestions arrived. Culling through the submissions, the seven-person Tennessee Coin Commission created by the governor identified three finalists.

One design finalist celebrated Tennessee's ratification of the U.S. Constitution's Nineteenth Amendment, which gave women the right to vote. In August 1920, thirty-five states had already voted to ratify the amendment, leaving Tennessee to deliver the suffragists with the so-called Perfect 36. Tennessee delivered, but only after a nail-biting 49–47 vote in the state legislature.

A second design finalist depicted Sequoyah, a Cherokee Indian born on the Little Tennessee River in present-day Monroe County. Sequoyah's single-handed invention of a written alphabet for his people—the first written language for Native Americans—played a critical role in fostering what amounted to a national identity for the Cherokee people.

The winning final design, however, was entitled "Musical Heritage" and was submitted by Shawn Stookey, a teacher at Lakeview Elementary in New Johnstonville, Tennessee. In its final form on the Tennessee state quarter, the design incorporates sheet music, a fiddle (representing the Appalachian music of East Tennessee), the trumpet (acknowledging the blues of Memphis and West Tennessee), and the guitar (symbolizing Central Tennessee, home to Nashville, the self-proclaimed capital of country music). Three stars emphasize the existence of Tennessee's three regions—east, central, and west.

When music scholars think of East Tennessee, the so-called Bristol Sessions of Ralph Peer come quickly to mind. As the new head of the General Phonograph Company's Okeh record label, Peer had realized that changing musical tastes and the easy availability of radio music threatened Okeh's traditional stable of classical musicians and opera singers. In response, Peer decided to give the American people what they wanted to hear—which seemed to be what Peer called "hillbilly music," the songs of Appalachia and the rural South.

Peer's success with his "hillbilly music" led him, in July 1927, to hold a recording session in Bristol, Tennessee, for aspiring Southern musicians. Renting an abandoned hat factory to serve as a makeshift studio, Peer, who now worked for Victor records, placed an ad in local papers declaring that "[t]he Victor Company will have a recording machine in Bristol for ten days beginning Monday to record records" and extending an open invitation to local musicians to perform.

Scores of local musicians responded to what became known as the Bristol Sessions. Their numbers included Alvin Pleasant (A. P.) Carter; his wife, Sara; and Sara's cousin Maybelle Addison—all of the soon-to-be-legendary Carter Family. When the Carters drove from Poor Valley, Virginia, into the town to join with the likes of Jimmie Rodgers to record for Peer, Bristol became known as the "birthplace of country music."

In total, the Carters recorded six songs in Bristol, earning a grand total of $300: Sara led the group on such songs as "Poor Orphan Child," singing alto, while A. P.'s voice provided the bass. Sara accompanied her singing on her autoharp; Maybelle played her guitar. Together, they, and the Appalachian folk music genre that they represented, ensured that East Tennessee earned its due acknowledgment on the state quarter—even if symbolized by a fiddle that none of the Carters played.

Fortunately, that oversight is remedied by the decision to allow a guitar to represent Central Tennessee. In central Tennessee, guitars have logged thousands of hours of playing time on Nashville's Grand Ole Opry, the longest-running radio show in U.S. history. Not only is the Opry Tennessee's preeminent stage, but it is the undisputed epicenter of American country music.

The *Opry* dates to October 1925, when the Nashville-based National Life and Accident Insurance Company opened radio station WSM (for the company motto, "We Shield Millions"). Based on his previous experience in Chicago with *The National Barn Dance*, WSM station manager George D. Hay started a similar program with an informal collection of local string bands and performers.

Hay's show scored his first big break with the appearance of fiddler Uncle Jimmy Thompson in November 1925. Responding to a delighted public, WSM began offering a regular Saturday night "barn dance." By the following spring, the barn dance had been renamed the *"Grand Ole Opry,"* and the show grew steadily in popularity, thanks to such performers as the banjo-picking, joke-telling David Harrison, a.k.a. "Uncle Dave" Macon.

In 1938, the *Opry*'s popularity surged with the arrival of Roy Acuff to join the show's regular repertoire of performers. Like the Carter family, Acuff's musical roots grew from a childhood in Appalachia. In Nashville, he specialized in sentimental and gospel songs carried by his high mountain tenor. Although Acuff shared the *Opry*'s stage with such legends as Kitty Wells and Eddy Arnold, it was Acuff who was still performing on the show and being revered as the "King of Country Music" even into the 1980s.

A year after Acuff's arrival, the *Opry* earned a slot on the NBC radio network and, in 1943, the show, which rotated through a wide selection of Nashville venues, settled into the venerable Ryman Auditorium. Designed originally as a "gospel tabernacle," the Ryman instead became famous as "the mother church of country music." For the next three decades, the *Opry* called the Ryman home, even as fiddle and banjo tunes and sentimental crooners gave way to steel and electric guitars, artists like Hank Williams and Ernest Tubbs, and the music of the modern honky-tonk.

Meanwhile, because of men like master guitarist Chet Atkins and extraordinary soundman and producer Owen Bradley, Nashville's growing record industry helped the *Grand Ole Opry* ensure that the city was synonymous with country music. Atkins helped craft the famed "Nashville sound," while studios such as Bradley's Quonset Hut helped build Nashville's soon-to-be-legendary Music Row.

The 1980s, 1990s, and the first decade of the twenty-first century witnessed further evolutions in country music. But all of those evolutions managed to simultaneously build on country music's past as the new styles, songs, and artists charted a course to country music's future. And whether one is speaking of country music past or country music future, it is difficult to imagine country music without a guitar—and equally difficult to think of a better instrument to represent the contributions of Central Tennessee on the state quarter.

In addition to the fiddle and the guitar, however, Tennessee's state quarter includes a trumpet, intended to symbolize the blues heritage of West Tennessee. It is a fitting choice, for the trumpet was the instrument of W. C. Handy, the "father of the blues." By the time Handy settled in Memphis in 1908, a variety of musical forms—ranging from Southern folk tunes to church music to minstrel shows to brass bands—had worked their influence on him. And when Edward H. "Boss" Crump commissioned him to write a campaign song, those influences found expression in a tune Handy first entitled "Mr. Crump" and later changed, in 1912, to "Memphis Blues."

"Memphis Blues" was Handy's first commercial success; two years later he scored his greatest with "St. Louis Blues." In the decade that followed, major record companies began staging what they termed "field sessions" in Memphis—much like Peer had done in Bristol. The years 1925 to 1935 marked a golden age of blues in the city, when groups such as the Memphis Jug Band recorded such infectious tunes as "Sun Brimmer's Blues" and "K. C. Moan." One of the highest compliments that could be paid to these musicians is to recognize that four decades later, they were still finding fans in the likes of Bob Dylan.

Meanwhile, another sub-genre of the blues, the so-called Delta Blues, found a commercial home in Memphis, where master bluesmen (and women) such as Furry Lewis, Frank Stokes, Mississippi Fred McDowell, and Memphis Minnie crafted their own national reputations. In doing so, they laid the groundwork for second- and third-generation efforts by the likes of the iconic Riley "B. B." King. As a disc jockey on Memphis's WDIA, King billed himself first as the "Blues Boy from Beale Street" and then "Blues Boy." But after crafting such classics as "The Thrill Is Gone" and "Lucille," King proved that simply "B. B." was more than enough to make his point while simultaneously ensuring that Memphis's Beale Street was synonymous with the blues across the country.

Of course, Memphis's musical heritage encompasses far more than the blues. Elvis Presley made his home in Memphis from 1948 to 1977. Aretha Franklin, the "Queen of Soul," began her musical career singing in the choir at her father's Memphis church. And speaking of soul music, Isaac Hayes solidified the city's reputation as a center for soul music, owing to his brilliantly original scoring of the movie *Shaft* in 1971. It was more than appropriate, therefore, that when the U.S. Mint celebrated the Tennessee state quarter's release on January 14, 2002, Isaac Hayes joined Ricky Skaggs, Marty Stuart, and Ruby Wilson in a series of musical performances that not only entertained but underscored the incredible diversity of Tennessee's musical heritage.

# 17

# OHIO
## *The Illegal Astronaut*

Does Ohio's quarter violate federal law?

Perhaps only U.S. Mint engraver Donna Weaver knows.

Public Law 105-124, also known as the 50 States Commemorative Coin Program Act, directed the U.S. Mint to launch the 50 State Quarters® Program. The act contains a number of restrictions and admonitions regarding the acceptable design of state quarters. In the case of Ohio's quarter, section 3(1)(4)(E) is particularly relevant. It directs that "no portrait of a living person may be included in the design of any quarter dollar" minted pursuant to the act.

And that leads to the question: Which astronaut on the Ohio quarter is superimposed over an outline of the state and standing alongside the Wright brothers' famed flyer? The phrase "Birthplace of Aviation Pioneers," which is also inscribed on the coin, seems to offer a damning answer—at least as far as section 3(1)(4)(E) is concerned.

Why? Because Ohio can not only claim to be the birthplace of Orville Wright but also to be the birthplace of two latter-day aviation pioneers, John Glenn and Neil Armstrong. But if it is Glenn's or Armstrong's face behind the anonymous astronaut's face visor, then there is a problem—if only in the most painfully legalistic of minds. Both Glenn and Armstrong are still alive—in fact, they both attended the official launch (no pun intended) of Ohio's state quarter—and are thus prohibited from depiction on a state quarter.

Nevertheless, if an exception to the rule is warranted, it would be difficult to think of two more exceptional men. Today, with space shuttles blasting off on increasingly routine missions to support the permanently manned International Space Station, it is far too easy to think of Glenn's and Armstrong's aeronautical accomplishments in terms of a historic fait accompli. But a look back at just what they accomplished—and what they overcame to do so—leaves no doubt that their courage and skill should continue to be celebrated today.

John H. Glenn, Jr., was born in Cambridge, Ohio, in 1921. He later attended primary and secondary school in New Concord, Ohio, where he also earned a Bachelor of Science degree in engineering from Muskingum College. Wartime service as a Marine Corps combat pilot followed during World War II and the Korean War and led to his selection as a Navy test pilot.

In 1957, Glenn set a transcontinental speed record in an F8U Crusader, streaking from Los Angeles to New York in three hours and twenty-three minutes. Glenn's was the first transcontinental flight to average supersonic speeds and offered a taste of things to come for the talented, charismatic pilot. Two years later, the National Aeronautics and Space Administration selected Glenn as one of the original seven Project Mercury astronauts, ensuring his place in history as one of America's most famous astronauts.

As the pilot of the Mercury capsule *Friendship* 7, Glenn was not the first man to enter space—Soviet cosmonaut Yuri Gagarin had claimed that honor ten months earlier. Nor was he the first man to orbit the earth; again, that honor went to a Soviet cosmonaut, Gherman Titov, on August 6, 1961. In fact, Glenn was not even the first American in space. Both Alan Shepard and Virgil "Gus" Grissom logged suborbital flights in the spring and summer of 1961.

But on February 20, 1962, Glenn became the first American to orbit Earth. For a nation that seemed to be losing the space race to the Soviet Union, Glenn's three passes around the globe—at a maximum altitude of 162 miles and at an orbital velocity of approximately 17,500 miles per hour—were just the tonic a thirsty American public craved.

In the end, Glenn earned every accolade that he received. First, a malfunction in the automatic control of the capsule's yaw caused Glenn to have to manually control the capsule in order to maintain its proper altitude. Then a faulty sensor mistakenly warned Glenn that the capsule's heat shield and landing cushion were not fully in place. In short, it was a very relieved Glenn who splashed down in the Pacific Ocean at the end of that five-hour flight.

Glenn's immediate award for his triumph included a ticker-tape parade through the streets of New York before 4 million spectators. Later, his fame helped launch a twenty-five-year career in the U.S. Senate, capped in 1998 by his triumphant return to space at the age of seventy-seven on board the space shuttle *Discovery*. As the oldest person to fly in space, Glenn again logged his name in the history books on a nine-day mission.

The success of Glenn's initial flight in 1962 imbued America's space program with a renewed sense of confidence. Confidence was an important quality, given that the previous spring, President John

F. Kennedy had committed to Congress that the United States would "land a man on the moon and return him safely to the Earth" before the decade was out. In light of the impressive, and seemingly superior, competition from the Soviets, Kennedy's challenge was decidedly bold. Nevertheless, as Kennedy later told NASA officials, "[W]e chose to go to the Moon in this decade and do the other things not because they are easy, but because they are hard."

To command its first mission to the moon, NASA looked to another Ohio native—in this case, Neil A. Armstrong, who was born in Wapakoneta, Ohio, in 1930. After graduating from Purdue University, he served as a naval aviator from 1949 to 1952, logging seventy-eight combat missions during the Korean War. He then joined the National Advisory Committee for Aeronautics (the predecessor to NASA) and, as a research and test pilot, pioneered many high-speed aircraft, including the sound barrier–breaking X-15.

In 1962, Armstrong became an astronaut and, four years later, served as the command pilot for the *Gemini 8* mission. At the controls of *Gemini 8*, Armstrong performed the first successful docking of two vehicles in space. In the wake of such success, Armstrong earned a spot on the upcoming Apollo mission to the moon.

By then, the danger of space flight was all too real to Armstrong and his fellow astronauts. On January 27, 1967, during a ground test of what would be a future moon mission's command and service module, an oxygen fire claimed the lives of *Apollo I* astronauts Gus Grissom, Edward White, and Roger Chaffee. Trapped inside their capsule as the fire raged within it, the three men never had a chance.

If memories of the *Apollo I* disaster were on Armstrong's mind on July 16, 1969, when he, Edwin "Buzz" Aldrin, and Michael Collins blasted off from Cape Canaveral on a mission designated *Apollo XI*, history does not reveal it. But three days later, as Armstrong and Aldrin piloted the lunar module *Eagle* down to a landing on the southern edge of the moon's Sea of Tranquility, disaster for the Apollo program loomed once more.

As *Eagle* descended, a series of alarms sounded, warning the astronauts and Mission Control back in Houston, Texas, that the rudimentary on-board flight control computers were being overwhelmed with data. Ignoring the alarms, Collins took manual control of the module as planned and began to guide it in for a landing.

At that point, the two astronauts realized that their prospective landing field was strewn with truck-sized boulders. In response, Collins brought *Eagle* to a hover 270 feet over the moon's surface. Nearly three minutes passed as he and Armstrong angled *Eagle* for a safer spot to land. When they finally did settle in for a landing on the moon's dusty surface, they had a mere seventy seconds of fuel remaining.

The close call on the landing did not rattle the two consummate professionals on board *Eagle*. Rather, they set about making preparations to set foot on the moon. Six and a half hours later, Armstrong squeezed out of the lunar module and, with a careful step off *Eagle's* ladder, became the first man on the moon. "That is one small step for man; one giant leap for mankind," Armstrong declared over the radio to Mission Control.

Once Aldrin joined him, the two astronauts planted an American flag, collected fifty pounds of moon rocks, and unveiled a commemorative plaque of poetic simplicity.

"Here men from the planet Earth first set foot upon the Moon, July 1969 AD," the plaque read. "We came in peace for all mankind."

After twelve hours on the moon, Armstrong and Aldrin blasted off to rejoin Collins orbiting overhead. They then turned for home, splashing down in the Pacific Ocean on July 24, 1969. Upon their arrival from mandatory quarantine two and a half weeks later, they were feted as international heroes.

"Because of what you have done, the heavens have become part of man's world," President Richard M. Nixon assured Armstrong and his comrades.

Thirty-two years later, Ohio's state quarter matched Nixon's rhetoric by, in turn, becoming part of the heavens itself. Astronauts Nancy Currie of Troy, Ohio, and Richard Linnehan—like Currie, a graduate of Ohio State University—carried four of the quarters into space on the space shuttle *Columbia*. Their pocket change provided a fitting tribute to the aviation accomplishments of the Buckeye State and its pioneering progeny.

# LOUISIANA
## *The Pelican Brief*

In 2001, Louisiana became the second—but certainly not the last—state that felt compelled to include its state bird on its state quarter. But in the case of the Pelican State's coin, the case for the brown pelican's appearance is indeed compelling.

The brown pelican *(Pelecanus occidentalis)* is a large, gray-brown bird tufted with white feathers around its head and neck. It can weigh as much as nine pounds and, in the case of larger individuals, boasts a wing span of over seven feet. Some have been known to live for as long as thirty-one years.

"One of the most interesting of our American birds," the eighteenth-century naturalist and artist John James Audubon wrote. "The Brown Pelican is a strong and tough bird, although not so weighty as the white species . . . . It seems never satisfied with food . . . and I must say that, much as I admire it in some respects, I should be sorry to keep it near me as a pet."

At one time, the pelican inhabited a range that stretched from North Carolina to Texas and Mexico, with a subspecies inhabiting the Caribbean and South America. In those regions, pelicans could be found soaring above the surf, loafing on off-shore sand spits, or nesting—sometimes on the ground, but usually in trees—on the small coastal islands that isolated them from such predators as raccoons and coyotes.

During the nesting season of early spring and summer, the male pelicans carry nesting materials—sticks, reeds, straws, palmetto leaves, and the like—to their mates, who in turn construct the pair's nest and lay a clutch of two to four white eggs. Upon hatching, the nestlings depend upon their parents for food for upward of nine weeks. During that time, a typical nestling consumes as much as 150 pounds of fish.

Nurtured in that manner, the nestlings grow to inherit the slightly comical appearance of their parents, thanks to the droopy underskin beneath their eighteen-inch bills. Designed for function rather than form, that underskin provides pelicans with a 2.5-gallon capacity scoop net for fishing. And when they soar into the air on a hunting expedition intended to put that bill to use, they leave their ungainly image on the ground. When describing their flight, it is difficult to best Audubon's prosaic observations:

The flight of the Brown Pelican, though to appearance heavy, is remarkably well sustained, that bird being able not only to remain many hours at a time on wing, but also to mount to a great height in the air to perform its beautiful evolutions.

Their ordinary manner of proceeding . . . is by easy flappings and sailings alternating at distances of from twenty to thirty yards, when they glide along with great speed. They move in an undulated line, passing at one time high, at another low, over the water or land, for they do not deviate from their course on coming upon a key or a point of land. When the waves run high, you may see them "troughing," as the sailors say, or directing their course along the hollows. While on wing they draw in their head between their shoulders, stretch out their broad webbed feet to their whole extent, and proceed in perfect silence. (Audubon 1844, 33)

Once airborne, pelicans glide gracefully over the open water, seeking fish such as mullet and menhaden with their sharp eyesight. But whether just off the beach or over the horizon, the pelicans' signature fishing maneuver remains the same. When they spot their prey, they dive like a Stuka dive-bomber, plunging from heights of as much as sixty feet to smash into the water, bill first. The resulting impact would kill ordinary birds. Pelicans, however, are equipped with air sacs just beneath their skin that cushion the otherwise punishing blow.

Unfortunately, pelicans were not so well equipped to confront the challenge of sharing their habitat with man. Even in his day, Audubon recognized the pressures human settlement placed on brown pelicans.

"The Pelicans," he wrote, "in fact are, year after year, retiring from the vicinity of man, and although they afford but very unsavory food at any period of their lives, will yet be hunted beyond the range of civilization, just as our best of all game, the Wild Turkey, is now, until to meet with them the student of nature will have to sail round Terra del Fuego."

In the mid-twentieth century, however, the brown pelicans confronted a menace from which they could not fly away—the widespread use of such pesticides as DDT and endrin. Those chemicals were impressive modern-day marvels and lethally effective at killing insect pests.

Unfortunately, those same chemicals posed both direct and, more insidiously, indirect threats to the pelicans. Misuse of endrin contributed to catastrophic population crashes, while DDT's metabolites found their way into the food chain, inexorably worked their way up it, and contaminated the fish ingested by the brown pelican. Those fish, in turn, contaminated the pelicans themselves.

The results, while indirect, were horrific. Female pelicans contaminated with DDT or equally insidious chemicals such as PCBs laid hopelessly thin-shelled eggs that, too often, were accidentally crushed by their distraught fathers or mothers long before being ready to hatch. By the mid-1960s, the population of pelicans in Texas and Louisiana had shrunk from some 50,000 birds to scarcely 100 pelicans fighting for survival along the Texas coast. In Louisiana—the so-called Pelican State—the species was virtually extirpated.

Confronted with this threat to the species' survival, the U.S. Fish and Wildlife Service, on October 13, 1970, listed the pelican as endangered pursuant to the Endangered Species Preservation Act—a predecessor of 1973's Endangered Species Act. Arguably, even more practical protection came in 1972, with the U.S. Environmental Protection Agency's banning of the use of DDT and its subsequent restrictions on the use, handling, and disposal of pesticides such as endrin.

Meanwhile, determined to take active measures to rebuild Louisiana's brown pelican population, the Louisiana Department of Wildlife and Fisheries joined with the Florida Game and Fresh Water Fish Commission to jointly implement a restoration project. From 1968 to 1980, the agencies reintroduced and monitored a total of 1,276 pelicans at three release sites in southeastern Louisiana. Eventually, restored nesting populations were established at North Island in the Chandeleur Island chain and at Queen Bess-Camp Island in Barataria Bay. Although the project suffered a tragic setback in 1975 when a pesticide spill killed 260 of the birds, the numbers of nesting pairs have generally trended reassuringly upward.

Elsewhere, the brown pelican staged an even more remarkable comeback and, in 1985, the U.S. Fish and Wildlife Service was able to declare that the species was no longer endangered outside of Texas and Louisiana. Meanwhile, progress continued to be made in Louisiana, where, in 1990, the state's Department of Wildlife and Fisheries surveyed approximately 1,333 nests. By 2007, there were 3,600 nesting pairs identified on Raccoon Island alone. The numbers offered a stirring testament to the successful reintroduction effort focused on the bird's recovery there.

Nevertheless, challenges remain. The U.S. Fish & Wildlife Service lists human disturbance of nesting colonies, birds being caught on fish hooks and subsequently entangled in monofilament line, oil or chemical spills, erosion, plant succession, heavy tick infestations, and hurricanes as continued threats to the species' survival.

In fact, in 2001, the pelican was not even assured of a place on Louisiana's state quarter. To select a design for the coin, Governor Mike Foster, Jr., established the Louisiana Commemorative Coin Advisory Commission, which solicited design suggestions from Louisiana residents. From the 1,193 residents (80 percent of them schoolchildren) who responded, Foster chose five finalists to submit to the U.S. Mint. In addition to the brown pelican, they included commemorative depictions of the Louisiana Purchase, an iconic Mississippi riverboat, and the Cabildo, the historic seat of the Spanish municipal government in New Orleans.

In the end, the final Louisiana quarter design incorporated not only the image of a brown pelican but also a trumpet with musical notes (symbolizing the state's jazz heritage). It also included an outline of the Louisiana Purchase territory (which, in 1803, delivered

not only New Orleans but also 828,000 squares miles of western territory to the United States at the bargain-basement price of three
cents an acre) and the explanatory inscription "Louisiana Purchase."

"The launch of the Louisiana quarter is one of those moments
that makes me proud of Louisiana," said Governor Foster at the
quarter's launch ceremony in New Orleans. Fittingly, that ceremony
was held at the historic site of the New Orleans Mint, where gold
dollars were first minted in 1838.

# 19

# INDIANA

## *Gentlemen, Start Your Engines*

Kudos to the state of Indiana. Without its foresight, that overwhelming symbol of American industry, economy, and individualism—the automobile—would never have found a place on any of the fifty state quarters.

Apparently, Indiana did not make its decision lightly. The Hoosier State's selection process began at the Indiana State Fair on August 17, 1999, when the first lady of Indiana, Judy O'Bannon, requested design concept submissions for the Indiana quarter. Her request garnered 3,736 submissions.

Culling through the responses, the Indiana Quarter Design Committee narrowed the field to seventeen semifinalists and asked

Indiana residents to vote for their favorites. The response of 160,000 voters led to a quartet of final designs being approved by the U.S. Mint. Two of the designs included a collection of sports icons and state symbols.

A third design depicted Michikinikwa—also known as Chief Little Turtle—hardly a household name but revered nonetheless as the last chief of the Miami Indians. In 1791, on the banks of the Wabash River near present-day Fort Wayne, Little Turtle inflicted arguably the bloodiest defeat on the U.S. Army at the hands of any Indian foe.

Even Chief Little Turtle, however, could not muster the historic horsepower capable of besting the final design selected by Governor Frank O'Bannon. O'Bannon's choice featured the inscription "Crossroads of America," a circle of nineteen stars signifying Indiana as the nineteenth state admitted into the Union, and a race car, intended to symbolize the Indianapolis 500 race, superimposed over an outline of the state.

"We are very proud of this coin, and we think people around the country will instantly think of Indiana when they see it," Governor O'Bannon said. "Our state played a significant role in the expansion and development of the United States at its crossroads, and this coin signifies that importance."

Do people around the United States really consider Indiana to be America's crossroads? One has to wonder. But it is hard to disagree that, if asked to identify the most legendary motor-racing event in the United States, the typical American would likely waste no time naming the Indy 500—the so-called greatest spectacle in racing. By choosing to commemorate what is officially called the Indianapolis 500-Mile Race, O'Bannon honored a racing tradition dating back over nine decades in Indiana's capital at the Indianapolis Motor Speedway.

Built in 1909, the speedway was a 2.5-mile track originally constructed for automotive research purposes. Although it is still used for research, the speedway's claim to fame comes from hosting the

Indy 500, which it first did in 1911. By then, the track's original surface of crushed stone and tar—a challenging and, frankly, deadly surface at high speeds—had already been replaced with 3.2 million bricks. Fittingly, approximately 90 percent of them were manufactured in Indiana by the Wabash Valley Clay Company. The bricks were laid on their side in a bed of sand, staggered in rows, and separated by an approximately one-inch gap filled with mortar. Eventually, they were paved over with asphalt, the current surface of most of the track.

Today, only three feet of bricks remain exposed at the start–finish line. Nevertheless, the nickname "the Brickyard" endures for what is arguably the largest and highest-capacity sporting facility in the world. The speedway has a permanent seating capacity of more than 257,000 people. Infield seating boosts capacity to an approximate 400,000 spectators.

Fewer spectators—but an impressive 80,000 nevertheless—attended the inaugural Indy 500 in 1911. With an intimidating forty cars crowding the field, race founder Carl Fisher reasoned that a standing start—as was usually done at the time—would be impracticable. Instead, he used a pace car to enable a rolling start, an innovation that was destined to become commonplace in races to come.

Other innovations could be found in the cars themselves. Ray Harroun, a talented race-car designer destined to win the first race, piloted a Marmon Wasp—a car believed to be the first to use a rearview mirror. With his newfangled rearview mirror in place, Harroun was able to dispense with a passenger-mechanic riding with him. Such co-pilots were a convention in racing at the time, intended not only to keep an eye on the car's gauges but also to serve as a lookout for other racers. Harroun's decision to go solo raised the ire of many of his fellow drivers, who felt he was compromising their safety.

The other drivers' mood did not improve when Harroun claimed the checkered flag after six hours, forty-two minutes, and eight seconds of racing. He averaged seventy-five miles per hour (today's racers reach speeds approaching 238 miles per hour) and took home a winner's purse of $14,000.

As the years passed, tradition seemed to become as important as innovation. Today, the Indy 500 is the oldest auto race in the world, having been run every year since 1911 except during the two world wars. The race, sanctioned by the Indy Racing League, is held every Memorial Day with a field of thirty-three racers. On race day, prior to the firing of the competitors' engines, the crowd is serenaded with "Back Home Again in Indiana." As the final notes fade away, a massive armada of multicolored balloons is released skyward.

Two hundred laps and 500 miles later, the winner is wreathed in a garland of thirty-three ivory-colored Cymbidium orchids with burgundy tips and thirty-three miniature checkered flags, intertwined with red, white, and blue ribbons. In homage to a tradition started in 1936 by three-time Indy winner Louis Meyer (whose mother had told him that buttermilk was good for him on a hot summer day), the winner chugs a cold bottle of milk. It was a tradition temporarily—and notoriously—upended in 1993, when winner Emerson Fittipaldi chose instead to drink orange juice to promote Brazil's citrus industry. Regardless of his drink of choice, the winner thereafter receives the Borg-Warner trophy, upon which the face of every winner is sculpted in bas-relief, and the keys to the race's pace car.

One tradition, however, may not be destined to survive. To date, every Indy 500 winner has been a man. Nevertheless, a female face may one day appear on the Borg-Warner trophy. Janet Guthrie became the first female driver to race in the Indy 500 in 1979, followed by Lyn St. James, and then Danica Patrick. In the 2007 race, a record number of women—Danica Patrick, Sarah Fisher, and Venezuelan Milka Duno—joined the field.

Nevertheless, tradition remains an integral component of the Indy 500, offering a stark contrast to the technologically cutting-edge attributes of a modern Indy car. An IRL IndyCar Series car, with horsepower four times that of an average car, accelerates from 0 to 100 miles per hour in less than three seconds. At 220 mph, it generates enough aerodynamic downforce so that, technically, it could run upside down if that speed were maintained. Its tires, with tread depth only slightly thicker than a credit card, approach the temperature of boiling water when running at speed—and actually become tarlike in consistency in order to help the car stick to the track. Of course, all of that speed and power comes with a price— which includes gas mileage figures of less than two miles per gallon.

On August 8, 2002, one of those same Indycars, joined by a lumbering Brinks armored car, rolled down the brickyard in a most unusual convoy. The Indycar delivered Governor O'Bannon; the armored car delivered the first of the Indiana state quarters to a waiting public.

On that celebratory day, however, an American racing fan might be forgiven for pointing out a fly in the proverbial ointment. Two months earlier at the Brickyard, Brazilian Helio Castroneves had claimed his second back-to-back victory in that year's Indy 500. But perhaps the Indiana quarter helped inspire America's racing cadre to rise to the challenge. Arizonan Buddy Rice won the race in 2003; Ohioan Sam Hornish, Jr., quaffed a celebratory glass of milk in 2006.

Nevertheless, foreign competition remains strong, as was evident in 2007, when Scotland's Dario Franchitti captured the checkered flag—but at least his wife (actress Ashley Judd) is an American. Franchitti's prize money amounted to $1,645,233, a mere drop in the bucket compared to the $172,450,000 worth of Indiana state quarters minted in 2002.

# MISSISSIPPI
## *Steel Magnolias*

Although the Civil War was the crucible of the modern United States, that episode in American history gets short shrift in the 50 State Quarters® Program. Not a single coin commemorates either the Blue or the Gray. Nevertheless, Mississippi's state quarter, with its blossoming bouquet of magnolia leaves erupting across the coin's reverse, provides an indirect but potent reminder of the bloody conflict that forged today's America.

The embers of that forge flared to life on January 9, 1861, when Mississippi became the first state to follow South Carolina's lead and secede from the Union. Two weeks later, on January 26, 1861, the state unveiled its new banner. Mississippi's flag was white, with a five-pointed white star in a blue canton. A magnolia tree was painted or embroidered on the flag's white field. Even in the nineteenth century, the romantic southern magnolia—*Magnolia grandiflora*, named after famed eighteenth-century French botanist Pierre Magnol—had already seduced the Southern psyche with its spectacular fragrant white flowers and lustrous green leaves.

In the spring of 1861, however, Mississippi was focused on war, not love. With enthusiastic companies of troops being raised for action across the state, a host of martial nicknames proliferated— such as the Rough and Readies, the Quitman Grays, the Pettus Rifles, and the Panola Vindicators.

Meanwhile, in northern Mississippi's Calhoun County, several dozen farmers, tradesmen, and laborers converged on the small hamlet of Sarepta. On April 23, 1861, they elected John M. Lyles as their commanding officer and, in homage to *Magnolia grandiflora*, christened themselves the Magnolia Guards.

Ordered to Corinth shortly thereafter, the company joined the Seventeenth Mississippi Infantry Regiment, was redesignated Company K, and immediately set forth to distant Virginia. Company K's baptism of fire came at the First Battle of Bull Run—a fight that cost its regiment two dead and ten wounded.

After Bull Run, both sides, unsettled by the chaos of that first battle, fell into a period of watchful unease and regrouping. The lull was shattered on October 21, when Union forces landed along the Potomac River at Ball's Bluff, near the town of Leesburg. In response, Company K and its regiment joined in a fearsome counterattack.

"The whole line marched forward in the most admirable order upon a vastly superior force," recalled Colonel Winfield S. Featherston, the Seventeenth's regimental commander, "reserving their fire until within the most effective range; then pouring it in with deadly effect and rushing forward over ground broken into abrupt hills and ravines, and covered with thick woods, without a single halt or waver, until the enemy was literally driven into the river."

At Ball's Bluff, the regiment again lost two men; this time, however, it captured over 300 dejected blue-clad prisoners in one of the most resounding Confederate victories of the war's early days. After the battle, Featherston left the regiment, leaving it in the command of W. D. Holder.

The following summer, Holder led his regiment through the Seven Days Battles outside of Richmond, Virginia, culminating in the desperate charge against Malvern Hill. A bloody cataract of shell, grape, canister, and minié balls poured into the attacking Mississippians, killing or wounding close to one-third of them and knocking Holder out of action with a broken thigh.

The regiment's next big fight came at Sharpsburg on September 17, 1862. Marching to the sound of the guns, Lieutenant Colonel John C. Fiser (barely twenty-four years old) led the foot-weary Seventeenth into battle, leaving its stragglers behind and pushing the Federal forces so far back into the woods to their front that, in the end, the regiment was in danger of being cut off and captured. The regiment suffered nearly 100 casualties that day.

Three months later, the battle of Fredericksburg saw the regiment and the men of Company K in the thick of the fight once again. This time, Fiser's regiment found themselves fighting one of the classic defensive battles of the war. Posted along the town's riverbank in or behind rifle pits, cellars, windows, and fences, for twelve hours the Mississippians fought off Union efforts to successfully bridge the Rappahannock River. Giving way only in the face of a punishing artillery bombardment, Fiser's men retreated street by street before joining the rest of the Confederate force arrayed along or on Marye's Heights.

In the summer of 1863, the Gettysburg campaign brought further hard fighting—the heaviest the regiment and the men of Calhoun

County had seen yet. On the second day of the Battle of Gettysburg, the regiment joined in the assault on the Union army's southern flank. Fighting like demons, the Mississippians tore into the peach orchard held by the Federal troops, only to be nearly overwhelmed by sheer numbers. In the end, the remnants of the Seventeenth had no choice but to retreat, leaving forty killed and 160 wounded on the field of battle.

Following General Robert E. Lee's retreat south, the Confederate high command shifted the Seventeenth into the war's western theater of operations, arriving in Georgia just in time to fight in the Battle of Chickamauga. Captain A. R. Govan was the acting regimental commander at the time; he paid for the honor with the loss of a leg. In all, the fight at Chickamauga cost the regiment twelve killed and seventy-five wounded.

Unbeknownst to the erstwhile Magnolia Guards, the Seventeenth Mississippi Infantry's toughest fight of the war still lay ahead of them.

In the wake of its defeat at Chickamauga, the Union army retreated to its bastions of Chattanooga and Knoxville. A fortification known as Fort Sanders protected the key approach to the latter. Undeterred by Fort Sanders's formidable defenses, Lieutenant Colonel Fiser pushed for a decision to storm the fort. Unfortunately, his argument was successful and an attack against Fort Sanders's southwest salient was ordered.

On November 29, 1863, the assault began, with two parallel columns of the Thirteenth and Seventeenth Mississippi Infantry Regiments leading the way. Ignoring snipers and cannon fire, the Mississippi troops hacked and twisted their way through 150 yards of a tangled abatis. Upon clearing the abatis, the regiments paused only momentarily to regroup before rushing across a patch of open ground toward the fort.

At that point, the men of the Thirteenth and Seventeenth encountered their most implacable obstacle yet—a six-foot-wide, ten-foot-deep ditch, fringed with a network of wire. Beyond it rose the fort's icy parapet, some twelve feet high. Undaunted, the regiments poured into the ditch, bridging it with their bodies as best as they could as they tried to clamber up the slippery parapet.

The result was a bloody disaster. From the parapet above, Union troops hurled axes, rocks, and even sticks of wood, while artillery and sharpshooters firing from another angle of the fort added to the carnage. Nevertheless, some of the Confederates somehow managed to plant their flags on the enemy ramparts. Eventually, though, it was all to no avail. Bloodied and battered, the remnants of two Mississippi regiments retreated back through the abatis. A good 140 of their comrades did not make it back with them, and Fiser paid for his aggression with his arm.

"Nowhere in the war," declared Confederate artilleryman Edward P. Alexander, "was individual example more splendidly illustrated than on that fatal slope and in that bloody ditch."

Deployed to Virginia the following spring, the regiment saw even more fighting at the Wilderness, Spotsylvania Courthouse, Cold Harbor, Petersburg, and in the Shenandoah Valley. After weathering the final winter of the war, the regiment joined in the Army of Northern Virginia's dash for freedom in the spring of 1865. Cut off at Sailor's Creek, the Seventeenth Regiment was decimated even further. By the time Lee surrendered at Appomattox, the regiment, which had started the war with 600 men, was down to sixty-two soldiers.

The cost of four years of fighting weighed even heavier on the ranks of Company K. The Magnolia Guards was reduced to only seven soldiers—scarcely a squad. Only Privates Aaron B. Carter, Henry Calvin, William Greer, Aaron Phillips, George Tankersly, Jonathan D. Williams, and musician Kirk H. Chilcoat were still on the company's muster roll.

In the years to come, time managed to heal at least some of the war's old wounds and varnished the horrific memories of Malvern

Hill, Gettysburg, and Fort Sanders. And in the place of the Magnolia Guards, there arose the phrase "moonlight and magnolias," a description, according to the *New Encyclopedia of Southern Culture*, of "one of the South's central myths—the story of the charmed and graceful society of the Old South."

Myth or not, Mississippi's schoolchildren voted overwhelmingly in 1900 to make the magnolia the state flower, beating out the cotton blossom and the cape jasmine. A similar election for state tree in 1935 gave the magnolia a landslide victory, one that was made official on April 1, 1938. On February 26, 1952, the Mississippi legislature finally adopted the magnolia as the state flower, opposed by only a single vote.

With the heft of such precedent weighing on him, Governor Ronnie Musgrove's decision in 2001 was likely not surprising to his constituents. He passed over a Magnolia flower with a branch and another with a mockingbird, choosing the one entitled "Mississippi: The Magnolia State."

"This is an exciting and historic day for Mississippi," Musgrove remarked at the quarter's official launch ceremony. "This coin showcases the beauty throughout our state and symbolizes our Southern heritage . . . . For years to come, Mississippians can be proud of this coin and its unique design."

# ILLINOIS
## *Lincoln's Hat Trick*

Nearly 100 years ago, Abraham Lincoln made his first appearance on a coin. In 1909, his bearded visage replaced the unidentified Indian princess who had adorned the penny for the previous fifty years. Eleven years later, in 1918, Lincoln's face again appeared on a coin—that time on the commemorative Illinois Centennial Half Dollar. And in 2003, a young, ambitious Lincoln, law book tucked under one arm, claimed not only the center of Illinois' state quarter but a third appearance on America's coinage.

Although Illinois' official motto is "The Prairie State," the moniker "Land of Lincoln" is more widely recognized, and deservedly so.

From Illinois, Lincoln sprang onto the national stage at one of the most critical moments in American history. Five years later, it was back to Illinois that a funeral train carried Lincoln's remains.

In truth, Lincoln was not a native of Illinois; rather, he was born in a one-room log cabin in Sinking Spring, Kentucky, in 1809, the first president to be born in a log cabin and the first to be born outside of the original thirteen colonies. Two years later, his family moved to nearby Knob Creek; when he turned seven, the Lincoln clan moved north to Indiana, near present-day Gentryville. There he would spend the next fourteen years.

In fact, it was not until 1830, when Lincoln was twenty-one, that his family moved to Illinois and settled along the Sangamon River, near what is now Decatur. Soon thereafter, he left home and moved to New Salem, where he worked as a clerk in one store, became part owner of another (which eventually failed), served as a postmaster, and worked as a surveyor.

Lincoln also served briefly with the Thirty-first Regiment of Illinois, a local militia unit, during the Blackhawk War. He saw no action—other than, as he noted with characteristic self-deprecation, "a good many bloody struggles with the musquetoes." Nevertheless, his election as his company's captain stoked dreams of a higher calling and, in August 1832, he ran for a seat in the Illinois General Assembly as a candidate for the Whig Party.

"Fellow citizens, I presume you all know who I am—I am humble Abraham Lincoln," he said at an early campaign speech. "I have been solicited by many friends to become a candidate for the legislature. My policies are short and sweet, like the old woman's dance. I am in favor of a National Bank, I am in favor of the internal improvement system, and a high protective tariff. These are my sentiments and political principles. If elected I shall be thankful; and if not, it will be all the same."

In the end, it was "all the same." Lincoln finished eighth in a field of thirteen candidates, a disappointing start to his political career.

Two years later, Lincoln rebounded from his earlier defeat by winning election to the Assembly from Sangamon County. He would go on to be reelected three more times, eventually become a member of the "Long Nine," a group of nine Whigs elected from Sangamon County noted for their remarkable height (for his part, Lincoln stood an impressive six feet, four inches).

Thanks in no small part to Lincoln's legislative work, Illinois' state capital relocated to Springfield. Lincoln himself followed suit. A contemporary newspaperman described Lincoln's new hometown in 1839 as containing "a throng of stores, taverns, and shops . . . and an agreeable assemblage of dwelling houses very neatly painted, most of them white, and situated somewhat retiringly behind tasteful front yards."

Meanwhile, Lincoln began studying to practice law and on September 9, 1836, received his license to practice law from the Illinois Supreme Court. He logged his first appearance in court on October 5, 1836, representing a defendant named Wooldridge who was accused of severely beating a man named Hawthorn. Hawthorn, incapacitated for six weeks and unable to work, had sued Wooldridge for $500 in damages. Although the jury returned a verdict for Hawthorn, it only awarded him $36 in damages.

The Wooldridge case marked the beginning of a successful but arduous law practice for Lincoln. He literally "rode the circuit" in the U.S. Eighth Circuit, a sparsely settled region that encompassed 12,000 square miles, with little more than a volume of the Revised Statutes, copies of Blackstone's *Commentaries* and Chitty's *On Pleadings*, and an extra shirt and change of underwear in his saddlebags.

In the meantime, Lincoln pursued an on-again, off-again courtship of Mary Todd, a Lexington, Kentucky, belle who had moved to Springfield to live with her sister Elizabeth. The courtship culminated in their wedding on November 4, 1842. "Nothing new here," Lincoln later wrote to a friend, "except my marrying, which to me, is matter of profound wonder."

Four years later, Lincoln had made enough of a name on the Eighth Circuit to be able to win election to the U.S. House of Representatives in 1846. In Congress, he earned a reputation as "a droll Westerner of average talents"; back home, his opposition to the Mexican War made him increasingly unpopular. Lincoln's opposition manifested itself most publicly in a series of resolutions that challenged President James Polk to admit that the "spot" where American blood was first shed was, in fact, in Mexican territory. In the end, however, all his so-called spot resolutions earned him was the nickname "Spotty Lincoln," so in May 1849, Lincoln returned home to Illinois and his law practice.

In the spring of 1854, Lincoln heeded the call of politics once again, this time energized by Senator Stephen Douglas's Kansas-Nebraska Act. Douglas's legislation repealed the Missouri Compromise that prohibited slavery north of Missouri's southern border. Motivated by his opposition to slavery's spread, Lincoln ran for the U.S. Senate in 1855 but lost—a defeat that did not prevent him, a year later, from being nominated (unsuccessfully) at the Republican national convention in Philadelphia for vice president.

The year 1858 brought another political race for Lincoln, this time against Senator Douglas when Douglas sought reelection. In accepting the Republican Party's nomination at the state capitol in Springfield, Lincoln warned, "a house divided against itself cannot stand. I believe this government cannot endure permanently half slave and half free." The famous Lincoln-Douglas debates ensued and, although Lincoln is credited with winning the debates (and the popular vote), Illinois' legislators, sitting in electoral college, sent Douglas back to Washington, D.C.

Nevertheless, the debates ensured Lincoln of a national reputation and, in 1860, he spoke to the Young Men's Central Republican Union of New York City at Cooper Union on February 27, 1860, an event that marked a watershed moment in his career. Speaking on the subject of slavery and its expansion into the new territories, he stated with characteristic eloquence: "Let us have faith that right makes might, and in that faith let us, to the end, dare to do our duty as we understand it."

Less than three months later, Lincoln secured the Republican Party's nomination for president at its convention in Chicago; in the general election that followed, he faced Stephen Douglas, John Breckinridge, and John Bell. Although he took only 40 percent of the popular vote, his clear majority of the electoral vote carried the day. Lincoln's time in Illinois was coming to a close.

On February 11, 1861, a day before his fifty-second birthday, Lincoln stood on the Springfield train platform, his family's luggage roped together with cards that read: "A. Lincoln, White House, Washington, D.C." As rain pelted a crowd of well-wishers, he emotionally bade his friends and neighbors farewell.

"My friends, no one, not in my situation, can appreciate my feeling of sadness at this parting," Lincoln said. "To this place, and the kindness of these people, I owe every thing. Here I have lived a quarter of a century and have passed from a young to an old man. Here my children have been born and one is buried. I now leave, not knowing when, or whether ever, I may return, with a task before me greater than that which rested upon Washington. Without the assistance of that Divine Being who ever attended him I cannot succeed. With that assistance I cannot fail."

Four years passed before Lincoln returned to Illinois—and on an even sadder occasion. On April 21, 1865, Lincoln's funeral train, carrying his remains and those of his son Willie (who had died in the White House of typhoid fever at the age of eleven), departed from Washington, D.C., bound for Illinois. After a twelve-day journey, the train arrived in Springfield. After his remains lay in state at the state capitol, he was buried at Springfield's Oak Ridge Cemetery on May 4, 1865, thereby ensuring that Illinois would always be "the Land of Lincoln."

But Illinois is a land of many people and many things, so in January 2001, Governor George Ryan announced the Governor's

Classroom Contest to solicit ideas for the state's quarter design. The contest generated more than 6,000 submissions, with approximately 5,700 coming from schoolchildren. After a fourteen-member committee reviewed the submissions, Illinois forwarded three concepts to the U.S. Mint for consideration: Illinois history; agriculture and industry; and state symbols.

In response, the Mint returned five designs based on the concepts for final selection by Governor Ryan. The final design, "Land of Lincoln—21st State/Century," with its depiction of a farm scene, Chicago's skyline, Lincoln's figure, and the phrases "Land of Lincoln" and "21st State/Century," was deemed to fully represent the history and future of Illinois, the twenty-first state to have entered the Union.

In the meantime, the U.S. Mint's Presidential $1 Coin Program has ensured that Lincoln will one day have yet another coin to his credit. That program, modeled on the wildly successful 50 State Quarters® Program, is releasing four one-dollar coins a year in honor of each of the nation's deceased presidents in the order in which they served. As the sixteenth president, Lincoln's turn will come again in 2010.

## 22

# ALABAMA
## *The Other Helen Keller*

One of the great ironies of the 50 State Quarters® Program is that Alabama, where the appellation "liberal" is, for the most part, a four-letter word, selected what one biographer described as a "rabid Socialist" as the subject of its state quarter. And the identity of that rabid Socialist? She is none other than Helen Keller.

In an earlier assessment of Keller, Mark Twain declared her to be, along with Napoleon Bonaparte, "one of the two most interesting people of the nineteenth century." In the century that followed, President Lyndon Johnson awarded her the nation's highest civilian recognition, the Presidential Medal of Freedom, honoring her in the twilight years of a life of remarkable accomplishments.

That string of accomplishments traced its beginning to Tuscumbia, Alabama, where Keller was born in 1880 at the family home known as Ivy Green. Her genteel life in the Tennessee Valley river town shattered, however, when, at the age of one and a half, a severe illness—possibly scarlet fever or meningitis—claimed both her sight and her hearing. Furious and frustrated by the resulting alienation from a speaking, seeing world, she degenerated into a half-wild child prone to fits of almost demonic rage.

In despair, Keller's parents sought the guidance of Dr. Alexander Graham Bell. In return, he dispatched Anne Sullivan—the "Miracle Worker" of Keller's life—to live with the Keller family in Tuscumbia. Sullivan's arrival promised hope of a better future for a troubled young girl snared in a life of darkness and silence. Hope turned to joy with seven-year-old Keller's fabled encounter with a garden water pump and the realization that there was a word to describe the water flowing through her small hands.

Freed of her isolation, Keller quickly displayed an astonishing intellect. Six months after she learned the simple word "water," she had learned to write. By the age of ten, she had mastered Braille, the manual alphabet, and even learned how to use a typewriter. Not stopping at English, she had learned French, German, Latin, and Greek by the time she turned thirteen. Determined to learn to speak, she mastered that challenge so successfully that she was able to attend Radcliffe College. She graduated cum laude in 1904 as the first deaf-blind person to ever graduate from college. A year earlier, she had published her best-selling autobiography, *The Story of My Life*.

Nevertheless, most Americans are acquainted only with the remarkable personal accomplishments during the earlier parts of Keller's life. Such familiarity owes, in large part, to the 1962 film *The Miracle Worker*. The truth of the matter, however, is that once

Keller mastered language and connected with the outside world, she directed her considerable intellect and personal drive in directions that she thought would lead to making the wider world a better place.

Viewed in the hindsight illuminated by several decades of intervening history, some of those directions seem naive. After reading Marx and Engels in German Braille, she joined the Socialist Party in Massachusetts in 1909. An active member of the party, she lectured and wrote compelling articles in defense of socialism, supporting trade unions and strikes, and even opposed American entry into World War I.

Today, such affinities might seem merely misdirected, considering the course of events to come. In the middle decades of the last century, however, such inclinations were deadly serious. In fact, Helen Keller's reputed ties to the Communist Party merited her own file at the Federal Bureau of Investigation.

Documents provided by the FBI in response to a Freedom of Information Act request produced a November 8, 1956, "name check request" that contained a variety of allegations about Keller "presumed to have been obtained from reliable sources." Rather ironically, many of those "reliable sources" seem to have been the *Daily Worker*, an East Coast Communist newspaper.

Issues of the *Daily Worker's* reliability aside, the FBI report cited several of the newspaper's articles in its discussion of Keller. One article claimed she had signed a petition drafted by the "American Friends of Spanish Democracy," an organization that supported the Loyalist forces in Spain's civil war. As the report noted, the Special Committee on Un-American Activities had subsequently decided that that "multifarious so-called relief organization" was thoroughly infiltrated by the Communist Party.

Another article noted her support of the Friends of the Abraham Lincoln Brigade, which the Special Committee had also decried as a "communist-front organization." In that case, Keller was in good company, sharing her support with such talents and intellectual luminaries as Albert Einstein, Dorothy Parker, Gene Kelly, and Paul Robeson—all of whom supported the military volunteers fighting the Fascists in Spain's civil war. Still another article identified her as sponsoring a dinner at the Hotel New Yorker held under the auspices of the Congress of American-Soviet Friendship—yet another Communist-front organization.

Other evidence of Keller's political proclivities included a letterhead from the United American Spanish Aid Committee—yet another reputed Communist organization—and a report of a congratulatory letter celebrating the twenty-fifth anniversary of the Red Army. Another source identified her arriving at a reception at the Soviet consulate in New York and declaring, "Finally, I am on Soviet soil." Still another reported friendly correspondence between Keller and the American Communist Mother Ella Reeve Bloor. Keller's signature on a March 1948 letter to the Speaker of the House of Representatives protesting the House Committee on Un-American Activities gained further unfavorable comment, as did her sponsorship of the Committee of One Thousand, another "Communist-created and controlled front organization." So did a warm 1957 letter to Elizabeth Gurley Flynn, the Communist leader, then in jail for violating the Smith Act.

In another touch of irony, Keller, who was apparently unaware of the FBI file compiled on her during the height of the Red Scare period, later included FBI chief Herbert Hoover in her mailing list of solicitations for donations for her American Foundation for the Blind. "Inasmuch as it is a form letter and in view of the large number of similar requests received by the Director, it is not felt that this letter should be acknowledged," an internal FBI memo stated.

Other aspects of Keller's social activism did not need to be ferreted out by the FBI. She publicly supported the socialist Eugene Debs in his quixotic race for the presidency in 1920 and even joined the militant labor union Industrial Workers of the World (IWW).

"I was appointed on a commission to investigate the conditions of the blind," Keller once said when questioned about her membership in the IWW. "For the first time I, who had thought blindness a misfortune beyond human control, found that too much of it was traceable to wrong industrial conditions, often caused by the selfishness and greed of employers. And the social evil contributed its share. I found that poverty drove women to a life of shame that ended in blindness."

Over the years, Keller's political and social views found voice in a number of her writings, notably 1938's *Helen Keller's Journal.* In it, Keller not only condemned Germany's Nazi Party but also encouraged the sitdown strikes of the Committee for Industrial Organization and berated Margaret Mitchell's *Gone with the Wind* for sentimentalizing Southern slavery.

Less controversial, at least to many modern sensibilities, were her campaigns for the right of women to vote and to have access to birth control. Furthermore, as a natural advocate for the blind and disabled, she traveled extensively to raise funds for the American Foundation for the Blind. It was no coincidence, therefore, that Alabama's state quarter became the first American coin to have Braille imprinted on it. Nor is it coincidental that the quarter bears the appellation "Spirit of Courage" emblazoned on a banner underneath Keller's straight-backed pose, where she sits on the reverse of the quarter between a longleaf pine branch and a sprig of magnolia.

Keller's appearance on Alabama's quarter resulted from a statewide competition for Alabama schools to submit concepts for the Alabama quarter. After a review of thousands of concepts submitted, Governor Don Siegelman forwarded three themes to the U.S. Mint for its consideration: Helen Keller, Alabama's role in social movements, and Alabama's social and economic history. The Mint reciprocated with five candidate designs; in the end, Governor Siegelman selected Helen Keller and the "Spirit of Courage" to grace what would one day be 457.4 million state quarters.

When it came time to unveil the new quarter on March 24, 2003, at Ivy Green, a new governor, Bob Riley, occupied the governor's mansion. Although his politics differed from those of the former governor, his speech that day made it clear that he shared his Democratic predecessor's affinity for the Helen Keller quarter—regardless of Governor Siegelman's, or Keller's, own politics.

"Her life and accomplishments cast a wonderful reflection upon the State of Alabama, the United States, and upon all mankind," Riley declared. "And having her image on a national coin—Alabama's coin—shall remind us all of the courage and strength that exists in the most unlikely places."

# 23

# MAINE

## *The Maine Attractions*

The year was 1635. It was less than thirty years after the English first settled Jamestown, scarcely a decade into the permanent settlement of what would one day be Maine, and at the height of the so-called Great Migration of some 70,000 English Puritans to New England and the Chesapeake Bay area.

Some of those Puritan migrants sailed westward in large, well-organized fleets, such as John Winthrop's 700-settler expedition of eleven ships to the Massachusetts Bay Colony in 1630. Other would-be colonists, however, trusted their lives, families, and fortunes to smaller ventures—as did the 100-odd men and women who, in the spring of 1635, booked passage on the galleon *Angel Gabriel* in Bristol, England, and sailed for the New World.

At the time, the hardy *Angel Gabriel*, crewed by twenty-three sailors, was a slow but steady 240-ton twenty-year veteran of the Atlantic. Sir Walter Raleigh had commissioned the vessel's construction in 1615 and named it *Starre;* two years later, for his expedition to Guiana, he renamed it *Jason.* The ship was renamed a third time, to become the *Angel Gabriel*, after Raleigh's arrest upon his return to England. An ancient sailors' superstition warns that it is unlucky to rename a ship; in the *Angel Gabriel*'s case, the superstition would prove tragically accurate.

A summer voyage brought the *Angel Gabriel*—separated during the voyage, owing to slow speed, from the other four accompanying ships—to the shores of Maine. For the surviving ninety-eight colonists, who had weathered seasickness, an outbreak of smallpox, and two months of close quarters with the twenty-six cows and calves that accompanied them on board the ship, Pemaquid Point must have been a welcome sight.

On the afternoon of August 14, the *Angel Gabriel*, battling increasing winds and a stiffening breeze, anchored off the Maine coast and began unloading passengers. Nightfall not only interrupted the unloading but cloaked the arrival of a catastrophic hurricane, one of the worst in New England's recorded history.

By the wee morning hours of the following day, the storm surge was running as high as twenty feet. The boiling surf and raging winds pushed the hapless galleon into John Bay, where it was slashed apart by the bay's treacherous shoals and split open beneath Pemaquid Point's granite cliffs. Fortunately, with many of the ship's party already ashore, the disaster only claimed the lives of one sailor, between two and four settlers, and most of the cattle and cargo. In return, it left a stern reminder of the perils of navigation along Maine's rocky coast.

Other stretches of shoreline witnessed similar disasters as the years passed, but it was not until 1716 that a lighthouse first illuminated America's shores, specifically, the Boston Lighthouse on Little Brewster Island. Nevertheless, Congress underscored the importance of lighthouses when, in only the ninth statute that it enacted, it passed "An Act for the Establishment of Lighthouses, Beacons, and Buoys" in 1789. Two years later, Maine's first lighthouse began operation at Portland Head.

Even after the passage of what became known as the Lighthouses Act of 1789, it took another quarter of a century for Congress to appropriate $4,000 to construct a lighthouse at Pemaquid Point in 1826. The first lighthouse, completed shortly thereafter, soon crumbled—a demise caused, some suspected, by its builder's use of saltwater in his lime mortar.

Learning from its earlier mistake, the government's subsequent contract specified that only fresh water be used, and by 1835, the thirty-eight-foot stone tower was in place, an edifice that still stands today. Because of its setting on a rock ledge, the lighthouse actually rises nearly eighty feet above the surf, and because of its fourth-order Fresnel lens (now fully automated), it can be spotted from fourteen nautical miles out to sea.

Back in the nineteenth century, however, lighthouses required rugged individuals such as Issac Dunham to serve as tenders and keep the lights lit. Dunham, Pemaquid Point's first tender, earned $350 a year for his work, a supplement to his income from a small farm nearby. As far as his lighthouse was concerned, though, Dunham was more than satisfied. Inspecting his new charge, he stated, "I will venture to say, a better tower and lantern never was built in the state."

By 1869, the lighthouse was in the capable hands of Marcus Hanna, a Bristol native and Civil War veteran. Hanna had served in both the U.S. Navy and in a regiment of Massachusetts volunteers during the war; while with the latter during the siege of Port Hudson, Louisiana, he earned the Medal of Honor. After his tour of duty at Pemaquid, he transferred to the Cape Elizabeth Light on Portland Head. There, he earned another medal—the Gold Lifesaving Medal—for rescuing two sailors from the shipwrecked schooner *Australia* in 1885.

Even with the Pemaquid Point Lighthouse in place and men like Marcus Hanna tending it, the waters off Bristol remained dangerous. Even the tenders tasked with keeping the lighthouse stocked with supplies rued their trips to Pemaquid Point, where they had to anchor amid the dangerous rocks and ferry the supplies ashore in launches. And on September 16, 1903, there was nothing that the lighthouse or its keeper, Clarence Marr, could do to prevent a terrible tragedy from occurring under its very nose.

That day, a sudden gale caught the fishing schooner *George F. Edmunds* at sea. The skipper decided to make a run for South Bristol harbor; it proved to be a fatal mistake. Caught on the same shoals that had claimed *Angel Gabriel* over two and a half centuries earlier, the *George F. Edmunds* was dashed to pieces on the unforgiving rocks. Thirteen men, including the schooner's skipper, lost their lives. Only two survived.

Despite such tragic undercurrents lurking in its history, Pemaquid Point and its lighthouse remain one of the most visited and photographed tourist spots in Maine. And unlike the *Angel Gabriel* and the *George F. Edmunds*, most of Maine's sailing stories have far happier endings, such as that of the *Victory Chimes*.

First launched at Bethel, Delaware, in 1900, the *Victory Chimes* is a three-masted schooner built of Georgia pine and Delaware oak with three Douglas fir spars soaring eight stories high above its decks. Originally named the *Edwin and Maud*, after the first skipper's two children, the 170-foot-long schooner earned its keep as a merchant ship for the first half century of life. Later, during World War II, the vessel performed patriotic duties in the waters of the Chesapeake Bay, helping to patrol and maintain the bay's defensive network of anti-submarine nets and minefields. In the end, however, the *Edwin and Maud* was ill-rewarded for wartime services. Peace brought with it a glut of surplus cargo ships, and an old sailing schooner like the *Edwin and Maud* was poorly equipped to meet the challenge they posed.

For a time, the old schooner survived as an excursion boat for vacationers in the waters off Annapolis. But in 1954, new owners provided a new lease on life. They brought the ship from Annapolis to Maine, newly christened the *Victory Chimes*, and put it to work as a Windjammer charter boat. In 1997, the schooner became one of only 127 vessels designated an American National Historic Landmark. Today, sailing out of Rockland, Maine, *Victory Chimes* remains the largest American flagged pure sailing vessel still in operation.

Given the prominent imprint of Pemaquid Point and the state's popular Windjammer fleet on Maine's subconscious, it was not surprising that in a popular vote, the citizens of Maine opted for the design featuring Pemaquid Point and the *Victory Chimes*. The design bested three other final concepts—"Nation's First Light," "Where America's Day Begins," and Mount Katahdin (the northern terminus of the Appalachian Trail).

According to some accounts, however, the accurate depiction of *Victory Chimes* only occurred following eleventh-hour changes to the U.S. Mint's proposed design. According to Paul DeGaeta, one of *Victory Chime's* two captains and owners, the original design looked suspiciously like the two-masted topsail schooner *Pride of Baltimore*.

"That was never going to fly," DeGaeta said. "People in Maine know their ships!"

Less controversial was the U.S. Mint's selection of Pemaquid Point to celebrate the quarter's official launch. "Pemaquid Point is a spectacular setting for this historic event," Governor John Baldacci declared at the ceremony on June 9, 2003, "and our state quarter depicts a scene that demonstrates part of what makes Maine such a special place."

Some had hoped that the ceremony's scene might include *Victory Chimes* sailing off the coast. Conflicts in the charter schedule, however, prohibited the schooner from making an appearance. Given the heavy fog that blanketed the area, it was unlikely that the ship would have been visible anyway. It was a fact not lost on DeGaeta, who telephoned his co-captain, Richard "Kip" Files, on the day of the event. DeGaeta was at sea; Files was in attendance at the launch ceremony as a guest speaker. Upon hearing of the fog, DeGaeta had a practical suggestion.

"I told Kip, hell, it's so damn foggy out there, just tell them that we're here—they'll never know the difference!"

# 24

# MISSOURI
*Show Me (the Money)*

Willard D. Vandiver represented Missouri in the U.S. House of Representatives from 1897 to 1905. In 1899, while attending a banquet, he was offered the podium to respond to an earlier speaker's comments. Vandiver, a former college president, stood up and, according to legend, said, "I come from a state that raises corn and cotton and cockleburs and Democrats, and frothy eloquence neither convinces nor satisfies me. I am from Missouri. You have got to show me." If the legends are to be believed, that moment marked the conception of Missouri's nickname as the "Show Me State."

Missouri's state quarter, however, does not include its famous nickname. Instead, it depicts Meriwether Lewis and William Clark's historic return to St. Louis down the Missouri River (seemingly paddling through an anachronistic Jefferson National Expansion Memorial [Gateway Arch] in the background). The inscription "Corps of Discovery 1804–2004" commemorates the expedition's bicentennial.

And for that reason alone, an inscription reading "The Show Me State" would be redundant. With his eye on a route to the distant Pacific, President Thomas Jefferson had ordered: "Show me." In response, Lewis and Clark responded magnificently with an epic 8,000-mile journey that began and ended in St. Louis and showed the young nation a Western landscape of unparalleled promise. Show me, indeed.

The genesis of the Lewis and Clark expedition lay in the late summer of 1802, when President Thomas Jefferson read of the Scots trader Alexander MacKenzie's journey from Alberta, Canada, across the Rocky Mountains to the Pacific Coast. Spurred by Great Britain's challenge for the Pacific Northwest, Jefferson decided to mount an American expedition overland to the Pacific. In requesting the $2,500 needed to finance such an expedition from Congress, he expressed his goals in the following terms:

> The interests of commerce [to wit, challenging Great Britain's fur trade in the Pacific Northwest] place the principal object within the constitutional powers and care of Congress, and that it should incidentally advance the geographical knowledge of our own continent can not but be an additional gratification. (Ambrose 1997, 78)

To head the expedition—which, by the spring of 1803, enjoyed the added impetus of the need to explore the recently acquired

Louisiana Purchase—Jefferson had to look no further than his trusted personal secretary and fellow Virginian, Captain Meriwether Lewis of the U.S. Army. Jefferson explained his decision simply:

> It was impossible to find a character who to a complete science in botany, natural history, mineralogy and astronomy, joined the firmness of constitution and character, prudence, habits adapted to the woods, and a familiarity with the Indian manners and character, requisite for this undertaking. All the latter qualifications Captain Lewis has. (Ambrose 1997, 76)

For his part, Lewis set about putting together a company of explorers—the so-called Corps of Discovery—to chart America's overland course to the Pacific. To help him lead the expedition, Lewis tabbed William Clark, a hardy army veteran, skilled at watercraft, mapmaking, and perhaps most important, leading soldiers. Like Lewis, Clark was a Virginian by birth; he had, however, moved to Kentucky as a young boy. At the time of Lewis's invitation to join the expedition, he was thirty-three years old, three years older than Lewis.

Traveling down the Ohio River from Pittsburgh by keelboat with the Corps' first three members—John Colter, eighteen-year-old George Shannon, and Seaman, a Newfoundland dog—Lewis rendezvoused with Clark and his slave York in Clarksville, Kentucky, on October 15, 1803. Joined by seven handpicked woodsmen, Lewis and Clark floated down the Ohio and then battled the current up the Mississippi to St. Louis.

The expedition members arrived in St. Louis in early December. They found 1,000 inhabitants in the town, which perched on a bluff over the Missouri's flood plain. The settlement had, in four short decades, become the vortex of the West's fur trade. It was just the place for the expedition to stock up on supplies and add new men, which Lewis and Clark did as they holed up for the winter at nearby Wood River.

The following spring heralded the official beginning of the expedition when, on May 21, 1804, Lewis, Clark, York, Seaman, three sergeants, and twenty-three men pushed off into the Missouri River from the small upriver settlement of St. Charles and pointed the bows of their boats north. George Drouillard, a seasoned frontiersman, born of a French Canadian father and Shawnee mother, sailed with them as well. So did a detachment of local soldiers and eight French Canadian voyageurs who would accompany them for part of the journey at least as far as the next winter's camp.

For the rest of that spring and summer, the Corps of Discovery edged its way up the Missouri River, skirting modern-day Iowa and Nebraska and finally crossing into the Dakotas. They covered 1,600 miles, suffering snakebites, battling grizzly bears, and finessing their passage among the region's Indian tribes. Despite the challenges, only the death of Sergeant Floyd, probably from a ruptured appendix, marred the first leg of the epic journey.

With the onset of winter, the Corps waited out the season in the realm of the Mandan Indians, near the site of present-day Bismarck, North Dakota. On April 7, 1805, Lewis and Clark resumed their journey. Toussaint Charbonneau, a French trapper, now aided them, as did his young wife Sacajawea. Sacajawea was one of Charbonneau's two Indian wives, a sixteen year-old Shoshone Indian with her infant son in tow. Her resolute nature and skill with languages would become an important asset in the months to come.

Crossing into modern-day Montana, the expedition reached the Great Falls of the Missouri by the middle of June. The Great Falls and associated rapids necessitated a grueling eighty-five-mile portage before they could rejoin the river and ascend up one of its tributaries (a river they named Jefferson in a moment of political astuteness). Eventually, the Corps left Mr. Jefferson's river altogether to climb toward the Continental Divide.

By August, the Corps had reunited Sacajawea with her Shoshone brethren. In early September, pressing up through the Bitterroot Mountains, the expedition encountered its first snowfall of the season as it crested the Continental Divide. It was a punishing march that brought it into the land of the Nez Perce and, finally, to the Clearwater River.

The Corps followed the Clearwater to the Columbia River, which in turn led them to its estuary on the Pacific. By November 7, 1805, Clark was able to write in his journal: "Great joy in camp we are in view of the Ocean, this great Pacific Ocean which we [have] been so long anxious to see." Several days later, Lewis carved into a tree overlooking the Pacific, "By land from the U. States in 1804 & 1805." In all, according to Clark's calculations, he and his companions had rowed, sailed, rode, marched, and climbed 4,121 miles to reach that point.

The Corps wintered at what it named Fort Clatsop, near modern-day Astoria, Oregon, and after four months of making salt to preserve meat for their return trip and otherwise replenishing their supplies, they set off for home in March. For the most part, the expedition retraced its route, splitting at the Great Divide to explore the Marias and Yellowstone rivers. By late summer, they rejoined one another and on September 22, 1806, paddled the last few miles to St. Louis.

At St. Louis, the town's 1,000 residents thronged the riverbank to see the return of the buckskin-clad adventurers. As Lewis, Clark, and their canoes landed, the crowd greeted them with three celebratory cheers. The Corps of Discovery, by beginning and ending in Missouri—the future Show Me State—had just shown America how to reach the Pacific.

Together, the two men had charted what seemed, in 1806, to be the most direct and convenient route across the continent to the Pacific's shores. They had discovered 178 new plants and 122 species and subspecies of animals and had established contact with Indian tribes that, until their arrival, had never seen a white man.

Quite simply, in the course of their 8,000-mile round trip, they had set the standard for expeditions to come.

Such a rote listing, however, threatens to reduce the Corps of Discovery's accomplishments to a mere ledger of objective achievement. The late Stephen Ambrose's prosaic cataloging of Lewis's (and Clark's) exploratory deeds does a far better job.

> [Lewis] had seen wonderful things. He had traveled through a hunter's paradise beyond anything any American had ever before known. He had crossed mountains that were greater than had ever before been seen by an American, save the handful who had visited the Alps. He had seen falls and cataracts and raging rivers, thunderstorms all but beyond belief, trees of a size never before conceived of, Indian tribes uncorrupted by contact with white men, canyons and cliffs and other scenes of visionary enchantment. A brave new world. And he had been first. (Ambrose 1997, 404–405)

Little wonder, then, that in 2001, when Missouri Governor Bob Holden asked his constituents to "show" him design concepts for the state's quarter, the more than 3,000 submissions he received in response included representations of the Pony Express, the nation's westward expansion, a riverboat, and a commemoration of Lewis and Clark crafted by noted Missouri watercolorist Paul Jackson. Those were among the concepts forwarded to the U.S. Mint, which responded with four candidate designs.

After an online vote, Missourians picked Jackson's "Corps of Discovery 1804–2004" concept. In 2003, after raising Jackson's ire by amending his original design, the U.S. Mint produced 453.2 million quarters. Such issues of design aside, the quarter nevertheless succeeded in showing the world that the Corps' great expedition began and ended in the Show Me State.

# ARKANSAS

## *Diamonds Are a State's Best Friend*

Millions of years before the idea of a state quarter was the merest flickering of an idea, a geologic formation known as a volcanic pipe—later named the Prairie Creek Pipe by modern scientists—began to form some 93 miles beneath today's Pike County, Arkansas. The pipe allowed red-hot magma—full of magnesium and volatile compounds such as water and carbon dioxide—to surge upward toward the earth's surface.

As the magma rose and pressure decreased, the volatile compounds transformed rapidly into gases. That sudden gaseous expansion propelled the magma through the earth's surface in a shallow supersonic eruption like a giant champagne cork. To carry the alcohol metaphor even further, the result was, if viewed cross-sectionally, a martini glass–shaped deposit of volcanic materials that included a remarkable garnish of diamonds carried up from the earth's lithospheric mantle and strewn across the pipe's extinct crater.

As time passed, the ancient volcano's crater eroded, exposing the volcano's payload of diamonds to the elements and, in the summer of 1906, to the amazed eyes of local farmer John W. Huddleston. Shortly after buying a farm atop the crater earlier that year, Huddleston caught sight of what he later described as a "glittering pebble" in the Arkansas soil.

"I knew it was different from any I had ever seen before," Huddleston later told the *Arkansas Gazette*. "It had a fiery eye that blazed up at me every way I turned it. I hurried to the house with the pebble, saddled my mule and started for Murfreesboro . . . riding through the lane, my eye caught another glitter, and I dismounted and picked it up out of the dust."

With his careful eye, Huddleston had managed to discover what state geologist John C. Banner and chemist Richard N. Brackett had failed to uncover nearly two decades earlier—the eighth-largest diamond deposit in the world.

Shortly after Huddleston's discovery, Charles S. Stifft, a Little Rock jeweler, broke the good news to Huddleston: The farmer had discovered two blue-white diamonds, one weighing 2.6 carats and the other 1.4 carats. Overnight, Huddleston earned the nickname "Diamond John."

In once-sleepy southwestern Arkansas, Huddleston's discovery sparked a veritable diamond rush. Thousands of hopeful prospectors besieged Murfreesboro, where the Conway Hotel was forced to turn away as many as 10,000 would-be guests. Not to be deterred, the overflow erected a tent city in the sand hills and pine forests on the outskirts of Huddleston's farm.

Meanwhile, a more well-heeled group, consisting of a collection of Little Rock businessmen led by Samuel W. Reyburn, took a more comprehensive approach in their prospecting. Paying Huddleston $36,000, the group secured options on most of his land and the adjacent properties and began tilling and sluicing the rocky, humus-enriched soil—what the mine workers called "black gumbo"—for diamonds.

Reyburn's venture, which eventually operated under the auspices of the Arkansas Diamond Company, enjoyed some initial success. In fact, in 1924, one of its workers, Wesley Oley Basham, unearthed a 40.23-carat diamond dubbed the "Uncle Sam"—after Basham's own nickname, rather than the government's. Basham's gem still holds the record as the largest diamond ever discovered in the United States. It still registered 12.42 carats after being cut.

Despite such successes, the Arkansas Diamond Company and its competitors, such as those spearheaded by Austin and Howard Millar, only managed to scratch out hand-to-mouth existences. The Arkansas Diamond Company's mining petered out in the late 1920s; bankruptcy and an arsonist's blaze in 1919 spelled the end of the Millars' efforts.

In the years following World War II, as Americans once again returned to the nation's highways and byways, the prospect of car-borne tourists promised another opportunity for landowners sitting atop the Prairie Creek Pipe to make a buck on its scattering of diamonds.

For a time, two competing operations—Crater of Diamonds and The Big Mine—waged a fierce billboard war in the battle for the attention and attendance of amateur rock hounds and passing tourists. The competition ended in 1969, when Texas-based General Earth Minerals bought both properties. Like so many of its predecessors, however, it also decided that mining—commercial or recreational—at the crater was simply not viable.

Three years later, in 1972, the State of Arkansas bought the land for $750,000 and created the 887-acre Crater of Diamonds State Park. In addition to riverfront along the Little Missouri River, the park includes a thirty-seven-acre diamond field. There, for a mere $6.50, visitors can enter the park, and if they want, they can rent the "basic diamond hunting kit"—a U.S. Army surplus folding shovel, a screen set, and a five-gallon bucket—for $7.75.

To date, prospectors have discovered 25,000 diamonds since the crater became a state park, some of which have sold for as much as $34,000. The largest stone discovered since the park opened remains the 16.37-carat Amarillo Starlight, discovered by a visitor from Amarillo, Texas, in 1975, and later cut into a 7.54-carat marquise shape.

Another impressive find came in 1990, when Shirley Strawn, of nearby Murfreesboro, discovered a 3.03-carat stone. Strawn added her great-great-grandfather's name to the stone, christening it the Strawn-Wagner Diamond, and sent the gem to Lazare Kaplan International of New York for cutting. There, Lazare Kaplan cut the gem to perfection into a 1.09-carat, round brilliant shape "Ideal Cut" diamond. The result was certified as a perfect D flawless diamond, the highest-quality stone to ever be so certified by the American Gemological Society.

Perhaps even better known is the uncut, triangular 4.25-carat "Kahn Canary" diamond, discovered in 1977 by George Stepp, a logger from Carthage, Arkansas. Stepp later sold the gem to Stan Kahn, who loaned it to First Lady Hillary Clinton to be worn in a special Arkansas-inspired ring setting at galas celebrating both of her husband's presidential inaugurals. President Clinton was born in Hope, Arkansas, approximately thirty miles south of the crater.

Meanwhile, diamonds continue to be discovered at the crater, where the rule remains "finders, keepers." In 2006 alone, 486 diamonds were discovered, ending with Gary Dunlap's discovery of a 2.37-carat white diamond on the last day of the year. He named the gem "Star of Thelma," in honor of his wife. Dunlap's was an impressive find; more typically, the average size of a diamond discovered at the site is a mere one-fifth of a carat.

It was in 2003, however, that Arkansas' diamond mining industry arguably enjoyed its greatest success. At the Crater of Diamonds that year, the park's 47,864 visitors enjoyed better than average luck, finding 641 white, brown, and yellow diamonds. Eighteen of them registered over 1 carat in size.

Nevertheless, none of those diamonds discovered that year could match the fame of the anonymous diamond selected to command the center of Arkansas' state quarter. Two years earlier, Governor Mike Huckabee had announced the Arkansas Quarter Challenge as a statewide competition, a challenge that garnered 9,320 entries. After several rounds of elimination, the governor eventually forwarded three concepts to the U.S. Mint.

Two of those final concepts were the work of Ariston Jacks of Pine Bluff and Kathy Basler of Berryville. The final was that of Dortha Scott of Mount Ida, a sixty-five-year-old who draws and sketches as a hobby. Scott's design celebrated Arkansas' natural resources and featured a mallard duck, rice, and, in its center, an iconic diamond to represent the Crater of Diamonds.

"My daughter gave me the form and told me to fill it out," Scott later explained. "She said I had only a few days left before the deadline. I sat down, drew a diamond, and worked around it."

Apparently, Scott—like a diamond—worked well under pressure. Her design and the others inspired four candidate designs by the Mint. The governor, asked to select one, chose Scott's natural resources motif.

"This design captures what we're about as a state and as a people," Governor Huckabee declared. "It promotes our heritage and will show America why we proudly call ourselves the Natural State. Dortha Scott has done exemplary work, and I'm confident every Arkansan will be proud of our quarter."

In the end, 457.8 million of Arkansas' state quarters—composed of 8.33 percent nickel, 91.77 percent copper, and 0 percent diamond—were minted in the final ten weeks of 2003. A launch ceremony held at the Crater of Diamonds—and, fittingly, attended by Shirley Strawn as well as Governor Huckabee—inaugurated the new minting.

# MICHIGAN

## Great Lakes, Great Drama,
## . . . and a So-So Quarter

At the risk of irritating Michigan's nearly 10 million citizens, it is difficult to ignore the obvious: Michigan's state quarter, the first of the
series to be released in 2004, is perhaps the most boring of the bunch.

Complementing a depiction of the outline of the state and the
Great Lakes system, the quarter declares "Great Lakes State." After
a twenty-five-member gubernatorial commission reviewed over
4,300 design concept submissions, which included proposals featuring such topics as iconic automobiles and the Mackinac Bridge, is a

cupro-nickel-plated hydrogeography lesson the best the country can get from Michigan?

That is not to say, however, that Michigan's nickname "Great Lakes State" is undeserved—in fact, far from it. Michigan is the only state that borders four of the five Great Lakes (Superior, Huron, Michigan, and Erie), and it guards those coasts and the waters that feed into them with an impressive 124 lighthouses—over half as many as Maine, for that matter.

Nevertheless, geography aside, it is difficult to get excited about a coin that, in reality, offers little more than a numismatic map. But if one is willing to delve into the history that played out on those same lakes, a series of dramatic tales awaits.

Arguably, the most dramatic of all came in the early winter of 1913. In November, a storm of such ferocity slammed into the Great Lakes that for later generations, it became known simply as the White Hurricane. It was the deadliest natural disaster to ever strike the Great Lakes. By the time the skies cleared, at least 248 people were dead, twelve ships were at the bottom of the Great Lakes, and thirty-one others were run aground.

The White Hurricane's origins lay in the convergence of two major storm fronts, their winds combining over the Great Lakes with disastrous effect as temperatures plummeted and snow began to fall. The result was what one modern weather historian termed a "meteorological monster." It was the kind of event another writer eventually called a "perfect storm."

On Saturday, November 8, however, it still seemed as though the storm might simply be a typical November gale—admittedly, no laughing matter in its own right. Centered over eastern Lake Superior, the storm covered the entire lake basin. Winds had reached gale strength on northern Lake Michigan and western Lake Superior.

Unfortunately, on Sunday, a false lull in the storm—a so-called sucker hole—convinced a number of ships to ignore the gale warning flags still flying at harbors throughout the Great Lakes and try their luck on the open water—or to keep pressing it altogether.

One such ship was the 504-foot-long *Charles S. Price*, a steel-hulled, straight-deck bulk freighter. The previous day, it had steamed from Astabula, Ohio, en route to Cleveland, with a load of coal. A crew of twenty-eight, including the steward's wife, manned the freighter under the command of veteran sailor William M. Black.

The *Price* sailed, however, without Milton Smith, first assistant engineer. Although the *Price* was relatively new, with such modern amenities as electric lights and hot-water showers, Smith had not been able to shake an ominous sense of foreboding about the ship's remaining two weeks of the year's sailing season. Instead, Smith had debarked and took the train home to Port Huron.

It was a decision he would recall—and thank—for the rest of his life.

Despite Sunday's lull, by that evening the two storm fronts were fully joined, spawning a storm of epic proportions as hurricane force winds screamed out of the north. White-out snow squalls and blizzards, wailing ninety mile per hour winds, and towering waves turned life on the Great Lakes into a matter of survival.

Meanwhile, on shore, as Sunday passed into Monday, November 10, the storm dumped record amounts of snow. Port Huron was buried under four- to five-foot drifts, while Cleveland received 17.4 inches of snow within twenty-four hours. Wires and telephone poles succumbed to the weight of the ice and snow, and in Detroit, winds gusted up to seventy miles per hour.

The storm's duration compounded the problem. "No lake master can recall in all his experience a storm of such unprecedented violence with such rapid changes in the direction of the wind and its gusts of such fearful speed," the Lake Carriers Association stated in a post-storm report. "[T]his storm raged for sixteen hours continuously at an average velocity of sixty miles per hour, with frequent spurts of seventy and over."

The storm's power was apparent even to those without sight. Trapped in a Cleveland hotel room, Helen Keller recalled, "I knew it was storming before I was told. The rooms, the corridors—everywhere within this building vibrates with the power of the storm outside. The storm waves, like sound waves or the waves of the wireless, will not be denied by stone walls and plate glass windows."

The *Cleveland Plain-Dealer* was equally eloquent in describing the storm's aftermath. Cleveland, it recorded, "lay in white and mighty solitude, mute and deaf to the outside world, a city of lonesome snowiness, storm-swept from end to end."

It was a description that could aptly be applied to scores of cities and towns from Ohio to Minnesota.

But it was on the waters of the Great Lakes where the greatest drama played out. Waves at least thirty-five-feet high, coming in rapid succession in series of three, pounded those ships unfortunate enough to be caught on the lakes. And because of the cyclonic effect of the storm, the wind often blew counter to the waves—a sure recipe for disaster for ungainly, underpowered bulk freighters like the *Price*.

If modern ships such as the *Price* were in peril, vessels such as the *Plymouth* seemed absolutely doomed. A fifty-nine-year-old wooden schooner vessel that had seen better days, the *Plymouth* was laboring humbly through the twilight years as a de-masted barge. When the storm first hit on Lake Michigan that Saturday, the *Plymouth* was being towed by the tug *James H. Martin*. When he had determined that the *Plymouth* was unable to make headway against the mounting waves and was threatened with foundering, the *Martin*'s skipper took the *Plymouth* to the safest waters he could find—near Gull Island—and beat a hasty retreat. He knew that the maneuver offered both ships a fighting chance; with the *Plymouth* under tow, neither had a hope of surviving.

Nevertheless, his logic was scant consolation to the seven men left on board the *Plymouth*—particularly Chris Keenan, an unlucky federal marshal who was on board only because the *Plymouth* was the subject of litigation. By Sunday, as the *Plymouth* wallowed helplessly in the wind and waves, Keenan hurled a bottle overboard. It contained a short, simple note:

> *Dear Wife and Children: We were left up here in Lake Michigan by McKinnon, captain James H. Martin tug, at anchor. He went away and never said goodbye or anything to us. Lost one man yesterday. We have been out in storm forty hours. Goodbye dear ones, I might see you in heaven. Pray for me. Chris K. P.S. I felt so bad I had another man write for me. Goodbye Forever.* (Bourrie 2005, 39)

Keenan, his six comrades, and the *Plymouth* were never seen again.

The modern lake freighters scarcely fared better, particularly on Lake Huron. The *John McGean, Isaac M. Scott, Argus, Hydrus, James Carruthers, Wexford,* and *Regina* all floundered in the vicious teeth of the white hurricane. The first sign of their demise came as the fierce storm moved off into Canada. As the cities and towns along the Great Lakes began to dig out of their massive snowdrifts, the icy bodies of those ships' crews began to wash stiffly ashore in the rough surf.

Even before the storm had fully receded, the waves offered up another sacrifice. Late in the afternoon of Monday, November 10, an unknown ship was spotted floating upside-down in the gray swells off Michigan's eastern coast. For the next five days, newspapers ran headlines pondering the identity of the mystery wreck, even after it sank beneath the waves.

Finally, on November 15, a diver named Baker reached the sunken wreck and, braving the cold underwater gloom, felt his way along the raised letters that spelled the ship's name on the bow. The front page of that day's *Port Huron Times-Herald* extra edition read: "BOAT IS PRICE—DIVER IS BAKER—SECRET KNOWN."

The wreck was indeed the *Charles S. Price;* all twenty-eight hands on board were lost, from Captain Black to the unfortunate assistant engineer who had signed on at the last minute to take Milton Smith's place.

"I am indeed a fortunate man," Smith told the *Port Huron Times-Herald.* "There is no doubt the *Price* is gone. It is awful to think of it."

Smith's part in the drama was not over. For the next several days, he took on the morbid task of visiting morgues and identifying the thawing bodies of his former shipmates.

The white hurricane's legacy lasted long after the snowdrifts were plowed and the sailors' bodies were buried. The demoralizing loss of so much tonnage on the Great Lakes—a major avenue of commerce for such staples as grain, coal, and iron—shadowed America's economy for the remainder of the winter.

Michigan had a happier legacy in mind, however, when the U.S. Mint celebrated the launch of the state's quarter on January 26, 2004.

"Everyone who sees our new Michigan quarter for the first time will get a fresh glimpse of our prized peninsulas and abundance of natural water," Governor Jennifer M. Granholm said. "A quarter that begins its journey here today in Michigan could very well, months from now, wind up in the hands of a beachcomber in Southern California or a fisherman off the coast of Maine."

"Most who look at the quarter will miss a lot of the symbolism that is implied in the design," added Patrick Heller, who owns a Lansing, Michigan, coin dealership and who served on the governor's commission. "The Great Lakes and the geography of Michigan are the main reason for the prosperity of the state in years past."

"The other distinctive feature is that the state of Michigan is the one state that can be positively identified from space," Heller added. "One of the members of the governor's commission was Jerry Linenger, an astronaut from Michigan who had spent time on Russia's Mir space station. His Russian co-workers were able to pick out Michigan from way out in space and identify it for him."

# 27

# FLORIDA
## *The Costliest Quarter*

America's history is replete with countless men and women who challenged the unknown, triumphed over adversity, and in the end, pushed forward the frontiers of knowledge. Florida's quarter, designed by artist Ralph Butler to depict a soaring space shuttle and a Spanish galleon, its sails billowing as it tacks toward a spit of land festooned with sabal palm trees, certainly reminds one of that manifest national drive. So does the quarter's inscription: "Gateway to Discovery"—a concept that beat out such competing designs as the Everglades, St. Augustine, and "Fishing Capital of the World."

But America's quest for knowledge is often a costly one—as the image of the space shuttle reminds anyone whose eyes fall on the coin's reverse. So, if the Florida design does nothing else, it offers the opportunity to remember the fourteen astronauts who gave their lives on board the *Challenger* and *Columbia* in 1986 and 2003.

The *Challenger* mission, identified as STS-51L (for "Space Transportation System"), launched from the Kennedy Space Center's Launch Pad 39B on January 28, 1986, on what should have been a weeklong mission. Much of the mission's prelaunch publicity focused on NASA's Teacher in Space program, which would take flight with this mission. The shuttle carried a TDRS-B satellite (to provide communications and data relays for spacecraft and satellites in Earth's orbit), a Spartan satellite (which would have been deployed and then retrieved by the shuttle's robotic arm after collecting spectrographic images of Halley's comet), and a variety of scientific experiments. Coincidentally, it also carried two complete sets of that year's newly minted U.S. Liberty coins—the first legal tender American coinage to make a trip into orbit.

Seventy-three seconds into the mission, *Challenger* exploded, the victim of an O-ring failure in its right-side rocket booster, believed to have been caused by Florida's unseasonably cold weather that week. The disaster cost seven astronauts their lives—lives well worth remembering here.

Francis R. "Dick" Scobee was the mission's spacecraft commander. A former U.S. Air Force pilot who flew combat missions in Vietnam, Scobee was a talented test pilot who had graduated from high school in Auburn, Washington, and in 1965, from the University of Arizona. He joined NASA in 1978; STS-51L would have been his second space shuttle mission. His official NASA biography listed a diverse number of hobbies—oil painting, woodworking, motorcycling, and racquetball, to name a few. Back on Earth, he left his wife, June, and two children.

U.S. Navy Commander Michael J. Smith served as *Challenger's* pilot. A native of Beaufort, North Carolina, who listed woodworking, tennis, and squash as his hobbies, he graduated from the United States Naval Academy in 1967. Like Scobee, he was a combat veteran of the Vietnam War and a former test pilot. He was survived by his wife, Jane, and three children.

Judith A. Resnik, a classical pianist who held a Ph.D. in electrical engineering from the University of Maryland, was born in Akron, Ohio, and later graduated from Carnegie Mellon University. Her engineering work included stints with RCA, the National Institutes of Health, and Xerox before she joined the astronaut program in 1978. On board as a mission specialist, STS-51L would have been her second shuttle mission.

U.S. Air Force Lieutenant Colonel Ellison S. Onizuka was another mission specialist and, like Resnik, was marking his second shuttle mission. A native of Kealakekua, Hawaii, Onizuka earned degrees from the University of Colorado before going on to become a test pilot for the Air Force. He was survived by his wife, Lorna, and two daughters and is remembered as America's first Japanese American astronaut.

Ronald E. McNair was born and grew up in Lake City, South Carolina. He graduated with a bachelor of science degree in physics from North Carolina A&T State University in 1971; he earned his Ph.D. from the Massachusetts Institute of Technology five years later. A fifth-degree black belt karate instructor and an accomplished jazz saxophonist, he had, in 1984, become the second African American astronaut to orbit Earth on shuttle mission STS-41B as a mission specialist. He was survived by his wife, Cheryl, and two children.

Gregory B. Jarvis, one of the shuttle's payload specialists and on board to conduct experiments on behalf of the Hughes Aircraft Corporation, was one of the mission's two rookies. Born in Detroit, Michigan, he graduated from New York's Mohawk Central High

School and later earned degrees from SUNY–Buffalo and Northeastern University. An avid squash player, bicyclist, and classical guitarist, he was survived by his wife, Marcia.

Sandra Christa Corrigan McAuliffe rounded out *Challenger's* crew as the other payload specialist. Born in Boston, Massachusetts, the thirty-seven-year-old economics, history, and law teacher from New Hampshire's Concord High School represented the culmination of NASA's Teacher in Space program. She was survived by her husband, Steven, and two children.

Regrouping in the wake of the *Challenger* disaster, NASA began launching shuttles again the following year. Nearly ninety missions helped fade the memory of the *Challenger* tragedy. The morning of February 1, 2003, however, brought a vivid reminder of the dangers—and the human cost—associated with space travel. As the shuttle *Columbia* reentered earth's atmosphere upon the completion of mission STS-107, it exploded over the skies of Texas. The disaster cost the lives of another seven astronauts.

U.S. Air Force Colonel Rick Douglas Husband served as *Columbia's* mission commander for the ill-fated flight. A native of Amarillo, Texas, he held degrees from Texas Tech and California State University, Fresno. His official NASA biography noted that the former test pilot enjoyed singing in his church choir, water and snow skiing, cycling, and spending time with his wife and two children. STS-107 was his second shuttle mission.

U.S. Navy Commander William C. "Willie" McCool was born in San Diego, California; he later graduated from Coronado High School in Lubbock, Texas, and the United States Naval Academy (as second in his class) in 1983 before earning a master of science degree from the University of Maryland. A test pilot like Husband, the former Eagle Scout was piloting *Columbia* on his first space shuttle mission and left a wife and sons behind.

With the *Columbia* disaster, U.S. Air Force Lieutenant Colonel Michael P. Anderson became the second African American astronaut to die in space. A graduate of Cheney High School in Cheney, Washington, and the University of Washington, the son of an Air Force officer called Spokane, Washington, home. Anderson served as the payload commander on board *Columbia*, his second shuttle mission, and was survived by a wife and children.

U.S. Navy Captain David M. Brown, a Navy flight surgeon in addition to a carrier jet pilot, joined NASA's astronaut program in 1996. Born in Arlington, Virginia, he held degrees from the College of William and Mary and Eastern Virginia Medical School. While at William and Mary, he was not only a collegiate varsity gymnast for all four years but also performed in the Circus Kingdom as an acrobat, seven-foot unicyclist, and stilt walker. STS-107 was his first shuttle mission; he served on board as a mission specialist.

Kalpana "K. C." Chawla, born in Karnal, India, later moved to the United States, where she earned a master's degree in aerospace engineering from the University of Texas and a Ph.D. in aerospace engineering from the University of Colorado. An aviator as well as a research scientist, she held pilot licenses for multi-engine aircraft, gliders, and seaplanes. On board *Columbia*, Chawla was a mission specialist tasked with operating the shuttle's robot arm. Back on Earth, she was survived by her husband.

U.S. Navy Captain Laurel Blair Salton Clark was, in addition to being a NASA astronaut, a naval flight surgeon, diving medical officer, and submarine medical officer who listed scuba diving and parachuting among her hobbies. She called Racine, Wisconsin, her hometown and was a graduate of Racine's William Horlick High School. She earned a bachelor of science degree in zoology from the University of Wisconsin, Madison, and later earned a medical degree from there as well. Survived by her husband and son, she served as a mission specialist on board *Columbia*.

Israel Air Force Colonel Ilan Ramon rounded out *Columbia's* crew as one of the shuttle's payload specialists. A fighter pilot with over 4,000 hours on a variety of jets, he was Israel's first astronaut and had been trained to work a multispectral camera designed to record. desert aerosol. A University of Tel Aviv graduate, Ramon was survived by his wife, Rona, and their four children.

Ironically, when U.S. Mint director Henrietta Holsman Fore joined Governor Jeb Bush and NASA administrator Sean O'Keefe at the John F. Kennedy Space Flight Center to mark the official launch of Florida's quarter on April 7, 2004, the space shuttle had not yet returned to flight. In fact, it would not do so until the following summer, when the *Discovery* blasted into space on a two-week mission—proving once again that Florida was indeed the "gateway to discovery."

# TEXAS

## *Texas Ties One On*

Let's be honest—did anyone really expect subtlety from Texas's state quarter? After all, it is a state that has enthusiastically embraced self-satisfied slogans that range from "Don't Mess with Texas" to "Texas: It's Like a Whole Other Country."

And at first glance, Texas's state quarter does not disappoint. Based on a design by Daniel Miller, the coin displays the width and breadth of the state—the largest in the continental United States—with, of course, a lone star prominently displayed. Roughly juxtaposing the quarter with a state map, it seems as if the star is fixed upon the town of Cleburne, the county seat of Johnson County.

If the star does indeed mark Cleburne, then it complements another subtle facet found on Texas's quarter—the lariat that encircles the perimeter of the coin. That length of braided rope symbolizes the state's cowboy heritage and the longhorn cattle those cowboys drove to market along routes like the famed Chisholm Trail—which, as fate or quarter design would have it, just happens to pass through Johnson County.

Despite popular misconceptions to the contrary, cattle drives did not begin in Texas—far from it. Even in colonial Massachusetts, New York, Pennsylvania, Georgia, Florida, and the Carolinas, Eastern "cowboys" collected free-ranging cattle and, often with the aid of dogs, drove the relatively tame beasts to market. In fact, some say that the origin of the pejorative term "cracker" came from descriptions of early Florida settlers who would crack their long bullwhips as they collected their cattle amid the longleaf forests of the future Sunshine State.

In Texas, however, settlers faced much wilder beasts and more challenging conditions. But early experiences with cattle driving demonstrated that the potential for handsome profits existed in the dusty wake of a cattle herd, as when an ambitious group of Stephen F. Austin's colonists drove a herd of surplus cattle through the treacherous swamp country of eastern Texas into New Orleans, where they fetched twice their Texas market value.

Texas became a state in 1845, and around that same time, cowboys mounted a series of successful but relatively small drives. They followed a trail that stretched through Austin, Waco, and modern-day Dallas, crossed the Red River near Preston, and then led north along what would one day be the eastern edge of Oklahoma. North of Fort Gibson, the trail split into various terminal branches that led to such cities as St. Louis, Independence, Sedalia, Kansas City, and other points east. In time, the trail became known as the Shawnee Trail.

In 1846, that trail bore Texas's first large cattle drive when Edward Piper herded 1,000 head from Texas to Ohio. But within seven years, trouble arose on the trail. The Texas cattle carried ticks infected with "Texas fever"; as the Texas herds passed through Missouri, those ticks found new hosts among the cows on Missouri's farms. The Texas cattle had developed immunity to the fever; their Missouri brethren were not so lucky. Missourians responded with quarantine laws and, in some cases, armed vigilante bands.

Meanwhile, on a happier note, the California gold rush generated enough demand for slaughter beeves that, during the early to mid-1850s, adventurous cowboys guided herds through the Rockies and across the West's deserts to hungry West Coast mining camps. To the hungry miners, cattle worth $14 in Texas sold for $100 or more. With the outbreak of the Civil War, New Orleans and Confederate commissary officers provided another destination.

The end of the Civil War found between 3 and 6 million head of cattle roaming the wilds of Texas. Locally, some were worth as little as $2 each, and with cattle demanding as much as $40 a head in the North, it did not take long for Texas cowboys to take to the trails once again. In the spring of 1866, Texans drove over a quarter million cattle to market.

Of those cattle, some headed east to Louisiana, where the cattle were shipped by boat to Cairo, Illinois, and St. Louis, Missouri. Heading in the other direction, Oliver Loving and Charles Goodnight blazed the Goodnight-Loving Trail through hostile Indian country to army posts in New Mexico and on to Denver.

For the most part, however, most drives headed up the Shawnee Trail, where, once again, they began meeting increasing resistance from local farmers still fearful of the dreaded tick-borne Texas fever. By 1867, six states had essentially barred herds of Texas cattle from crossing their borders.

Fortunately, Illinois cattle buyer Joseph G. McCoy stepped into the picture with the vision to establish a marketplace away from settled areas—and vulnerable local cows. For his new market, he picked Abilene, Kansas, near the center of the mostly uninhabited

Great Plains. Amid this sea of grass, McCoy convinced the Kansas Pacific Railroad to not only provide him with rail yard facilities but even to pay him a commission on each carload of cattle it shipped from Abilene.

Equally important, McCoy persuaded Kansas officials not to enforce the state's quarantine law at Abilene in order to attract trail herds. McCoy also successfully lobbied the Illinois legislature to allow entry of Texas cattle that had been "wintered" in Kansas—a key proviso that enabled McCoy to ship his cattle to Chicago's stockyards.

In response, Texans began driving their cattle north along what became known as the Chisholm Trail. In 1867, O. W. Wheeler, his partners, and 2,400 steers blazed the way. Originally, Wheeler had planned to drive his herd up the Shawnee Trail from San Antonio through Austin and Waco, and then, after striking north, to winter his steers on the Great Plains before driving them on to California.

But at the North Canadian River, Wheeler spotted wagon tracks— a trade route established by the Scot–Cherokee Indian trader Jesse Chisholm that led north to Wichita, Kansas—and decided to press on for the railheads of Kansas. Eventually, Chisholm lent his name to the entire trail that stretched from the Rio Grande to central Kansas. That larger trail split from the old Shawnee Trail in Waco, ran north (through Johnson County) to Fort Worth, and passed east of Decatur to cross the Red River. Today, U.S. Highway 81 parallels the old trail's path as it runs on to Newton, Kansas, although eventual destinations of a cattle drive coming up the trail could include Ellsworth, Junction City, Wichita, Abilene, or Caldwell as well.

Spurred on by Wheeler's success and McCoy's aggressive advertising of his railhead in Abilene, a veritable flood of cattle followed in the months and years to come. Some 35,000 cattle arrived in Abilene in 1867 for shipment; McCoy's numbers continued to double every year until 1871. By 1873, more than 1.5 million cattle had reached the railhead, as well as rival railheads in Wichita and Ellsworth.

In total, before the Chisholm Trail was finally closed by barbed wire and an 1885 Kansas quarantine law, it had been followed by more than 5 million cattle and 1 million mustangs. Some have called it the greatest migration of livestock in world history. Even railroad connections with Northern and Eastern markets, available in Texas after 1873, did not immediately diminish trail traffic because freight rates were two to three times more expensive than drovers' fees.

Such a massive migration would have been impossible but for the cowboys—or, less romantically, simply "drovers"—who shepherded the vast herds up the trail to Kansas. On a typical drive, a trail boss (or "ramrod"), ten cowboys (or "waddies"), a cook, and a horse wrangler (in charge of the extra mounts, called "remudas") were capable of trailing 2,500 cattle on drives that lasted three months and covered ten to fifteen miles a day. For a greenhorn waddie tasked with riding "drag"—following in the dust at the rear of the herd—it made for a long, monotonous journey.

As the encyclopedic *Handbook of Texas* observed, "the gun-totin' image of cowboys owes more to Hollywood than to history." Nevertheless, the *Handbook* could not help but also declare that "youthful trail hands on mustangs gave a Texas flavor to the entire range cattle industry of the Great Plains and made the cowboy an enduring folk hero."

In time, the Chisholm Trail, stymied by new quarantines enacted by Kansas, relinquished its prominence to the new Western (also known as the Dodge City or Ogallala) Trail blazed to Dodge City. And despite its success for several years, even the Western Trail eventually fell victim to quarantines and barbed wire, leading Texas cattlemen to turn to railroads to transport their animals to market.

Nevertheless, the ramrods, wranglers, and waddies of the Shawnee, Chisholm, and Western trails wrote a critical and colorful page in the history of the Lone Star State and earned a place for a symbolic lariat on the 541.8 million Texas state quarters eventually minted. It was quite an accomplishment in the face of stern competition from nearly 2,600 initial alternative designs, some of which featured such iconic images as the Alamo.

"The Texas quarter will serve as a timeless representation of our state's proud and storied history," said Governor Rick Perry at the quarter's official launch. "When Americans reach into their pockets, this quarter will remind all of the proud and rich history of the state that was once its own sovereign nation."

# 29

# IOWA

## An Education in Art

When Iowa picked a design for its state quarter, it followed the lead of New Jersey and relied on a famous painting to best illustrate and create an emblem for the Hawkeye State. Whereas *Washington Crossing the Delaware* was the work of German-born Emanuel Leutze, Iowans could count on native son Grant DeVolsen Wood to provide its iconic image.

Even Wood's home-field advantage, however, did not assure him of victory. Tasked with developing a series of candidate designs for the U.S. Mint's initial consideration, Governor Thomas J. Vilsack established the sixteen-member Iowa Quarter Committee in May 2002 to aid him in that endeavor. Working with libraries, banks, and credit unions to solicit ideas for the state quarter design, the committee eventually received nearly 2,000 submissions. It winnowed those submissions down to five finalists and submitted them to Vilsack for his consideration that August.

Two of the ultimately unsuccessful designs were, like the eventual winner, based on Grant Wood paintings. One depicted the farm couple—actually, Cedar Rapids dentist Byron H. McKeeby and Wood's younger sister, Nan—featured on Wood's *American Gothic*, standing in front of the soon-to-be famous (and still standing) white farmhouse in Eldon, Iowa.

The other Wood-inspired design, labeled "Beautiful Land," relied on his painting *Young Corn*, painted in 1931, to illustrate an idealized Iowa landscape of softly rolling hills and the promising growth of neat rows of spring corn.

Corn also featured in a competing design, "Feeding the World," submitted by Lennis Moore. Moore, an artist, illustrator, and designer living in Mt. Pleasant, Iowa, grew up on a small family farm in northeastern Iowa. Loyal to his family's livestock, Moore's design worked a cow and a pig into the mix as well.

Equally stiff competition, however, came from Waterloo, Iowa, artist Kim Behm, who crafted a design featuring Waterloo's five Sullivan brothers. The Sullivan brothers were all lost at sea during World War II when their cruiser, the USS *Juneau*, was sunk by a Japanese torpedo.

The loss of the Sullivan brothers came to symbolize the sacrifices being made by America's families during World War II. However, the legislation that enacted the Mint's 50 State Quarters® Program specifically excluded imagery of busts or portraits of any person, living or dead, on state quarters. The brothers' row of heads apparently fell too close to the mark.

In the end, therefore, a Grant Wood–inspired design triumphed, one based on Wood's painting *Arbor Day*. On its face, the painting, which depicts the planting of trees in front of a wooden-frame schoolhouse, readily complements the quarter's explicitly proclaimed theme of "Foundation in Education." But Wood's own ties to public education in Iowa run even deeper than the quarter suggests.

Wood was born on a small farm outside Anamosa, Iowa, in 1891, the second of four children. His father was a farmer; his mother, Hattie, was a teacher. Grant's father died in 1901, sparking Hattie to sell the family land and move to Cedar Rapids.

In Cedar Rapids, Wood—nicknamed "Gussie"—attended Washington High School, where his extracurricular activities included work for the *Pulse*, an artistic journal published by the school's students every six weeks. He also worked on the school's yearbook, drawing comics and designing headings and frontispieces.

Even as a high school student, Wood's artistic talents were so evident that Emma Grattan, the art director of city schools, often conspired to have him excused from other classes so that he could repair to her office to work on his art. At age fourteen, he won third prize in a national contest for his crayon drawing of oak leaves. Later, Wood said that the prize inspired him to become an artist.

Wood graduated from Washington High in 1910, and the very night of graduation, he caught a train for Minneapolis to study wood and metal techniques with Ernest Batchelder. That fall, he began pursuing a teaching degree at the University of Iowa and later attended the Art Institute of Chicago. Despite being exempted from the draft, Wood waived his exemption and spent most of World War I putting his artistic skills to work designing army camouflage at stateside bases.

Back in Iowa following the armistice, Wood earned his teaching credentials by teaching for a year at the Rosedale country school, a one-room building near Cedar Rapids. Later, he taught at Jackson Junior High School (1919–1922) and at McKinley High School (1922–1925). Shy, quiet, but with a disarming sense of humor, Wood earned a popular reputation with his students and inspired them to take on such projects as completing a frieze for McKinley High's cafeteria.

During breaks from teaching, Wood spent his summers in Europe, traveling the continent, taking art classes at the Academie Julien in Paris, and in Munich, being inspired by the German primitive movement and the work of such northern Renaissance masters as Jan van Eyck.

But Wood's heart remained in Iowa, as is evident in one of his most enduring, and endearing, quotes:

> I found the answer [about what I knew] when I joined a school of painters in Paris after the war who called themselves neo-meditationists. They believed an artist had to wait for inspiration, very quietly, and they did most of their waiting at the Dome or the Rotonde, with brandy. It was then that I realized that all the really good ideas I'd ever had came to me while I was milking a cow. So I went back to Iowa. (Roberts 1995, 32)

Back in Iowa, Wood found increasing popular and critical success, even as he worked as an interior designer, led an amateur theater group, and promoted the local art community. In 1927, he earned a commission from the city of Cedar Rapids to design the stained-glass windows for its Veterans Memorial Building, now the Cedar Rapids City Hall.

Meanwhile, a number of his early artistic works underscored Wood's own foundation in education. The Cedar Rapids School District began commissioning Wood to produce art for its school buildings; one of the first was a mural for the Harrison School, entitled *Democracy Leading the Way onto Victory*. Later commissions included *Pine Tree* and *Back of the Pantheon at Sunset* for Jackson School; *Paris 1924—Bridge at Moret* for Roosevelt School; and *Indian Creek* for Franklin School.

Wood broke onto the national scene in 1930 when his oil painting *American Gothic* captured a $300 prize at the Art Institute of Chicago. From that point on, his fame and commercial success seemed assured. Nevertheless, his artistic path remained intertwined with education in Iowa.

In 1931, students at Wilson Junior High School mounted a penny campaign and commissioned Wood to paint a memorial for favorite teacher Linnie Schloeman. Wood and the students selected a landscape outside of Amana, where the rich soil nurtured young corn in the same way that Schloeman had nurtured his students. The result was 1931's *Young Corn*. Although it did not make it onto Iowa's state quarter in 2004, Wood devotees could take some solace in the fact that it represented the state on the U.S. postage stamp that commemorated the state's sesquicentennial in 1996.

The following year, the school district commissioned Wood for a work in honor of two of McKinley School's teachers, Catherine Motejl and Rose Waterstradt. According to legend, Wood put a female friend behind the wheel of his car and, with a quart of whiskey in hand, combed the Iowa countryside one cold winter day, looking for just the right schoolhouse for what would become the inspiration for *Arbor Day*—and, as it turned out, Iowa's future state quarter.

That same year, Wood and others founded the Stone City Art Colony in 1932, intent on providing a laboratory and venue for participating artists to create artworks capable of expressing the unique character of his beloved Midwest. "A true art expression," Wood wrote, "must grow up from the soil itself." With such words, Wood easily articulated why he became not only one of America's outstanding regional painters but an articulate spokesman for the Regionalism art movement as a whole.

By 1933, Wood was a University of Iowa art professor and, the following year, received an appointment as the director of all Iowa Works Progress Administration (WPA) art projects. Making the most of the opportunity, he gathering his team of artists and began design-ing the murals for Parks Library at Iowa State University.

Ironically, Wood's longstanding ties to art education could not shield him from bitter battles with the more traditional academics in the University of Iowa's art department. From such antagonists, Wood faced increasingly vehement criticism regarding his lack of formal education, his teaching style, and his ideas about mural proj-ects for public schools and buildings. Turning back to his art, he opened a studio in Clear Lake, Iowa, where he focused on lithogra-phy, book illustration, carpentry, metalwork, and painting.

Toward the end of his life (which came in 1942, from liver can-cer), Wood offered the following observations about his work: "In making these paintings, as you may have guessed, I had in mind something which I hope to convey to a fairly wide audience in America—the picture of a country rich in the arts of peace; a homely lovable nation, infinitely worth any sacrifice necessary to its preservation."

One wonders if the same could not be said of the 50 State Quarters® Program in general.

# 30

# WISCONSIN
## *Got Milk? Got Cheese?*
## *Got Corn?*

"Forward!" That is the intrepid declaration on Wisconsin's state quarters, all 453.2 million of them. They echo the state motto, adopted in 1851, that is intended to "reflect Wisconsin's continuous drive to be a national leader," according to the state's Web site.

After voicing its motto so boldly, however, the excitement quotient on the Wisconsin coin drops precipitously. In addition to the state motto, the quarter features an ear of corn, a round of cheese, and, most apparently, the head of a Holstein cow. It is not clear which of the trio the coin is exhorting to move along.

The agricultural theme wended its way to Wisconsin's quarter starting in December 2001, when Governor Scott McCallum appointed twenty-three people to the Wisconsin Commemorative Quarter Council to review and recommend candidate design themes. The committee collected 9,608 suggestions, eventually narrowing the concepts down to a total of six finalists (and rejecting suggested submissions that would have featured, among other ideas, beer mugs, bratwurst, and the Green Bay Packers).

The six finalists were: "Early Exploration and Cultural Interaction" (honoring such early explorers as Jean Nicolet, Jacques Marquette, and Louis Joliet); "Scenic Wisconsin" (paying homage to the state's scenic lakes, bluffs, rivers, and metropolitan skylines); "State Capitol Building"; "Old Abe" (the live eagle mascot that accompanied the Eighth Regiment of the Wisconsin Volunteer Infantry into battle during the Civil War); "Badger" (symbolizing not only the University of Wisconsin but also the early "burrowing" lead miners who ranked among the state's first settlers); and "Agriculture/Dairy/Barns."

Subsequent consultations with the U.S. Mint reduced the options to three—"Scenic Wisconsin," "Early Exploration and Cultural Interaction," and "Agriculture/Dairy/Barns." In an online poll, Wisconsin's citizens voted for the last one, trumping the quarter council's favored design, "Early Exploration and Cultural Interaction." Bowing to his constituents, Governor Jim Doyle opted for "Agriculture/Dairy/Barns."

In the end, the inclusion of such agricultural components on Wisconsin's state quarter makes eminent sense—although reliance on a cow, cheese, and corn to represent the state's agriculture would certainly have surprised a farmer in mid-nineteenth-century Wisconsin. Back then, wheat was king.

At the time, wheat's popularity could be traced to the territory's early settlers from New York, Pennsylvania, and Ohio. Those settlers brought with them an appreciation of wheat's advantage (namely, its relatively low labor demands and ability to be readily stored), sowed their fields with that grain, and, in the 1850s and early 1860s, reaped healthy profits. Cyrus McCormick's reaper, J. I. Case's thresher, and enthusiastic investment in railroads spurred the enthusiasm for wheat farming.

In 1860, wheat production in Wisconsin peaked at over 27 million bushels in what farmers called "the golden year." But then the bottom fell out. Prices began dropping, just as the effects of years of sowing wheat on the same fields (which depleted the soil of essential nutrients) began to be felt. Plant diseases and pests added to the farmers' woes. In short, it became harder and harder to grow wheat that was worth less and less.

Fortunately, the same climate and soil that had produced large wheat crops were ideal for forage crops, and the land that was unsuitable for cultivation was good for pasture for livestock. Furthermore, many of the newest wave of immigrants—New Englanders, New Yorkers, and European immigrants (particularly those from Northern Europe) were skilled dairymen.

By 1867, Wisconsin was home to 245,000 dairy cows. The work of the Wisconsin Dairymen's Association, founded in 1872, helped fan milk production in the state, as did the opening of the University of Wisconsin's Dairy School in 1887 (the first in the nation). In 1912, Wisconsin could boast of 1.46 million dairy cows; it was home to more than 2 million by 1925.

By World War II, the reputation of Wisconsin's cows was such that the state legislature placed the slogan "America's Dairyland" on automobile license plates—a reputation sullied only by California replacing Wisconsin as the nation's top milk-producing state at the end of the twentieth century.

Nevertheless, today Wisconsin is home to approximately 17,000 dairy farms and 1 million cows, which on average produce an annual

17,306 gallons of milk each. Fifteen percent of the country's milk comes from those cows, earning the unnamed bovine a well-deserved spot on Wisconsin's state quarter.

The demands of Wisconsin's cheese industry are directly related to the cow that shares the quarter with the round of cheese. Ninety percent of milk produced by Wisconsin's dairy industry is used for cheese production, and those cows boosted Wisconsin to its ranking as the nation's top cheese-making state, producing as many as 500 different varieties, types, and styles of cheese.

In total, Wisconsin leads the nation in production of cheddar, American, mozzarella, Muenster, and Limburger cheese and at the same time can claim to be the origin of such varieties as Colby, baby Swiss, and brick cheese. That litany does not even count the foam headpieces seen adorning the noggins of Green Bay Packers fans.

Cheese-making in Wisconsin owes much of its success to the state's diverse immigrant heritage. Swiss immigrants introduced Swiss cheese; Italians brought mozzarella, provolone, and gorgonzola. From the French came Camembert, Brie, and a variety of blue cheeses. The Germans, for their part, brought Muenster and Limburger; the English, cheddar, and the Dutch immigrants brought Gouda and Edam.

Historians credit Charles Rockwell as ranking among the state's earliest cheese makers. He began production at Koshkonong near Fort Atkinson in 1837, eleven years before Wisconsin became a state. In those days of limited transportation and storage capabilities, cheese, which kept longer than milk or butter, simply made economic sense.

Over the course of the next two decades, the potential for cheese production in Wisconsin had reached such a point that J. I. Smith, of Sheboygan County, erected the state's first cheese vat in 1858. He then became the first cheese maker to market outside the state when he shipped barrels of cheese to Chicago.

By the end of the Civil War, thirty cheese factories operated in Wisconsin; by 1870, the number had grown to fifty-four, with the state producing over 3 million pounds of cheese. That number more than quadrupled within ten years as cheese production eventually concentrated in three counties: Sheboygan, Green, and Jefferson. By the 1920s, there were over 2,800 cheese factories in the state.

Today, cheese remains a primary focus of Wisconsin's dairy industry; 90 percent of the state's total milk production is directed to cheese-making. In fact, Wisconsin's government Web site serves up 5,234 hits in response to a search for the word "cheese." And in the Wisconsin Historical Museum in Madison, the treasured artifacts include a round copper kettle, five feet in diameter, capable of holding 2,500 gallons of milk—enough to make one 200-pound round of Swiss cheese at its original home at the Tuscobia Cheese Factory.

Corn also earned its place on the state quarter—and, like the cow, arguably at the expense of wheat. The collapse of the state's wheat market in the 1860s encouraged crop diversification. Innovative farmers learned how to grow corn in the state's higher latitudes and added oats to their agricultural portfolios as well. In total, the production of corn and oats rose from slightly over 5 million bushels in 1849 to more than 67 million bushels in 1879.

In the years to come, Wisconsin's corn farmers never looked back. In 2002, Wisconsin led the United States in corn silage production and, with 391.5 million bushels produced, ranked fifth in the production of corn for grain. In total, corn production contributed $882.4 million to the state's economy in 2003 and accounted for roughly one-third of Wisconsin's 12 million acres of cropland.

Thanks to the growing demand for ethanol, the prospects for the Badger State's corn farmers continue to look bright. Corn is the main ingredient for ethanol, and it takes 1 bushel of corn to make 2.8 gallons of the fuel. By 2010, U.S. ethanol plants will need 2.6 billion bushels of corn a year—the kind of demand that, in the summer of 2006, helped propel corn prices to their highest prices in a decade.

Even the corn on the Wisconsin state quarter promises to be valuable. Due to a brief problem with one of the Denver Mint's coin presses in November 2004, 50,000 of the Wisconsin state quarters were minted with an unusual flaw—an apparent extra leaf on the left side of the bottom of the ear of corn.

By the time the error was noticed and corrected, the flawed quarters had been commingled with quarters from the other four presses. Before long, they began appearing in cash registers and coin purses mainly in the Tucson and San Antonio areas—and sparking a renewed collecting interest in the already popular 50 State Quarters® Program. According to an article in *USA Today*, a set of three Wisconsin quarters—two flawed and one in good condition—sold the following January on eBay for $2,800.

"These days, a coin pulled out of circulation is probably worth $100 to $300, and a coin pulled out of rolls before entering circulation is probably worth $300 to $500," said Patrick Heller, who owns Liberty Coin Service in Lansing, Michigan. "It all depends on the coin's condition."

# 31

# CALIFORNIA
## *California Dreaming*

Over the course of a life focused in its latter half on preserving America's greatest natural treasures, Sierra Club founder John Muir never shied away from contentious controversy. It was only fitting, therefore, that the California state quarter that bears his image sparked heated debate as well.

Perhaps aware of the threat of such disagreement, Governor Gray Davis began California's design selection process by forming the twenty-member California State Quarter Commission. The commission then solicited design concepts from California citizens. Californians responded enthusiastically, offering up 8,000 designs.

After culling the list to twenty semifinalists, the commission forwarded its recommendations to Davis.

Davis picked his own five finalists from the twenty—no easy task for any politician, particularly one leading a state as diverse and expansive as California.

One image, designed by San Diego artist Jon Louie, featured a giant sequoia tree. Another design, crafted by James Cody of Santa Barbara, featured a coastal scene of sun and waves. A third design, submitted by San Diego artist Sarah Bailey, included the iconic Hollywood sign. A fourth candidate, designed by David Biagini of San Francisco, depicted a miner panning for (and discovering) gold. The fifth finalist, submitted by Garrett Burke of Los Angeles, featured John Muir gazing at Yosemite's Half Dome.

By the winter of 2004, when the U.S. Mint returned the five designs, revised to reflect the challenges of converting artistic designs to a coin engraving, Arnold Schwarzenegger was California's new governor. Some thought, perhaps only half-jokingly, that the former actor's presence in the governor's mansion meant that the Hollywood sign design would have the inside track to a historic place on the state quarter. Others surmised that his bodybuilding nickname the "Austrian Oak" might favor the sequoia design. Skeptics wondered if the Hummer-driving governor would give serious thought to a design featuring naturalist John Muir.

To hear Schwarzenegger tell it at the unveiling of the final design, it was a tough decision.

"This was one of the first decisions, I remember, that I had to make after I was elected into office," Schwarzenegger said. "And we had these five designs there, and for a week we went back and forth, debating over which one it should be, and we couldn't make up our minds."

"And all of a sudden," he continued, "one day we got a phone call from Kevin Starr, who was the state librarian at the time. He was on the phone, and he said, 'Governor, it is extremely important you make up your mind. The people of California are looking at you now; they want to decide how quick are you with the decision-making process. And remember that the decision is very, very important, because this is not like the financial situation, the crisis California is in. This is a much more important decision. We need it right away.'"

"So, talk about putting pressure on someone," the governor lamented. "My wife and I were scrambling, because we couldn't make a decision right away, because there were five beautiful designs there. And of course California is an incredible state that has so much to offer."

"So anyway," Schwarzenegger continued, "I was thinking about calling the Mint and to just tell the Mint, 'What's wrong with all five designs? Let's just produce all five designs. I mean, we are an incredible state, we are the most spectacular state in the Union, and we are the sixth largest economy—we deserve five designs.'"

"Maria, as usual, held me back, not to make the phone call," the governor admitted. "And so therefore we went back and forth again. And the more we went through the five designs the more we decided that Garrett's design is really the most beautiful one and it says it all. With Yosemite, with the California condor, with John Muir—I thought it was spectacular. A beautiful, beautiful design and a beautiful coin."

Not everyone agreed, however. The dissidents' ranks included David Biagini, who had submitted the miner design—a design entitled "A Golden Moment" and that had actually claimed the majority of votes in an Internet poll commissioned by the California State Quarter Commission. In response to the Muir selection, he created a Web site, www.caquarter.com, to press his arguments for his miner in cyberspace.

"The facts are that the people chose 'A Golden Moment' for the California quarter, and there were great efforts to ensure that the people's choice would never become the California quarter," Biagini argued.

John Muir, on the other hand, would have been delighted with the outcome—an outcome that, one might say, represented the culmination of a chain of events that began in 1849. That year, a year before California gained statehood, Muir's family emigrated from Scotland to the United States, bringing the eleven-year-old Muir with them. He grew up on a farm near Portage, Wisconsin, and later studied at the University of Wisconsin. A talented woodworker and inventor, he worked odd jobs around the northern and midwestern United States and Canada for several years.

But in Indianapolis, Muir suffered a frightening eye injury. Reflecting back on the incident, Muir said, "I felt neither pain nor faintness, the thought was so tremendous that my right eye was gone—that I should never look at a flower again." Accordingly, once his eyesight returned, Muir resolved to focus on the natural world. He tramped from Indianapolis to the Gulf of Mexico, sailed first to Cuba and then Panama, crossed the Isthmus of Panama, and sailed up the West Coast. He landed in San Francisco in March 1868.

Taking a job as a sheepherder, Muir soon made his home in the Yosemite Valley. He famously described the Sierra Nevada Mountains as "the Range of Light . . . the most divinely beautiful of all the mountain chains I have seen . . . . I came to life in the cool winds and the crystal waters of the mountains, and were it not for a thought now and then of loneliness and isolation the pleasure of my existence would be complete."

Suitably inspired, Muir devoted the rest of his life to the conservation of natural beauty in Yosemite and elsewhere, ranging as far afield as Alaska and South America. He published more than 300 articles and ten books that expanded his naturalist philosophy. Some would later christen him "The Father of Our National Parks" and "Wilderness Prophet." Considerably less seriously, Muir described himself as a "poetico-trampo-geologist-botanist and ornithologist-naturalist etc. etc."

Despite Muir's self-deprecation, his accomplishments were indeed serious and long-lasting. His writings, particularly a series of articles in *Century* magazine, contributed greatly to the creation of Sequoia, Mount Rainier, Petrified Forest, and Grand Canyon National Parks, and, perhaps most famously, Yosemite. To help protect such creations ("to do something for wildness and make the mountains glad," in his words), Muir helped form the Sierra Club in 1892, serving as that organization's president until his death in 1914.

In 1901, Muir published *Our National Parks*, bringing him to the attention of President Theodore Roosevelt. In response, Roosevelt visited Muir in Yosemite two years later. Over the course of a legendary camping trip, the two men sat beneath the trees and laid the foundation of Roosevelt's conservation programs.

Muir did not always meet with success, however. Perhaps his most painful failure came in the Hetch Hetchy Valley, when the Tuolumne River was dammed to create a water reservoir for San Francisco. Years of polarizing debate followed—to no avail. Congress approved damming the river in 1913; Muir died the following year in Los Angeles after a sudden bout with pneumonia.

"John Muir was best known to the general public as a great lover of nature," his obituary in the *New York Times* noted. "But aside from being a naturalist—'more wonderful than Thoreau,' according to his good friend Ralph Waldo Emerson—Mr. Muir was a geologist, an explorer, philosopher, artist, author, and editor, and to each of his avocations he devoted that deep insight and conscientious devotion which made him its master."

After Muir's death, some went so far as to claim that the naturalist had died of a broken heart in the wake of the loss of the Hetch Hetchy. If so, then it would be of no small consolation to Muir to know that because of the perpetuation of his image on California's state quarter, he might survive to see the Tuolumne River flow free once again. In 2004, the same year that Governor Schwarzenegger picked Muir to stand astride California's quarter, he directed the state's resources agency to review the idea of draining the Hetch Hetchy Reservoir and restoring what Muir once called a "second Yosemite."

# 32

# MINNESOTA

*10,000 Lakes,*
*488 Million Quarters*

"Land of 10,000 Lakes," Minnesota's state quarter declares. In addition to an outline of Minnesota, the quarter features one of those same lakes, with a loon paddling contentedly in its foreground. Behind the state bird, a fishing boat floats. Seated in it, two anglers try their luck.

Fishing is big business in Minnesota, whose 15,000 (rather than 10,000) lakes boast a total shoreline that exceeds 90,000 miles, a remarkable figure that tops California, Hawaii, and Florida combined.

Sport fish include walleye, northern pike, smallmouth bass, crappie, lake trout, bluegill, and whitefish. According to one report, those fish are stalked by 1.5 million resident and nonresident anglers every year.

Minnesota's anglers contribute mightily to the state's economy—as much as $1.8 billion, in fact. Most is spent on boats, gas, and lodging, although bait ($50 million), lures, lines, and tackle ($34 million), and ice fishing equipment ($8 million) demand impressive expenditures as well. In short, fishing—and the 15,000 lakes and rivers that support it—makes a significant contribution to Minnesota's coffers.

But 300 years ago, Minnesota's lakes—in particular, the so-called Boundary Waters of the state's northern border with Canada—yielded an equally rich bounty. In doing so, those waters helped write some of the greatest tales of endeavor and adventure in America's history.

The adventure began in 1679 when the French explorer Sieur Duluth (or Du Lhut, born under the name Daniel Greysolon) pushed westward from Montreal and into modern-day Minnesota. There, he found a land full of economic potential. Covered in great boreal woods, latticed with innumerable lakes and ponds scoured by the glaciers of the region's last great ice age, it contained forests of pine, birch, balsam fir, white spruce, and white cedar, which sheltered thriving populations of moose, wolves, bears, muskrat, bobcats, falcons, loons, caribou, and, perhaps most enticingly, beaver.

Other explorers followed Duluth's lead. Some, like Father Hennepin, a Jesuit priest, sought converts. Others, such as Nicholas Perrot, came for national glory. The latter formally took possession of the entire Upper Mississippi region for France in 1689. At that same time, another explorer, Jacques de Noyon, pushed into what would one day be known as the Boundary Waters and wintered along the Rainy River.

Further exploration followed in the first half of the eighteenth century and on its heels came the canoes of the hardy French Canadian *coureur des bois*—literally, "runners of the woods." These men, operating outside of the auspices of France's colonial government, began trading guns, copper kettles, blankets, and other trade goods with local Indians for fur pelts, notably beaver.

As French Canada found itself in increasing economic competition with Great Britain's Hudson Bay Company, the French realized that dramatic steps would need to be taken to open up North America's interior to French traders.

In 1731, Pierre Gaultier de Varennes, sieur de la Vérendrye, responded. Leading a brigade of canoes that included his three sons, a nephew, and fifty men, la Vérendrye forged a watery path that linked Lake Superior, Rainy Lake, Lake in the Woods, and Lake Winnipeg. Establishing a network of forts and a patchwork of Indian alliances, he helped ensure the next three decades of French fur trade in the region.

An important part of that trade involved the legitimizing of the individual efforts of the *coureur des bois*. Montreal merchants began licensing and funding increasingly large-scale fur expeditions to Minnesota and beyond. The men once called "runners of the woods" became known as "voyageurs."

For the voyageurs, the scattered French forts offered isolated outposts on a remarkable 3,000-mile canoe route that stretched from Montreal, along the Great Lakes, through the Boundary Waters of northern Minnesota, and on to Fort Chipewyan on the shores of remote Lake Athabaska. With challenges that included 120 back-breaking portages, 200 treacherous rapids, and fifty lakes capable of being whipped into an oceanlike frenzy in a storm, the route was not for the timid.

The hard-paddling, hard-fighting, and, at times, hard-loving voyageurs could, and would, be called many things. "Timid," however, would not be one of them. They responded enthusiastically. Piloting their birch-bark canoes, companies of voyageurs struck out in the spring from Montreal for distant Fort St. Pierre, on the banks of Rainy Lake. Sometimes paddling for as long as sixteen hours a day, the voyageurs would pause along shore to trade with local Indians, wait out a summer storm, dab fresh pitch on their canoes, or perhaps cook a quick meal or enjoy a pipe.

Such stops, however, were brief. The voyageurs knew that they could not tarry for long. It would take them until midsummer to reach Fort St. Pierre; after a final exchange of trades, the voyageurs faced an arduous journey back to Montreal before winter descended upon the North Country.

As they traveled along what some have called the Voyageurs' Highway, the network of forts succored the weary traders with welcome shelter and provisions of grain, vegetables, and wild rice. They also offered defined trading posts for the voyageurs to swap their European trade goods for beaver pelts with the local Indians.

Without the cooperation of the region's Indian tribes, a fur trade on the scale of the one that eventually developed would have been impossible. The Chipewyan and Cree were willing, skilled trappers. So were the numerous Ojibwe, who, in addition to hunting, raised corn, vegetables, and wild rice that helped to keep the forts adequately provisioned. For their part, the Huron and Iroquois often made appearances as middlemen and brokers.

Regardless of the tribe, one can only imagine the amazement those Indians would have felt had they seen the eventual destination of so many of those same pelts—the fashionable hat shops and salons of distant Paris and Europe.

France's defeat in the French and Indian Wars spelled the end of its organized political–economic endeavors in the north of Minnesota. The British, however, stepped readily into the void, as personified by two competing companies—the upstart North West Company and the venerable Hudson Bay Company.

The former was, according to historian Daniel Francis, "a restive partnership of aggressive colonial merchants," one that was managed for its partners by a hardworking collection of English or Scottish clerks—called *bourgeois*—who supervised the work of their French Canadian voyageurs. Interracial unions between the voyageurs and local Indian tribes created a race of offspring known as *metis*, who in turn further solidified the so-called Nor'Westers key relationships with their Indian trading partners.

The Hudson Bay Company, on the other hand, was headquartered in London and organized "in the traditional mould of the imperial trading company, chartered by the British monarch and given a monopoly to exploit the resources of its far-flung possessions." Its ranks were made of English "officers" and lower-class English and Scottish "servants." The company compensated for its rigid, class-based structure with strong internal discipline and the confidence born of years of successful experience.

"If a Hudson Bay Company trading house resembled a military barracks," Francis observed, "a Nor'Wester establishment had more in common with a rowdy tavern."

For nearly three decades, the two companies waged one of the fiercest economic wars North America had ever witnessed, vying with each other and with smaller rivals. And to use the phrase "war" is not mere hyperbole. In 1816, for example, the Hudson Bay Company even relied on a force of *meurons*, Swiss mercenaries imported from the recent Napoleonic Wars, to subjugate troublesome North West Company forts. It was not until 1821, when the Nor'Westers merged into the Hudson Bay Company, that such hostilities subsided.

By then, American traders were offering their own competition—particularly in the form of New York financier John Jacob Astor's American Fur Company. But the American traders were no match for the wealth of experience and organization that the British Canadian traders brought to the table. The American Fur Company declared bankruptcy in 1842.

Other forces, however, were afoot that spelled the end of the large-scale, organized fur trade in Minnesota. In particular, the movement of Indians onto federal reservations and increasing governmental efforts to limit the traders' influence over Indians played a key role in emasculating the industry.

"Without exaggerating greatly," one historian commented, "one might argue that the Upper Mississippi Valley fur trade in its final stages collapsed not from depletion of the wild game but for lack of Indians."

Great Britain's Red River Expedition of 1870, which successfully subjugated a rebellion of *metis*, sounded another death knell for the organized trade. The British army sent an expeditionary force westward from Toronto to crush the revolt, which, as a side effect, led to the completion of a road network into the former wilderness. With a road in place, a fur-trading industry once dependent on organized canoe traffic and isolated trading posts fragmented and dissipated by 1871.

Today, where voyageurs once paddled and isolated trading forts hosted colorful gatherings of traders and Indians, Minnesotans (and others) avail themselves of those same bountiful waters—although in far more recreational pursuits. Perhaps that was why, when Governor Tim Pawlenty's Minnesota State Quarter Commission offered him a variety of designs that included such concepts as "State with Symbols" (which included the state outline, snowflake, loon, and plow; "Mississippi River Headwaters"; and "Fisherman/Lake Recreation," the governor chose the latter to grace Minnesota's 488 million state quarters in 2005.

In the end, even Minnesota's quarter may yield its own bounty. According to published reports, minting errors found on some of the state quarters have resulted in images that look like additional trees along the coin's lakefront image. If that is the case, then the additional timber may make those quarters worth more than a mere twenty-five cents to savvy collectors.

# 33

# OREGON
## *Hillman's Richest Find*

In the spring of 1853, a twenty-year-old gold prospector named John W. Hillman convinced a band of fellow miners—namely, Isaac G. Skeeters, Henry Klippel, J. S. Louden, Pat McManus, and three others named Dodd, McGarrie, and Little, and possibly two more—to strike out into Oregon's Josephine County in search of a legendary seam known as the Lost Cabin Mine. Within a matter of days, however, Hillman's group, along with a party of Californian prospectors they joined, was hopelessly lost in the rugged terrain of southcentral Oregon's Cascade Mountains.

Visions of gold temporarily forgotten, Hillman took Skeeters, Klippel, and some others with him and began climbing the long, sloping flanks of a nearby mountain. From its summit, they hoped to be able to establish their location and chart a course out of the mountains.

As evening approached on June 12, 1853, the group reached the top of the mountain. Fifty years later, Hillman described the moment to the *Portland Oregonian*:

> [W]e suddenly came in sight of water, and were very much surprised, as we did not expect to see any lakes . . . and not until my mule stopped within a few feet of the rim of Crater Lake did I look down, and if I had been riding a blind mule I firmly believe I would have ridden over the edge to death and destruction . . . . Every man of the party gazed with wonder at the sight before him, and each in his own peculiar way gave expression to the thoughts within him; but we had no time to lose, and after rolling some boulders down the side of the lake, we rode to the left . . . I was very anxious to find a way to the water, which was immediately vetoed by the whole party, and . . . we decided to return to camp; but not before we discussed what name we should give the lake. There were many names suggested, but Mysterious Lake and Deep Blue Lake were most favorably received, and on a vote, Deep Blue Lake was chosen for a name. (Unrau 1987, n.p.)

Back in camp, the miners reported their discovery, although it failed to excite much interest, particularly in light of growing Indian troubles in the area and the ongoing quest for gold. Little did Hillman realize, however, that he had discovered a future gem of America's national parks—parks that, one day, would be treasured far more than all of the gold Hillman and his fellow prospectors were ever destined to find.

The idea of national parks did not fully germinate for another two decades. In 1870, an expedition financed and led by Henry Washburn, Nathaniel P. Langford, and under U.S. Army escort led by Lieutenant Gustavus C. Doane built upon the groundwork laid by earlier explorers and thoroughly combed and documented the Wyoming Territory's Yellowstone region. It was their expedition, for example, that christened "Old Faithful."

The Washburn Expedition included in its ranks a Montana writer and lawyer named Cornelius Hedges. Hedges was, according to one modern chronicler of the expedition, "not really an outdoors person." Nevertheless, his visit to Yellowstone fired him with awe and appreciation for the region's natural wonders. Once back in Helena, Montana, Hedges began vocally espousing setting aside the region as a national park. Hedges idea was not original. In fact, it had been first proposed by former acting Montana territorial governor Thomas Francis Meagher—but Meagher had died in a suspicious drowning in the Missouri River three years earlier.

On this occasion, however, the timing could not have been better. Both Hedges and Langford had the ear of William H. Clagett—Montana's newest delegate to Congress—and, upon reaching Capitol Hill, Clagett introduced a bill to make Yellowstone a national park on December 18, 1871. He found a ready ally in Dr. Ferdinand V. Hayden, who had led one of two U.S. Geological Survey expeditions into the region that same summer. Because of Hayden's work, Yellowstone was, by this time, national news, as is evident in the following musings of the *New York Times*:

> There is something romantic in the thought that, in spite of the restless activity of our people, and the almost fabulous rapidity of their increase, vast tracts of the national domain yet remain unexplored. As little is known of these regions as of the topography of the sources of the Nile or the interior of Australia. They are enveloped in a certain mystery, and their

attractions to the adventurous are constantly enhanced by re-markable discoveries . . . . Sometimes, as in the case of the Yellowstone Valley, the natural phenomena are so unusual, so startlingly different from any known elsewhere, that the inter-est and curiosity excited are not less universal and decided. (Haines 1974, n.p.)

Clagett's bill (introduced in the Senate by Samuel C. Pomeroy) passed in the House on January 30, 1872, and in the Senate on Feb-ruary 27, and was signed by President Ulysses S. Grant on March 1. "Conservation," for the first time, had a new meaning—one that stretched beyond simply conserving coal, iron, timber, and the other raw ingredients of American industry. Now it applied to mountains, lakes, forests, geysers, canyons, and the creatures that inhabited them.

It was not until 1890 that more national parks were created. That year ushered in Yosemite (which had been deeded to California in 1864 as a state park), General Grant (today's King's Canyon), and Se-quoia National Parks in California; Mackinac, in Michigan, followed three years later, although it was later abolished. In Washington, Mount Rainier National Park was established in 1899.

Meanwhile, similar efforts were underway in Oregon. William Gladstone Steel, a postmaster, newspaperman, railroad promoter, and publisher in Portland, Oregon, had first visited Crater Lake in 1885. At the time, he linked up with an expedition in southern Oregon led by Joseph LeConte and U.S. Army captain Clarence E. Dutton and, fulfilling a dream that he had harbored since first reading about the lake in a Kansas newspaper fifteen years earlier, trekked with the ex-pedition to its shores. The following year, writing for the literary jour-nal *The West Shore*, Steel recounted his initial impression:

Not a foot of the land about the lake had been touched or claimed. An overmastering conviction came to me that this wonderful spot must be saved, wild and beautiful, just as it was, for all future generations, and that it was up to me to do something. I then and there had the impression that in some way, I didn't know how, the lake ought to become a National Park. I was so burdened with the idea that I was distressed. (Unrau 1987, n.p.)

Steel need not have been distressed; thanks to his tireless publication and exhortation, Crater Lake became a national park in 1902. Today, we know that it was formed more than 7,700 years ago by the collapse of Mt. Mazama. At 1,949 feet, it is the deepest lake in the United States, the seventh-deepest in the world, and, isolated from incoming streams and rivers, possesses a record clarity depth of 134 feet.

Fourteen years after Crater Lake became a national park, President Woodrow Wilson signed legislation in 1916 that formally created the National Park Service. Today, there are 391 areas within the National Park System (in every state except Delaware) encompassing 4 million acres—national parks, monuments, battlefields, lakeshores, seashores, historic parks and sites, and the White House. To date, the newest area remains Colorado's Sand Creek National Historic Site, dedicated on April 28, 2007, to commemorate the massacre of nearly 160 Cheyenne and Arapaho Indians there on November 29, 1864.

Ironically, the year 2005 was one of the few years in which no new areas were added to the National Park System—an irony, given that on June 6, 2005, the U.S Mint released the first of 720.2 million quarters featuring Crater Lake. The design reflected the endorsement of the eighteen-member Oregon Commemorative Coin Commission, which had also considered such historical themes as the Oregon Trail, Mt. Hood with the Columbia River, and a wild Chinook salmon.

"Crater Lake is one of the natural wonders in the world. Steeped in thousands of years of history, and considered sacred land to the

Native Americans, it is Oregon's only National Park enjoyed by thousands every year," said Governor Ted Kulongoski in 2004 when he opted for the Crater Lake design. "Crater Lake represents all that is good in Oregon: beautiful scenery and a hardiness that is represented in its citizenry."

# 34

# KANSAS

## *Buffalo Soldier*
## *in the Heart of America*

On August 29, 2005, the U.S. Mint released the first of Kansas' 563.4 million state quarters. The quarter featured a sunflower and, most prominently, the hulking bulk of an American bison—better known as a buffalo. The sunflower is Kansas' state flower; the buffalo the official state animal. Together, they combined to beat out such competing design finalists as an image of the statue that sits atop the state capitol (an American Indian archer aiming his bow skyward, toward the North

Star); an image of a sunflower with wheat; and a design that featured a single sunflower.

A week later, on September 6, First Sergeant Mark Matthews (U.S. Army, retired) passed away at a nursing home in Washington, D.C. Matthews was 111 years old when he died. The army buried him with full military honors at Arlington National Cemetery.

So what could the Kansas state quarter and First Sergeant Matthews possibly have in common? More than the casual observer might think.

Matthews, as it turns out, was the last surviving member of the U.S. Army's fabled "Buffalo Soldiers" of the Tenth U.S. Cavalry, a hard-riding, hard-fighting cavalry unit that, as coincidence would have it, traced its origins to Fort Leavenworth, Kansas.

An act of Congress entitled "An Act to increase and fix the military peace establishment of the United States" was approved July 28, 1866, which authorized the U.S. Army to add four additional cavalry regiments to the six already in existence. Of those four, it was directed that "two . . . shall be composed of colored men, having the same organization as is now provided by law for cavalry regiments."

The two regiments "composed of colored men" became the U.S. Army's Ninth and Tenth Cavalry Regiments. Both were manned by African American soldiers and sergeants, though for the most part, they had white officers. The Ninth formed in New Orleans and soon relocated to Texas; the Tenth formed in Fort Leavenworth.

Although African Americans had long played an important role in the exploration and settling of the American West—arguably, dating back to William Clark's slave, York, who accompanied the Lewis and Clark expedition—the arrival of all-black cavalry regiments in Kansas and Texas made a quick and lasting impression on the Cheyenne Indians.

Confronted by the new regiments, Plains Indians—some say Cheyenne, others Kiowa—christened their new foe "Wild Buffalo," a nickname that evolved into "Buffalo Soldiers." Some say that the nickname was given out of respect for the fierce fighting ability of the Tenth Cavalry. Others argue that the nickname derived from the soldiers' dark curly hair, which resembled a buffalo's coat.

Regardless of the origin, the nickname "Buffalo Soldiers" not only stuck but was proudly embraced by the troopers of the Ninth and Tenth Cavalry Regiments. It was not long before the army's two new African American infantry regiments, the Twenty-fourth and the Twenty-fifth, were known as Buffalo Soldiers as well.

A deadly cholera epidemic at Fort Leavenworth in the summer of 1867 taught the new recruits of the Tenth Cavalry that, on the Plains, disease could be as much of a foe as the region's Indians. But shortly before the regimental headquarters moved on to Fort Riley, Kansas, the Buffalo Soldiers had an opportunity to test their mettle against the Indians as well.

In late July, the regiment's F Troop, under the command of Captain George Armes, deployed to Fort Hays, Kansas, to offer protection to construction crews laying the tracks of the transcontinental Union Pacific Railroad nearby. On August 1, 1867, Armes received word that a party of workers had been killed and scalped at nearby Campbell's Camp. In response, Armes mounted his forty-four-man company and rode out to investigate.

Upon arriving at the camp, Armes not only found seven scalped bodies but also realized that he needed reinforcements. He dispatched a squad of six back to Fort Campbell with the request. By daylight of the next day, however, no reinforcements had arrived. Undeterred, Armes, a lieutenant named Bodamer, two civilian guides, and thirty-one Buffalo Soldiers rode after the Indians, leaving four sick soldiers behind.

By 9:00 AM, F Troop had covered twenty-five miles and reached the banks of the Saline River. Spotting a group of seventy-five Indians—and the railroad crew's stolen horses—Armes dismounted his troop and intrepidly, perhaps even rashly, attacked along the bank of the small river. Within a matter of minutes, as he began to receive fire from the bluffs overhead, he realized he was surrounded. Armes's concerns grew when he realized that a herd of nearby bison was, in fact, actually another group of Cheyenne warriors creeping up disguised in buffalo robes.

At that point, Armes realized that discretion would be the better part of valor. He ordered a withdrawal and, for fifteen miles, beat a fighting retreat, leading his horses on foot as charges of Indians repeatedly swept against—and at times, through—his command. Later, Armes estimated that his troop of thirty-some men battled between 350 and 400 Cheyenne warriors.

In the fighting, one of F Troop's sergeants, a soldier named Christy, was shot through the head as he organized a line of defense. Meanwhile, the company's first sergeant, Thornton, had his own horse shot out from underneath him. Armes himself took a rifle shot to the leg and had to be placed upon his horse. By the time the Cheyenne finally ceased their attacks, many of Armes's men had run out of ammunition. Adding to the misery, six of the troopers were so debilitated by attacks of cholera that they had to be strapped to their horses and led to safety as the fighting raged.

In his memoirs, Armes candidly assessed his narrow escape: "It is the greatest wonder in the world that my command and myself escaped being massacred, as we had to retreat fifteen miles through a hilly country, full of canyons, rocks, and gullies, fighting our way foot by foot, the Indians dodging from one gully and rock to others and firing on us at every chance."

What became known as the Battle of the Saline River marked the Buffalo Soldiers' baptism of fire. In the years to come, however, they would carry their regimental flag and guidons into combat many more times. Eventually, twenty-two officers, men, and Indian scouts assigned to the Buffalo Soldier regiments earned the Medal of Honor during the Indian Wars throughout the West and in conflicts further afield.

Among their foes, the Buffalo Soldiers could count Cheyenne, Arapaho, Kiowa, Comanche, Oglala Sioux, and Apache. They even battled white outlaws, such as when Sergeant Benjamin Brown, of the Twenty-fourth Infantry Regiment, helped fight off a band of robbers attacking a paymaster's convoy in Arizona in 1889. Brown, shot in the stomach, kept fighting until shot through both arms. He survived to be awarded the Medal of Honor the following year.

In later years, the Buffalo Soldier regiments, or companies of those regiments, also participated in the Spanish-American War, the Philippine Insurrection, and the relief of the foreign legations in Peking during the Boxer Rebellion. Several units of the Ninth Cavalry, along with a company of the Twenty-fourth, even garrisoned Yosemite, Sequoia, and General Grant (King's Canyon) parks in California—arguably making them some of the nation's first park rangers.

By then, the Tenth Cavalry's ranks included Mark Matthews. The Alabama native had met a detachment of the regiment's troopers at a racetrack in Lexington, Kentucky, where he had worked in the stables and, inspired by their stories, enlisted into their ranks, even though at age sixteen, he was underage. His first assignment took him to Fort Huachuca, Arizona. From there, he and his regiment pursued Pancho Villa into Mexico.

Matthews made a career of the army, eventually retiring in 1949. The days of a segregated U.S. Army had officially ended the previous year, when President Harry S. Truman's Executive Order 9981 officially ordered the American military desegregated.

The legacy of the Buffalo Soldiers lived on, however, and is particularly evident in Fort Leavenworth, Kansas, and in Junction City, Kansas, outside of Fort Riley, where monuments to the African American regiments now stand. But thanks to the Kansas state quarter—and the soldiers' namesake buffalo that adorns it—a reminder of Buffalo Soldiers and their accomplishments may be closer than you think.

# 35

# WEST VIRGINIA
## *A Bridge Too Far*

The fifth quarter released in 2005 commemorates, on a total of 721.6 million coins, the state of West Virginia. Possible designs for that quarter included concepts entitled "Appalachian Warmth," "River Rafters," and "Mother's Day/Anna Jarvis," the latter celebrating the native of Taylor County, West Virginia, who was credited with inventing the idea of Mother's Day. In all, more than 1,800 design concepts had been submitted to and considered by a committee of students at the state's Governor's School for the Arts.

In the end, West Virginia Governor Bob Wise opted for a design entitled "New River Gorge." On its reverse, it captures the scenic beauty of the self-proclaimed Mountain State with an intricate en-graving of West Virginia's New River and the New River Gorge Bridge, located a few miles north of Fayetteville, West Virginia.

What the quarter fails to capture, however, is sheer excitement that has descended on—and leaped off—that same bridge every au-tumn since 1980 (with the post–9/11 exception of 2001) with the annual celebration known as Bridge Day, which draws as many as 200,000 spectators to Fayetteville, West Virginia, every third Satur-day in October.

There would, however, be no Bridge Day without the bridge, and until 1977, there was no bridge spanning West Virginia's New River Gorge. Before then, local travelers had no choice but to snake their way along winding rounds on a dangerous forty-minute journey down into and then out of the gorge. In 1973, however, the West Virginia Department of Highways decided to remedy the situation. The de-partment accepted a bid from the American Bridge Division of U.S. Steel Corporation and directed American Bridge to begin work on a structure designed by the Michael Baker Company's engineers.

In June 1974, construction began. Matching pairs of 330-foot-high towers were constructed on opposite sides of the gorge, with three-inch-thick cables running the 3,500 feet between them. Once the cables were secure, trolleys running on those cables began guiding the first steel into place over the gorge.

Three years and $37 million later, American Bridge's work over the New River Gorge was done, with the bridge opening for traffic on Oc-tober 22, 1977. The result was a 3,030-foot-long steel arch bridge (with an arch measuring 1,700 feet in length, making it the longest in the Western Hemisphere) that soared 876 feet above the New River be-low. As such, it was the second-highest bridge in the United States, with top honors in that category remaining with Colorado's Royal Gorge Bridge over the Arkansas River. Despite its second-place status, however, the New River Gorge Bridge could fit the Washington Monu-ment underneath it and still have 325 feet to spare.

With its completion, the New River Gorge Bridge joined the ranks of legendary American bridges. For example, the span length of the Verrazano-Narrows Bridge, completed in New York City the previous decade to connect Brooklyn with Staten Island, is so great that its suspension towers had to be designed to compensate for the earth's curvature. At 4,260 feet, its span tops that of America's second-longest suspension bridge, California's Golden Gate, and dwarfs the 1,595 feet of the longest span of New York's iconic Brooklyn Bridge.

In other categories, the main span of Philadelphia's Commodore Barry Bridge in Chester, Pennsylvania, at 1,644 feet, gives it top honors as the nation's longest steel-truss girder bridge. Meanwhile, ongoing construction of the nearly 2,000-foot-long Hoover Dam Bypass Bridge (also known as the Colorado River Bridge) promises to give the United States its longest concrete arch bridge when completed in 2010. Not to be outdone, Louisiana natives continue to point proudly to their own Lake Pontchartrain Causeway outside of New Orleans. At over twenty-four miles in length, its champions claim that it is the longest overwater highway bridge in the world.

Taking its place in such good company, the bridge, not surprisingly, quickly became not only a means of getting from one side of the gorge to the other but a destination in its own right. Three years after the bridge was completed, the local community held the first New River Gorge Bridge Day on November 8, 1980. The day's events included two parachutists who jumped from a plane onto the bridge. Starting an even more enduring tradition, five other parachutists jumped off the bridge into the gorge below, free-falling for three to four seconds before deploying their chutes and enjoying the remaining thirty seconds of their descents.

The latter daredevils were practitioners of a relatively new extreme sport called "BASE jumping." BASE stands for "Building/Antenna/Span (as in bridge span)/Earth," and BASE jumpers' sport—on paper, anyway—is a relatively straightforward one: to jump off such fixed points (as opposed to jumping out of an aircraft) and parachute to the ground below. Jumpers use special ram-jet parachutes—devices that resemble kites as much as conventional parachutes–and self-deploy the chutes by first holding and then releasing a pilot chute that drags out the main chute to deploy. In the few seconds of free-fall, jumpers reach speeds of seventy-five miles per hour.

Arguably, the sport of BASE jumping can be traced to the summer of 1966, when two California skydivers, Brian Schubert and Michael Pelkey, scaled Yosemite National Park's 3,000-foot El Capitan and, in an unprecedented feat of daring, parachuted off the great monolith.

In the course of their descent and landing, Shubert suffered a broken ankle; Pelkey fractured several bones in his feet. Upon their landing, the National Park Service added insult to injury by search- · ing for regulations that prohibited such conduct. That particular search was unsuccessful, although later legal penmanship would soon fill that regulatory void—so successfully, in fact, that events such as Bridge Day would one day represent one of the few legal opportunities for BASE jumping in the United States.

As Bridge Day grew in popularity, so did the number of BASE jumps—and rappels and bungee jumps—from the bridge's span. Bridge Day in 1981 featured a dozen parachutists; by 1984, the number had surged to 300 and, in 1986, to 400. Even a jumper's death in 1987 did not deter the enthusiasm. In 1998, sixteen jumpers—twelve followed immediately by another serial of four—set a world record for a simultaneous BASE jump.

In the autumn of 2006, however, an accident of tragic irony reminded the world of BASE jumping's dangers. On that October day, some 400 jumpers made approximately 800 jumps off the bridge, much to the delight of the 175,000 spectators in attendance.

BASE pioneers Brian Schubert and Michael Pelkey also attended that year's event as an encore to their visit of the previous year. The year 2006 marked the fortieth anniversary of their leap from Yosemite, an anniversary that the two men intended to mark with ceremonial jumps from the New River Gorge Bridge's steels spans.

The sixty-six-year-old Schubert, a veteran of the Pomona, California, police force, jumped first, shortly before noon. He had 141 skydives to his credit but, according to the *Los Angeles Times*, it was his first jump in years, a gap in experience that perhaps proved fatal. He deployed his chute too late, failing to give it enough time to fully inflate and provide him with adequate deceleration before he slammed into the New River. The resulting impact killed Schubert—and convinced Pelkey to forgo his own jump.

In the end, Schubert's BASE jumping career spanned a continent—and two quarters. California's quarter features John Muir gazing at Yosemite Park, where Schubert first jumped into fame. And West Virginia's quarter offers the deceptively tranquil image of what became his last jump.

"My father died with a smile on his face because he had so much passion for what he loved," his daughter Cynthia Lee later told the *Los Angeles Times*. "And that's our saving grace."

# 36

# NEVADA
## *Horse Sense*

If Brian Schubert and the West Virginia state quarter offer one vision of courage, then Nevada's Velma Johnston offers another—the courage of one's convictions. And although Johnston is not featured on the Silver State's quarter, it is difficult to imagine anyone who would have been happier with its imagery—a trio of wild mustangs, galloping in the foreground of a snowcapped mountain range, with the sun at their backs and sagebrush at their flanks.

Johnston was born in 1912 into a family tree already intertwined with the wild horses and burros of the Old West. Johnston's father, Joseph Bronn, had arrived in Nevada as a pioneer infant; according to family legend, the milk of a mustang mare succored the crying baby as his immigrant family crossed the region's burning deserts in their covered wagon. Later, in Reno, he operated a freight service that relied on a large number of horses, including some of mustang lineage. It was not long before Johnston herself was in the saddle.

In 1923, however, at the age of eleven, Johnston contracted polio. Sent to San Francisco for treatment, she spent months in a cast that, in the end, disfigured her terribly. At the same time, though, the experience engendered in Johnston a special empathy for confined or hurt animals. The taunting of cruel classmates made school a nightmare; in response, the softhearted Johnston turned her attention to drawing, poetry, and caring for the animals on her father's ranch, the Double Lazy Heart, on the Truckee River.

On the Truckee, one of the Bronn family's neighbors was a strapping, kindhearted rancher named Charlie Johnston. He courted and eventually wed Johnston, and in time the couple took over the Double Lazy Heart. Unable to have children of their own, they found a place for children in their lives by operating an informal dude ranch for youth at the Double Lazy Heart. Many of the dude ranchers included troubled children from nearby Reno, where Johnston worked as a secretary for a local insurance company executive.

Johnston's life took a dramatic turn one day in 1950 when, driving to Reno for work, she pulled behind a truck crammed with frantic wild horses. The sight of blood dripping from the back of the trailer aroused both curiosity and concern. She trailed the trailer to its destination—a slaughterhouse where the horses were rendered into pet food.

To Johnston, the truck and its gory destination unveiled an ugly truth about federal land use management in the mid-twentieth century. Some 85 percent of Nevada's land was actually owned by the federal government and was managed for the most part by the Bureau of Land Management, or BLM. That same land was home to the BLM herds of wild horses and burros—some were wild mustangs of Spanish or Indian lineage, others simply equines that had been let loose from failed Depression-era homesteads—that it simply classified as feral. In the 1950s, it routinely issued permits to companies to round up horses and burros. The lucky ones found service as bucking broncos; the majority, however, were destined for rendering plants. Similar activities took place on state, county, and private lands.

In Nevada, the roundups occurred with all of the efficiency of the modern age. Aircraft and trucks combined with cowboys on horseback and in jeeps to effect industrial-sized roundups of the wild horses. One hundred thousand horses were captured in the 1950s; those numbers had dwindled to 17,000 across nine Western states by the late 1960s.

Spurred to action, Johnston quickly found herself fighting what seemed to be little more than a desperate rearguard action. Fortunately, however, she combined her passion for the horses' plight with the organizational and communication skills of a talented executive secretary.

Starting in Storey County where she lived, she charmed and cajoled local civic, community, and political leaders. At times, her cause put her at odds with many of her rancher neighbors who viewed the wild horses as simply pests. They disparaged her as "Wild Horse Annie." In return, Johnston embraced the name as a compliment, and in 1955, she claimed her first victory when the Nevada state legislature banned aircraft and land vehicles from capturing wild horses on state lands.

Unfortunately, the mustangs unlucky enough to roam the vast tracts of federally owned land in Nevada remained unprotected. But buoyed by her earlier successes, Johnston convinced U.S. Representative Walter S. Baring of Nevada to introduce legislation in Congress in 1959 that not only prohibited the use of any form of motorized vehicle to capture wild horses but also outlawed the poisoning of water holes. Recorded as Public Law 86-234, it was more popularly known as the Wild Horse Annie Act.

However, stymied by episodes of lax enforcement, even P.L. 86-234 seemed unable to promise that viable populations of the wild mustangs would remain on Nevada's public lands. In response, Johnston launched her most far-reaching and vocal campaign yet to agitate for greater protection for the West's wild horses and burros. Some have even said that Congress, in the 1960s, received more letters from constituents regarding the plight of the mustangs than on any other topic save the Vietnam War.

In 1962, Johnston's efforts began to bear fruit. That year, the government established the Nevada Wild Horse Range within the vast expanse of Nellis Air Force Base outside Las Vegas. BLM built watering holes throughout the area, and in the absence of competing livestock on the base, the horses grew in number from about 200 in 1962 to more than 1,000 by 1976. Similar sanctuaries would eventually include the Pryor Mountain refuge, established in 1968, on the Montana-Wyoming border, and the Little Bookcliffs refuge near Palisade, Colorado.

Further legislative relief came in 1971, with the unanimous passage of the Wild Free-Roaming Horse and Burro Act (P.L. 92-195). The new law gave the wild horses and burros protection on BLM and U.S. Forest Service lands "where found" at the time of the passage of the act—in total, 303 areas. Such animals, the act declared, are "living symbols of the historic and pioneer spirit of the West and shall be protected from harassment or death."

Even with the passage of the Wild Free-Roaming Horse and Burro Act, Johnston's work did not diminish. She established Wild Horses Organized Assistance (WHOA), designed to document horse locations through meticulous field notes, maps, and photographs of horse and burro spottings, witness affidavits, and other documents.

Johnston's final fight, however, was with her toughest foe yet—cancer. It was a fight she was destined to lose. On June 27, 1977, she passed away at the age of sixty-five, scarcely a year after the BLM implemented the nationwide Adopt-a-Horse program as part of its wild horse management efforts. Had Johnston survived, she would no doubt have taken great pride in knowing that by 1980, the public had adopted 20,000 wild horses and 2,000 burros. That same year, BLM estimated that on its lands, wild horse numbers exceeded 52,000 and burros 12,000, with some herds growing by 15 to 20 percent each year.

Such success presented—and continues to present—challenges in America's West, where cattlemen and ranchers depend upon the BLM land to forage and graze their own herds, particularly as the herds of wild horses grow. To their frustration, those ranchers often find themselves in competition with the wild horses and burros.

Nevertheless, such controversy was not enough in 2004 to prevent the mustang design from galloping away with a winning percentage of the 60,000 votes cast in a statewide poll to determine Nevada's state quarter design. The trio of mustangs left the four other candidate designs—"Nevada's Early Heritage," featuring a petroglyph and native artifacts; "Silver Miner," with a miner holding a pickax in front of a Comstock mine; "Nevada Wilderness," featuring an image of a bighorn sheep above snow-capped mountains; and "Battle Born Nevada," featuring a pair of crossed pickaxes fronted by a stylized star—in the proverbial dust.

On January 31, 2006, the U.S. Mint issued the first of 589.8 million Nevada state quarters bearing the mustang design, one of the largest mintings to date.

Chalk up another victory for Wild Horse Annie.

# NEBRASKA

*A Rock by Any Other Name . . .*

Admit it—you never thought the U.S. government would mint a coin with an elk penis on it. But in 2006, it did—some 591 million of them, in fact.

But before you scribble an angry letter to your Representative or Senator, rest assured that if ever an elk penis deserved to be on a piece of U.S. currency, it is the one featured on Nebraska's state quarter along with a pioneer's covered wagon.

Today, the feature in question—actually, a 325-foot-tall pillar rising out of the broad and dusty North Platte River Valley—is far better known as Chimney Rock, the name given to it by passing pioneers. But if you had asked a Native American to name the geologic formation, he would have told you "Elk Penis"—a far earthier appellation coined by tribes that, unlike the pioneers, had never even seen a chimney. At the same time, however, many of those pioneers passing Chimney Rock must have wondered if they would ever see a real chimney again.

Chimney Rock stands astride what some historians have called the Great Platte River Road. It was a kind of pioneering superhighway that served as a conduit for a host of trails that would one day be synonymous with the settling of the American West. The Oregon Trail, the California Trail, and the Mormon Trail all followed the same dusty path along the North Platte River at the point they passed Chimney Rock. And although their destinations differed, they all demanded a high, and sometimes fatal, toll in blood, sweat, and tears of those who traveled them.

Consider the Oregon Trail, for example. Army explorers and fur traders first blazed the path in the 1820s; it wasn't until the spring of 1842 that the first organized wagon train of settlers set out for Oregon's fertile Willamette Valley. That original party numbered between 100 and 160 settlers, and it was a number that would be readily eclipsed within a year.

The following spring, the so-called Great Migration of 1843 occurred when Marcus Whitman led a party of 800 immigrants westward to the as yet unorganized Oregon Territory. Their reports of a verdant paradise sparked "Oregon Fever," leading to 5,000 new immigrants within two years. Such a surge in settlement sparked a diplomatic crisis with Great Britain, which had its own interests in the Pacific Northwest. In 1846, diplomacy settled the so-called Oregon question; by 1848, Oregon was a vast territory (which originally included modern-day Washington and parts of Montana and Wyoming). In 1859, Oregon became the thirty-third state.

Statehood encouraged further settlement. The numbers of pioneers increased steadily every year until 1869, when the transcontinental railroad was completed and offered a far faster—and safer—route west to California. The completion of the Northern Pacific Railroad in 1883 almost completely outdated the notion of a 2,000-mile wagon journey to the Pacific Northwest.

But before the railroads were completed, the Oregon Trail was the way west. And for most of the trail's travelers, their journey would have truly begun in St. Louis, where they would have hopped a steamship to capitalize on a 200-mile run westward in relative comfort and ease. But the Missouri eventually turns northward, which meant that the would-be emigrants had to debark at any one of a number of small towns along the river—the "jumping off" places, like Independence, Westport, St. Joseph, Omaha, and Council Bluffs.

Once ashore, the pioneers usually found themselves cooling their heels in vast encampments, waiting for the grass on the springtime prairies to grow high enough to support their wagon trains' oxen, mules, and horses. It was a delicate decision. Go too soon, and there would not be enough forage for the oxen and mule teams pulling the settlers' wagons. Go too late, and the winter snows would catch the wagon train before it made it through the Rockies.

Oxen, mules, and horses dragged the wagons, which were typically hardwood boxes about eleven feet long with bows for the cover five feet above the bed; they could typically carry a load of 1,600 to 2,000 pounds. "No pen can adequately describe our start," wrote one pioneer. "Half-a-dozen circuses combined in one would have been tame in comparison. Not one of our 300 mules . . . had ever had a bit in its mouth or a collar on its neck."

Six hundred miles into their journey—a long month on the trail, but barely one-fourth of the way to Oregon—they would have spotted Chimney Rock. "This is the most remarkable object that I ever saw, and if situated in the states would be visited by persons from all parts of the world," one emigrant wrote. "No conception can be formed of the magnitude of this grand work of nature [until] you stand at its base and look up. If a man does not feel like an insect, then I don't know when he should," said another.

"Raising camp at daylight we resumed our way, and soon afterwards arrived opposite the 'Chimney,'" wrote pioneer Rufus B. Sage in 1841. "How came such an immense pile so singularly situated? What causes united their aid to throw up this lone column, so majestic in its solitude, to overlook the vast and unbroken plains that surround it?"

Still others, perhaps more thirsty and less philosophic, were less enthused. "This afternoon we sighted at a distance, the so-called Chimney Rock," wrote Charles Preuss, a frontier artist. "Nothing new otherwise. Oh, if there were a tavern here!"

After Chimney Rock, there were still several hard days of travel to Fort Laramie. After that came the long uphill climb along the Sweetwater River to the Rockies' South Pass. Beyond the mountains lay the blazing alkali deserts of Wyoming, the winding Snake River with its treacherous river crossings, and finally, the nearly impassable Blue Mountains that guard the entrance to the fertile Willamette Valley.

In 1852, 50,000 emigrants funneled through South Pass, participating in what some historians have called the greatest western migration in the history of the United States. To quote an observation reportedly made by famed mountain man Kit Carson, "the cowards never started and the weak died on the way."

Apocryphal or not, the sentiment reflected in Carson's statement was absolutely true. Hunger, thirst, blizzards, disease, and hostile Indians claimed the lives of thousands of pioneers along the length of the Oregon Trail. The passages recorded in a pioneer woman's diary illustrate the gruesome realities her wagon train faced in 1854.

"Here we found a man's skull and bones, and a bullet hole in the forehead, and a short distance from it found his clothing, an oil coat and some shirts and 2 or 3 pounds of tobacco, a knife, a pair of goggles, ink stand and so forth. We think if Indians killed him they would have taken his things, but the circumstance is unknown to us at present." Later, she reported that her train "noon'd at a grave yard where there is 10 died . . . great has been the suffering of man and beast at this place."

Shortly after passing the fur trading post at the Snake River's Fort Hall, the Oregon Trail continued down the Snake. The California Trail, at that point, turned left and plunged southwest toward the goldfields of California. From 1848 to the end of 1849, California's Anglo and Hispanic populations swelled from 14,000 to over 100,000. The migration to California raged at torrent-like proportions from 1848 to 1852, as emigrants rounded Cape Horn by boat, debarked in Central America to cross to the Pacific by land, or spent between sixteen and twenty-two weeks on the trail to California. A total of 20,000 died from 1841 and 1859, ten graves per mile on the overland route, as they tried to reach California.

The Mormon Trail, blazed in 1847, added to the westward flow. Seeking religious sanctuary for his people, Mormon leader Brigham Young led a party of 148 people and seventy-two covered wagons along the Platte River Road, into the Rockies, and south into modern-day Utah. Within three years, their capital of Salt Lake City had grown to 5,000.

But like the California and Oregon Trails, the Mormon Trail took a toll in human life as well. In 1856, a Mormon emigrant wrote, "At first the deaths occurred slowly and irregularly, but in a few days at more frequent intervals, until we soon thought it unusual to leave campground without burying one or more persons. . . . " "Sixty-seven died on the journey," he eventually tallied, "one-sixth our number."

With its selection of Chimney Rock and a pioneer wagon on its winning design, Nebraska chose to honor the hardships and travails of such men and women. It was a design that topped 6,500 others. Other finalists for the state quarter honor included "The Capitol"; "The Sower," depicting the statue standing atop the Nebraska capitol; and

"Chief Standing Bear," the Ponca Indian whose landmark 1879 trial established that Native Americans were "persons within the meaning of the law" and thus entitled to the rights of citizenship.

In the end, though, the days of Chimney Rock topping anything may be numbered. Records indicate that the spire has lost about thirty feet in the past 150 years. The formation is composed of Brule clay with layers of Arickaree sandstone and volcanic ash interlaced within it, a combination susceptible to erosion and catastrophic rock falls. New Hampshire may have jinxed its Old Man of the Mountains with its quarter selection; Cornhuskers can only hope they have not done the same.

# COLORADO

## *Secret(s) of the Mountains*

When the U.S. Mint unveiled the design for Colorado's state quarter, the Centennial State's citizens learned that their commemorative coin would provide a sweeping view of the rugged Rocky Mountains, complemented by evergreen trees and a banner carrying the inscription "Colorful Colorado."

In the selection process, Colorado's first lady, Frances Owens, chaired a committee that reviewed 1,500 suggestions and then narrowed the field to five for Governor Bill Owens's final selection. Unsuccessful designs included "Mesa Verde," featuring Mesa Verde National Park with cliff dwellings; "10th Mountain Division

Birthplace," depicting a ski soldier of the famed World War II division; "The Centennial State," featuring a stylized letter "C" entwined with a mountain columbine flower; and "Pikes Peak," displaying the slogan "Pikes Peak or Bust" and a gold prospector's tools.

Reportedly, the governor's decision was not easy. And when he opted for the "Colorful Colorado" design, he sparked a good-natured but growing controversy: Precisely what mountain peak did the quarter depict? In Colorado, where the Rockies are home to fifty-four mountains that soar above 14,000 feet, mountains can be an intensely personal issue.

Initially, the official story was that the quarter's final design was simply a generic but emblematic portrait of a Colorado mountain. But wilderness-savvy Coloradans wasted little time in identifying the likely model—Longs Peak (named, for some reason, with no apostrophe), which is, at 14,259 feet, the highest peak in Rocky Mountain National Park.

For weeks, the controversy grew until artist Len Buckley, of Damascus, Maryland, stepped forward on the eve of the quarter's official launch ceremony on June 14, 2006, and told the Associated Press that he based the design on a photo he took of Longs Peak during a family vacation in the 1980s.

For his part, Governor Bill Owens was unfazed by the revelation. "We're told it was an emblematic mountain, but it turns out the artist may have actually drawn a specific mountain," he assured the crowd at the quarter's unveiling at the state capitol, five short blocks from the U.S. Mint's Denver facility. "I don't know which mountain the artist looked at. It's indicative of all the mountains of Colorado, and if an artist back at the mint happened to look at one and feature it, that's fine with me."

If the secret identity of Buckley's mountain only lasted a matter of months, Coloradans could take solace in the fact that, for decades, their mountains did a far better job of concealing one of the great secrets of the Cold War.

A secret of the Cold War? You may be tempted to guess the Cheyenne Mountain Operations Center. Built in the early 1960s, the center is located 1,000 feet into the mountain, protected behind thirty-ton iron blast doors designed to shield the famed war room of the North American Air Defense Command (NORAD) from a nuclear attack.

But after being featured in such movies as *War Games* and *The Sum of All Fears*, Cheyenne Mountain has become somewhat passé. Besides, the month after the Colorado state quarter was released, the *Washington Post* reported that NORAD was shuttering the operations center and moving it to a nondescript office building at nearby Peterson Air Force Base.

Instead, the secret in question—and, admittedly, although still shrouded by the weight of history, it is not a secret anymore—was a Central Intelligence Agency operation known by the deceptively dull code name of "ST Circus."

"ST Circus" was a project born of the hottest days of the Cold War, when the United States, the Soviet Union, and China sparred at one another across the globe in any number of shadowy proxy conflicts.

One such conflict raged in Tibet, which had been invaded by the Chinese People's Liberation Army in 1951. The capital of Lhasa was occupied; the Dalai Lama was forced to sign a "Plan for the Peaceable Liberation of Tibet."

Before long, however, it became clear to the Tibetans that in Communist China's eyes, "peaceable liberation" was synonymous with exploitation, collectivization, repression, and forced acculturation. A resistance movement—Chushi Gandrung, or "Four Rivers, Six Mountains"—arose in the country's outlying regions, organized and led by a Tibetan trader named Gompo Tashi Andrugtsang. In February 1956, after the Chinese bombed ancient Buddhist monasteries at Chatreng and Litang, Tibet erupted into open revolt.

On the other side of the world, in Washington, D.C., the U.S. intelligence community could not help but take notice—even if, at the CIA's highest levels, Tibet hardly seemed a compelling cause. CIA officer John Greaney's recounting of his visit with CIA director Allen Dulles to discuss the situation in Tibet seems illustrative.

"Dulles asked me, 'Now where is Tibet?'" Greaney recounted. "We stand up on the leather couch in his office, and he has a National Geographic map up there, and he's pointing to Hungary, and he says, 'Is that Tibet?'" And I say, 'No, sir, it's over here by the Himalaya.'"

Issues of geographic literacy aside, the CIA soon decided that Chushi Gandrung and the revolt in Tibet presented a golden opportunity to make life difficult for the Chinese Communists. In the spring of 1957, it spirited six of Gompo Tashi's men out of Tibet and to, of all places, the sweltering Pacific island of Saipan. At a military base on Saipan, the six expatriate warriors took to their training in modern guerilla warfare, explosives, and communications remarkably well—so well, in fact, that the CIA decided to undertake a larger-scale training operation at a more appropriate location.

The assignment fell on the capable shoulders of Roger McCarthy, the head of the CIA's Tibetan Task Force. Casting about for a suitable training site, McCarthy's eyes settled on forgotten Camp Hale, Colorado.

Fifteen years earlier, Camp Hale had gained fame as the training camp of the U.S. Army's famed Tenth Mountain Division. Constructed out of whole cloth at the outbreak of World War II, the camp eventually housed some 16,000 soldiers and 3,900 animals. The army shuttered the camp at the end of the war, however, and by 1958, it was unoccupied and almost forgotten. But in McCarthy's eyes, it was perfect.

"Camp Hale," McCarthy recalled, "offered everything: mountains, valleys, the Eagle River, remoteness, yet near enough to support facilities to make it ideal. In 1958, there was nothing there. The closest town was Leadville. We could shield our effort easily. The entrance was just off a good road, used primarily by tourists."

In the winter of 1958, the army enthusiastically supported the CIA endeavor, constructing classrooms, barracks, and mess halls. All it knew was that it was building a training facility for foreign nationals, although the CIA was kind enough to suggest what ended up being a highly effective cover story—the base was being used for "atomic-related research." For its part, the CIA staffed the camp with a dozen intelligence officers and military trainers, a medic, and a pair of army cooks.

Camp Hale was an immediate hit with the Tibetan freedom fighters who soon arrived to train there. One of the Tibetans, Tashi Chutter, recalled: "We drove up to the camp after dark. When I got out of the truck, I saw snowy mountaintops all around me and I was shocked for a moment. The Americans called Camp Hale 'The Ranch.' But we Tibetans came up with our own nickname. We called it 'Dumra,' Tibetan for 'flower garden.' It really did feel like we were back home."

The Tibetans took quickly to their training—parachuting, radio communications, even the manufacturing of homemade munitions. Eventually, 259 of them would train at Camp Hale.

"I've never seen anything like it," Greaney said. "After dinner, they would go back to practice Morse code. Really, we used to comment back and forth that we were working with the Tibetans instead of the Central American problem, which was the Bay of Pigs. We knew we were involved in a good program."

In September 1959, the first eighteen Camp Hale graduates parachuted back into Tibet. Only five would survive, the victims of air attacks the following January on the Tibetans massed around Pembar monastery. As the Chinese crushed the revolt at large, resistance fighters turned to staging hit-and-run raids out of Nepal's Mustang Province, from which they still managed to score a number of impressive intelligence coups for the CIA.

Nevertheless, as the 1960s wore on, the prospects for success in Tibet dimmed. The CIA ended its clandestine airdrops of arms and munitions in 1965; it shut down Camp Hale that same year. The following year, control of the camp reverted to the U.S. Forest Service, in whose hands it remains today. But for those in the know, Camp Hale stands as a reminder that Colorado's declaration of "Colorful Colorado" on its state quarter was absolutely correct—Colorado and its history are and have been colorful indeed.

# 39

## NORTH DAKOTA
### *Where the Buffalo (Still) Roam*

The American bison—a.k.a., the buffalo—has a long tradition of appearing on American coinage that dates back to 1913. That year, U.S. Mint facilities in Philadelphia, Denver, and San Francisco began minting what became known as the Buffalo nickel. On one side the coin features an Indian head; on the other, a buffalo reportedly patterned after a bison named "Black Diamond" that lived in New York City's Central Park Zoo in the early part of the twentieth century.

The Buffalo nickel, which was generally considered to be among the most aesthetic of American coins, continued its run until 1938.

By Black Diamond's day, however, it was looking as though the Buffalo nickel might be one of the few places one could still find an American bison—the unfortunate result of America's westward expansion colliding head-on (sometimes literally) with the woolly beasts.

Although the buffalo is generally thought to be a resident of the Great Plains and the sheltered valleys of the Rocky Mountains, it once roamed a far larger range. In fact, the great mammal once called much of North America home, as is evident in Mark Catesby's pre-Revolution masterpiece, *Natural History of Carolina, Florida, and the Bahama Islands*, which includes a drawing of a bison head-butting a locust tree. Buffalo could be found from Alaska and Canada south into Mexico, undertaking great seasonal migrations that could be several miles wide. Some have estimated that as many as 40 million buffalo could, at one time, be found on the Great Plains.

Not surprisingly, the presence of a game animal of the numbers and size (some weighing over 2,000 pounds) made the buffalo popular prey for the Plains Indians. But even the lances, arrows, and bullets of the Plains tribes—which, it could be fairly said, built an entire culture centered on hunting the buffalo—could not rival the impending massacre of the species that would accompany white settlement of the American West.

In the eyes of the pioneers, settlers, ranchers, and the U.S. Army, the buffalo offered a ripe resource at best and a frustrating problem at worst. The army, tasked with provisioning a scattering of isolated forts across the frontier, turned to buffalo hunters to supply meat for their hungry troops. So did the growing number of railroad construction camps. In many ways, this need for buffalo meat marked the beginning of commercial buffalo hunting.

The buffalo was as much of a problem as it was a resource, however, at least as far as the settlers were concerned. The massive buffalo herds made farming and ranching across wide swaths of the Great Plains impossible. The massive migration of the herds blocked wagon train and railroad traffic for days at a time.

"We saw them in frightful droves as far as the eye could reach; appearing at a distance as if the ground itself was moving like a sea," one emigrant traveling along the Platte River wrote. "Buffalo extended the whole length of our afternoon's travel, not in hundreds, but in solid phalanx. I estimated two million," another added.

Those same herds served as a mobile commissary for those Indian tribes unwilling to accept life on reservations. In fact, the strategic significance of the buffalo herds was such that General Philip Sheridan once remarked, "Let them kill, skin, and sell until the buffalo is exterminated, as it is the only way to bring lasting peace and allow civilization to advance."

The completion of the transcontinental railroad in 1869 not only divided the Plains buffalo into what was loosely characterized as a northern and southern herd but also provided an industrialized vehicle for what became known as "the great slaughter." Thanks to the Union Pacific, it became possible to profitably ship hides back to the East, where a variety of uses developed for the buffalo. Buffalo robes were used as coats and lap robes for people riding in sleighs and carriages. Buffalo hides made durable drive belts for industrial machines. Buffalo bones were ground into fertilizer; their tongues were considered high cuisine in fine restaurants.

Spurred by such demand, large-scale hunting of the southern herd began in 1874; it was all over in four years. In the north, the great hunts began in 1880 and were over by 1884. Shipment inventories from those days tell a sobering tale of the intensity of the carnage. In 1882, hunters shipped 200,000 hides out of the Dakota Territory. The following year, the number was down to 40,000, and in 1884, only one carload was shipped east. Even more disturbingly, some estimated that for every two hides shipped, three were lost on the range.

Such productivity, if one can call it that, depended upon a hardy breed of man—willing to endure punishing weather, hostile Indians, and the ugly reality of hours of backbreaking work to skin his prey. Precise numbers are not known, but some estimate that as many as 5,000 hunters and skinners worked the buffalo's northern range in 1882.

A typical hunting operation would number four men (two hunters, a cook, and a skinner) on a three-month hunt. They operated out of two light wagons—one to haul the provisions and camping equipment, the other to carry bedding, a grindstone, ammunition, and extra guns. One calculation reports the ammunition required for an expedition included 250 pounds of lead to be molded into .50-inch bullets, 4,000 primers, and three twenty-five-pound cans of powder.

Most of the time, a day's hunt followed a relatively uniform plan of attack. After locating the herd in the morning, the hunters would single out a small group to target. Approaching from downwind, the hunters would attempt, through careful shooting, to create what they called a "stand" of buffalo by first carefully picking off the animals on the perimeter of the group. The buffalo, with their notoriously poor eyesight and penchant for traveling into the wind, made the hunters' jobs at this stage relatively easy. In fact, faced with so many targets, the hunters had to take care not to overheat their rifle barrels by firing too rapidly or too often.

As the hunters worked their way through the stand, careful shooting was important—the goal was to drop each buffalo with one shot. Otherwise, a wounded animal would spook the rest of the buffalo and the stand would disintegrate. Eventually, of course, the buffalo would sense their danger and the survivors would bolt, leaving the hunters to trail behind and shoot down the remainder one at a time. A good hunter would shoot as many as 100 buffalo in an hour or two. By the end of the season, he would have killed from 1,000 to 2,000. William F. "Buffalo Bill" Cody was among the most successful buffalo hunters, reportedly killing 4,128 buffalo in an eighteen-month stretch.

Trailing the hunters came the skinners. They removed the buffalo hides from the carcasses with skinning knives and a forked dragging contraption rigged to their wagon's rear axle, loaded the hides onto the wagons, and brought them back to camp. There they stretched, staked, dried, and piled the hides over the course of several days.

As they cured the hides, the skinners would pile them into four categories: bull hides, cow hides, robe hides, and kip hides (hides from younger animals). Bull hides fetched the highest prices—between $2.00 and $3.00 per bull hide—from the traders who came out to the camps, bought the hides, and arranged for their shipment east. It was good money in an era when a typical laborer was lucky to earn a dollar a day and when an army private barely made $13 a month.

Eventually, the massacre was such that a pioneer traveling along the Platte River could write of "the valley of the Platte for 200 miles; dotted with skeletons of buffalos." "Such a waste of the creatures God had made for man seems wicked," he added, "but every emigrant seems to wish to signalize himself by killing a buffalo."

By the mid-1880s, the damage was done, with barely 1,200 to 2,000 buffalo surviving in the United States. And although their numbers would eventually rebound as a result of federal protection, they would never reach the gargantuan proportions of that earlier era. For many Americans, therefore, the closest that they will ever come to a buffalo may be on the reverse of North Dakota's 664.8 million state quarters, first issued on August 28, 2006.

In North Dakota itself, the best bet for seeing a wild buffalo is in Theodore Roosevelt National Park, located in the same Badlands depicted in the background of North Dakota's quarter. Today, the park is home to more than 400 wild buffalo, the offspring of a herd reintroduced to the Badlands in 1956.

# 40

# SOUTH DAKOTA

## *"What Matter of Men*
## *They Were"*

In 1885, investors dispatched a New York attorney named Charles E. Rushmore to the Black Hills of the Dakota Territory to check legal titles on properties associated with a promising new tin mine in the area. One day, on his way back to the town of Pine Camp, Rushmore asked his guide, Bill Challis, the name of a 5,725-foot granite peak rising above what would one day be Harney National Forest.

"Never had a name," Challis replied laconically, "but from now on we'll call it Rushmore."

Little did the attorney know the contribution his simple question would one day make to his nation's cultural history.

Four decades later, on August 20, 1924, Doane Robinson, the superintendent of South Dakota's Department of History, typed a letter to the sculptor Gutzon Borglum. At the time, Borglum was trying to complete his work on Georgia's Stone Mountain, although disagreements with the project's backers threatened to derail the effort. Perhaps aware of the problems, Robinson offered Borglum a straightforward proposition.

> In the vicinity of Harney Peak, in the Black Hills of South Dakota are opportunities for heroic sculpture of unusual character. Would it be possible for you to design and supervise a massive sculpture there? The proposal has not passed beyond the mere suggestion, but if it be possible for you to undertake the matter I feel quite sure we could arrange to finance such an enterprise. (Taliaferro 2002, 54)

Upon receiving Robinson's letter, the fifty-eight-year-old Borglum, who had returned to his home in Stamford, Connecticut, responded immediately. "Your letter forwarded to me from Stone Mountain," he telegrammed. "Very much interested in your proposal. Great scheme you have; hold to it; the North will welcome it. Am two years ahead in my Southern work. Can get to Black Hills during September."

Borglum, an Idaho-born sculptor of Danish immigrant parents, had at the time already earned an international reputation. After studying for two years in France and befriending the great French sculptor Auguste Rodin, he had returned to the United States and set to work creating what he called "American art." His works eventually included the Metropolitan Museum of Art's *Mares of Diomedes*, the sculpture of General Phil Sheridan in Washington, D. C., and the marble bust of Lincoln that today sits in the Capitol Rotunda.

Less successful, however, was Borglum's work at Georgia's Stone Mountain. Although his initial carving of Robert E. Lee was so life-like that it reportedly moved surviving veterans to tears when it was unveiled in 1924, business disagreements with the project's backers led to his abrupt dismissal. Borglum destroyed his models; the Georgians swore out a warrant for his arrest. Borglum fled to Stamford; the Georgians eventually removed Borglum's original work from the mountain altogether.

Still wanting to steer clear of Georgia, Borglum left Stamford for North Dakota on September 24, 1924, with his twelve-year-old son, Lincoln Borglum, in tow. The two met Robinson and agreed in principle to undertake a "heroic sculpture." Originally, however, Robinson showed Borglum the Gothic cathedral-like granite spires of South Dakota's so-called Needles area. It was there that Robinson had envisioned carving the images of American Indians and explorers on the Needles spires, an idea that, not surprisingly, sparked firm opposition. "Man makes statues," one local conservationist scoffed, "but God made the Needles."

Fortunately, Borglum determined that the Needles would not suffice for his sculpting needs. Equally fortunately, on a visit the following August, he and his son came upon Mount Rushmore. Looking at its soaring granite face, Borglum knew he had found what he needed.

With a site selected, all Robinson and Borglum needed was the federal and state legislation to authorize the work and the funding to make it happen, which was (forgive the pun) an equally tall order. Senator Peter Norbeck and Congressman William Williamson threw their legislative weight behind the project, with Williamson in particular playing a key role. He convinced President Calvin Coolidge to visit the Black Hills in the summer of 1927, a visit that paid handsome dividends when Coolidge agreed to provide federal funding to support the project, the cost of which eventually totaled $989,992.32.

On October 4, 1927, Borglum set to work, motivated by an almost spiritual drive to create what would one day be called a "Shrine of Democracy." "A monument's dimensions should be determined by the importance to civilization of the events commemorated," he declared. "Let us place there, carved high, as close to heaven as we can, the words of our leaders, their faces, to show posterity what matter of men they were. Then breathe a prayer that these records will endure until the wind and the rain alone shall wear them away."

Borglum's sculpture was, however, as much a massive construction project as it was an artistic endeavor. Over the course of the project, he employed nearly 400 men and women, typically paying them $8.00 a day. For many, it was work of a kind they had never seen before and would never again. Enduring conditions that ranged from bitterly cold and windy to blazingly hot, jackhammer operators and dynamite powdermen would climb 700 stairs to the top of the mountain and punch in on the site's time clock. Then, relying on ⅜-inch-thick steel cables, they would be lowered by hand-cranked winches over the front of the 500-foot face of the mountain in a "bosun chair."

While working on Stone Mountain, Borglum had learned the technique of utilizing dynamite for even relatively precise carving work in granite and, at Mount Rushmore, he carved 90 percent of the sculpture using dynamite. Dangling from the mountain's ledges, powdermen would cut and set charges of dynamite of specific sizes to remove precise amounts of rock until only three to six inches of rock was left. With the final carving surface revealed, the drillers and assistant carvers would drill closely placed holes into the granite in a process known as honeycombing. Once weakened by the holes, the rock could often be removed by hand.

After the honeycombing, the workers smoothed the surface of the faces with a hand facer or bumper tool to create a surface as smooth as a sidewalk. All the while, Borglum and, in the project's final two

years, his son, Lincoln, guided the work—sometimes hanging in bo-
sun chairs themselves to join their workers.

As such work unfolded, adequate communications were essential
for both accuracy and safety. Accordingly, the work crews relied on
"call boys," who perched on the edge of the mountain to shout the
necessary messages back and forth. Apparently, the system
worked—over the course of fourteen years of construction, not a single fatality occurred. It was a feat that easily surpassed other construction projects of the era. The contemporaneous construction of
the Hoover Dam, for example, claimed 96 lives.

Even Borglum's best efforts, however, could not prevent one mis-
step. He started the figure of Thomas Jefferson on Washington's
right side. After eighteen months of carving, Borglum changed
course and ordered Jefferson's visage to be dynamited off the mountain. In the end, Jefferson appeared on Washington's left, followed in
order by Theodore Roosevelt and Abraham Lincoln.

By March 1941, Borglum's project was nearing completion after
nearly fourteen years of work. In that time, the sculptor had worked
tirelessly not only on the mountain but in the halls of government to
ensure adequate funding—particularly during the depths of the
Great Depression. Tragically, he never lived to see his dream's completion. On March 6, 1941, Borglum died following surgery in
Chicago.

In the wake of his father's passing, Lincoln Borglum carried on
the work and, on October 31, 1941, Mount Rushmore National
Memorial was completed. But one piece of Borglum's vision remained unfulfilled. Borglum wanted to create a "Hall of Records," a
large repository carved into the side of the canyon behind the carving of the presidents, to tell the story of Mount Rushmore and of
America. Work was stopped in 1939 (and never resumed) because of
the threat of losing all funding if the money was not used on the
carving of the faces as had been intended.

Thanks to South Dakota's 510.8 million state quarters, however, the tale of Borglum's "heroic sculpture" continues to be told. In addition to Mount Rushmore, the South Dakota quarter is bordered by heads of wheat and features a Chinese ring-necked pheasant in flight above the memorial. Other design concepts considered during the quarter's final selection process were "Mount Rushmore National Monument," featuring a three-quarter view of the famous mountain carving; "American Bison," depicting the classic animal symbol of the West; "Chinese Ring-necked Pheasant," featuring an image of the state bird in flight; and "Mount Rushmore and Bison," which placed an American bison in the foreground and Mount Rushmore in the background.

But before Mount Rushmore graced South Dakota's quarter, the departed Borglum faced one more battle for his work of art. In fiscal year 2004, the Citizens Coinage Advisory Committee considered the slate of prospective designs for the South Dakota quarter. As the CCAC's annual report noted, "Committee members liked the artistry of the Mount Rushmore image, but were concerned about the appropriateness of this theme in light of Native American opposition to the monument's creation."

Charles E. Rushmore, on the other hand, would likely have supported the quarter design wholeheartedly. Although he went on to have a successful career as an attorney with the Wall Street law firm Rushmore, Bisbee & Stern (and argued before the U.S. Supreme Court on at least one occasion), he always appreciated his connection to Borglum's masterpiece. In fact, before he died in 1930, he donated $5,000 to the cause—reportedly the largest single private donation the project ever received.

# MONTANA
## *Where the Buffalo*
## *Roam (Again)*

On December 26, 2006, the first of Montana's 513.24 million new buffalo came to life as they jangled out of the Denver and Philadelphia mints' stamping presses and fell into the machines' collection boxes. Admittedly, "came to life," might be a stretch, as the buffalo in question (technically, American bison) were actually those depicted on Montana's state quarters. Furthermore, they were not even images of a live buffalo. Instead, they depicted the hollow-eyed and horned visage of a bison's skull.

Nevertheless, enthusiasm reigned in Montana for the state's newest buffalo coins, officially launched at a ceremony in Helena on January 29, 2007.

"This quarter captures the sense of our history, our culture and the truest sense of the allure of our 'Big Sky Country,'" declared Governor Brian Schweitzer. He occasionally referred to it as the "Charlie Russell design" in homage to Charles M. Russell (1864–1926), the Montana-based cowboy artist whose signature work many believed inspired the image.

Some of the governor's enthusiasm might have been based on his knowledge of irreverent designs that had *not* made the cut over the course of a statewide design solicitation held during the summer of 2005, such as a three-wheeled ATV charging up a mountain, or the legendary "Pork Chop John sandwich," a breaded, fried pork sirloin sandwich invented by John Burklund of Butte, Montana, in 1924.

In the end, more serious contenders included the three other finalists: "Bull Elk," featuring a bull elk standing on a rugged rock formation; "State Outline," showing mountains tapering to the eastern Montana plains under a rising sun; and "Big Sky with River," prominently featuring a river emerging from a mountain range. Following an Internet poll of 30,000 votes (not including the 20,000 votes that a Bozeman-based teenage hacker reportedly cast for the bull from his home computer), the bison skull prevailed by netting 34 percent of the vote, thereby encouraging Governor Schweitzer to give the nod to that design.

Despite the plebiscite, Schweitzer's decision showed no small amount of political courage. According to the Helena *Independent Record*, the governor's own mother publicly favored the design that depicted the sun rising over a Montana prairie.

"My mom, she's a person of the prairie," Schweitzer offered in explanation.

Mrs. Schweitzer's opinion aside, the buffalo design's success was mirrored by a quieter triumph for the species playing out on the prairies of eastern Montana—but whose genesis could be found across the state line in South Dakota at Wind Cave National Park.

Wind Cave National Park was established on January 3, 1903, making it the nation's seventh-oldest national park. In 1912, Congress set aside land adjacent to Wind Cave to form the Wind Cave National Game Preserve (an area that was later incorporated into the larger park in 1935). The following year, the New York Zoological Society, in coordination with the American Bison Society, dispatched fourteen bison (six bulls and eight cows) from the Bronx Zoo to the preserve. At the time, there were scarcely 1,000 bison left in the wild, and the society hoped to nurture the buffalo's struggling presence in the American West. Six additional bison arrived from Yellowstone National Park in 1916.

Eventually, Wind Cave's bison herd grew to contain between 350 and 400 animals. In time, it gained renown as the only genetically pure herd on federal lands in the United States, and for two decades, it was an important source of bison for relocation elsewhere in the West to repopulate other preserves, parks, and refuges.

Concerns about brucellosis, however, terminated Wind Cave's ongoing redistribution of bison in 1943. Brucellosis, a contagious disease caused by a nasty species of bacteria, causes abortions, infertility, and lowered milk production in cattle and bison and is transmissible to humans as undulant fever. In people, the disease causes severe flu-like symptoms that can last for months or years and cannot always be treated successfully. In short, the prospect of bison spreading brucellosis to the cattle herds of the Great Plains sent cold shivers down the spine of many a rancher.

Two years later, testing confirmed that 85 percent of the park's herd was either reactors or suspect. Several vaccination and eradication programs followed. It was not until 1986, however, that brucellosis was eradicated from the herd. With the quarantine lifted, redistribution of the bison could—and did—resume.

On October 17 and 18, 2005, even as the Montana Quarter Design Selection Committee was mulling over designs for the state quarter, the park's annual roundup again took place. Park staff, with the assistance of two helicopters, rounded up 293 buffalo and eventually culled 153 from the park's herd. Of those, 117 were dispatched to the Intertribal Bison Cooperative (ITBC); another twenty headed for a South Dakota ranch run by The Nature Conservancy.

The remaining sixteen, however, endured a 500-mile truck ride to an expanse of grassland south of Malta, Montana, the county seat of Philips County. There, the American Prairie Foundation (APF) and the World Wildlife Fund (WWF) hoped the bison would become the nucleus of a successful return of free-ranging, genetically pure bison to Montana. Although the APF reports that 500,000 bison can now be found in North America, only about 19,000 bison, or 4 percent, live in fifty conservation herds. Furthermore, because of decades of crossbreeding cattle with bison, fewer than 7,000 of today's bison are non-hybridized. In short, the APF's plan for Montana—to establish a free-ranging herd of genetically pure bison—was ambitious.

APF's bison arrived at their new home shortly after midnight on October 21, 2005. As the trucks' tailgates dropped down, the sixteen bison stepped gingerly down the ramps and into the cold, rainy night. For the first time in 120 years, the hooves of a bison stepped on Montana soil.

A few weeks later, the bison were released from their holding enclosure onto a larger expanse of 2,600 acres. In time, the herd's range may expand even more, as the APF already owns or leases grazing rights to 60,000 acres of land in the area. Meanwhile, the herd's numbers are already increasing. In April 2006, five new baby bison were born on the reserve and in October 2006, a second echelon of twenty bison arrived from Wind Cave National Park. The herd marked the end of the minting of the Montana state quarter by bearing seven more calves in April 2007. Today, the Montana herd consists of forty-five healthy animals—with more on the way.

Plans for the APF's project in northeastern Montana are even bolder. Spurred by visions of a vast expanse of unbroken mixed-grass prairie, the foundation's leadership speaks in terms of "bringing the African Serengeti to America's backyard" and creating a home where the buffalo—and also other indigenous wildlife, such as elk, antelope, and bighorn sheep—can roam.

The plan is not without its skeptics. Some local ranchers and farmers in Philips County, for example, harbor fears about a brucellosis outbreak. Others question whether the APF's well-intentioned efforts will shoulder many of the region's already struggling family-owned farms and ranches out of existence. Still others worry about the influence of so much land being controlled by one organization, particularly in a corner of the country that values rugged individualism as highly as Montana's ranchers and farmers do.

Nevertheless, the APF so far controls two 30,000-acre tracts, with plans for obtaining 250,000 acres (nearly 400 square miles) over the next four years. The APF's ultimate goal is even more grandiose: to piece together between 3 and 4 million acres across eastern Montana, an expanse of land that would be bigger than even Yellowstone National Park's 2.2 million acres.

The APF's preserve would be centered, coincidentally, on the 1.1-million-acre Charles M. Russell National Wildlife Refuge, named after the artist many credit for inspiring the Montana state quarter bison skull design in the first place. And as far as the subject of the state's quarter design is concerned, the APF and the WWF could not be happier. "The bison is a superlative symbol for Montana's quarter," said Dr. Curt Freese, managing director of the WWF's Northern Great Plains Program. "This majestic animal once roamed in immense herds over the state's prairies and mountain valleys, and, after a close brush with extinction a century ago, wild herds of bison are roaming once more in eastern Montana."

# 42

# WASHINGTON
## *Profiles in Courage*

On Washington's state quarter, a king salmon breaches defiantly out of water that, in the distance, laps against a shoreline stand of evergreen trees. The date 1889 denotes Washington's year of entry into the Union; the inscription "Evergreen State" reminds one of the state nickname coined (pardon the pun) by newsman and real estate pioneer C. T. Conover.

In the background of that scene, U.S. Mint sculptor Charles Vickers engraved a profile of snow-capped Mount Rainier rising grandly to the heavens above. The "episodically active" volcano—called Tahoma, or "mother of all waters," in the language of the region's

Native Americans—soars to 14,411 feet in the Cascade Mountains. Its snow-capped peaks are visible from the dry high plains of eastern Washington to the verdant San Juan Islands in the west.

Mount Rainier does more, however, than simply provide a magnificent profile in its own right. For those in the know, its history reflects other profiles as well—profiles in courage both physical and moral.

Take, for example, U.S. Army lieutenant August Valentine Kautz. Kautz, who was German-born and a 1852 graduate of West Point, was stationed at nearby Fort Steilacoom. Intrigued by the mountain looming in the fort's backyard, he hired a Nisqually Indian guide named Wahpowety and, with a collection of companions, set off in July 1857 to scale the still unconquered (by white men, anyway) mountain. For a man who had already been twice wounded in battles with local hostile Indians during the Washington Territory's Indian Wars of 1855–1856, it was an audacious undertaking.

For six days, Kautz and his party forged through forest and thicket, picking their way up the slopes of the mountain before making a final push for the icy summit. Two days later, Wahpowety, stricken by snow blindness, gave up. Kautz's companions faltered as well. Undaunted, he pressed on alone, only to finally give up 400 feet from the summit. It would be another thirteen years before anyone else climbed as high.

In those intervening years, Kautz had other opportunities to display his mettle. During the Civil War, he rose from the rank of captain to the rank of major general and ended the war leading a division of United States Colored Troops into Richmond in April 1865. After the Civil War, he served on the military commission that tried the Lincoln assassination conspirators, commanded the Department of Arizona, and served throughout the Western frontier and California, ending a nearly forty-year military career in 1891.

One of Kautz's most memorable fights, however, was a legal one. In the early stages of the territory's Indian War of 1855 to 1856, when the

Nisqually chief, Leschi, battled efforts to move his and other local tribes onto reservations, a band of Nisqually and Klickitat warriors ambushed and killed A. Benton Moses, an officer in the territory's militia, on October 31, 1855. Moses was the U.S. surveyor of customs for the port of Nisqually and a highly respected local citizen; his death shook the territory's white settlers to the core.

The following August, negotiations ended the war at the Fox Island Peace Council, where the Indians obtained concessions concerning their reservations' locations. Leschi, however, was still a wanted man, and when a relative betrayed his location, he was captured and charged with murder for Moses' death in November 1856. In response, Leschi argued that not only was he not present at Moses' ambush, but regardless of such facts, the death occurred between lawful combatants during a time of war. Buoyed by such defense arguments, Leschi's first trial ended in a hung jury.

Determined to try again, the territory's prosecutors kept Leschi confined at Fort Steilacoom until the following March, when Leschi was tried a second time. This time, however, he was not allowed to offer his "time of war" defense—a fatal hindrance to his case. On March 18, 1857, Leschi was sentenced to hang. Ezra Meeker, a hops farmer who sat on Leschi's first jury, recorded his last statement to the court.

"I do not see that there is any use of saying anything," Leschi declared. "My attorney has said all he could for me. I do not know anything about your laws. I have supposed that the killing of armed men in war time was not murder; if it was, the soldiers who killed Indians were guilty of murder, too. The Indians did not keep in order like the soldiers, and, therefore, could not fight in bodies like them, but had to resort to ambush and seek the cover of trees, logs and everything that would hide them from the bullets. This was their mode of fighting, and they knew no other way."

Ironically, in the wake of his trial, Leschi found some of his strongest supporters among the ranks of those same soldiers, among them August Kautz. In the spring of 1857, Kautz was nursing both a bullet wound in his leg from an encounter with Indians the previous year and the memory of a close friend killed in the conflict. Nevertheless, his conscience was troubled by the prospect of Leschi's impending execution, so during the chief's confinement at Fort Steilacoom, the two struck up an unlikely friendship.

Seeking exonerating evidence, Kautz rode out onto the prairie to the place where Leschi reportedly ambushed Moses and, putting his West Point cartography training to use, sketched out a map demonstrating that Leschi could not have been present at the attack. Kautz's map could not be considered during Leschi's appeal; nevertheless, it convinced Kautz of Leschi's innocence. In fact, many think that Kautz was author of the anonymously published broadside, *The Truth Teller*, that circulated throughout the territory immediately thereafter and urged Leschi's release.

If Kautz was indeed *The Truth Teller's* author, it was a brave position to take in a territory where many still feared and resented the local Indians. After all, Seattle itself had come under attack during the recent war and had to rely on the gunfire of the U.S. Navy ship *Decatur* to beat back the attackers. In short, it was not surprising that some 700 settlers rejected Kautz's pleas and urged the territorial governor, Fayette McMullen, to proceed with the hanging.

McMullen bowed to the settlers' increasingly angry demands and, on February 19, 1858, Leschi was hanged outside of Fort Steilacoom. The army, still convinced that he should be treated as a prisoner of war, refused to let the execution occur within the fort's stockade. For his part, Leschi went to his death both stoically and steadily, pausing only to receive last rites from a priest.

A dozen years after Leschi's execution, another party of adventurers challenged Mount Rainier's slopes in a bid for its summit. This time, their ranks included General Hazard Stevens, Philemon Van Trump, and Edmond T. Coleman. Guided by a Yakima Indian, they followed a trail blazed to the final inclines by a settler named James

Longmire. Longmire's trail allowed the three men to get in position for a final ascent on August 17, 1870. The ensuing climb took Stevens and Van Trump (Coleman dropped out) slightly under eleven hours to reach the summit. Although Indian legends spoke of the mountain having been climbed in earlier days, Stevens and Van Trump were the first men known to have conquered the scenic peak.

In the end, there was no little irony in Stevens's accomplishing what Kautz failed to do thirteen years earlier. Stevens's father, Isaac Stevens, was the first governor of the Washington Territory and, as such, was the man responsible for the Indian treaties that sparked the armed resistance of Leschi's tribe. But like Leschi and Kautz, Hazard Stevens was a man whose bravery eclipsed even the ascent of Mount Rainier. When the Civil War broke out, he joined his father—who had just finished two terms in Congress—in volunteering for military service.

By September 1, 1862, the elder Stevens had reached the rank of brigadier general; his son Hazard was one of his aides-de-camp. On that day, however, the Stevenses found themselves in the fight of their lives in Chantilly, Virginia, when the Confederates attempted to cut off the Union Army's retreat from the Second Battle of Bull Run. Rallying his troops, Isaac Stevens grabbed the regimental banner of his old command, shouting, "Highlanders, my highlanders, follow your general!" A Confederate bullet to the brain killed him instantly. His son Hazard, standing nearby, fought on until he succumbed to a pair of wounds himself. By the following spring, Hazard Stevens had recovered enough to lead a successful assault on Fort Huger and earn the Medal of Honor. He was destined to end the war as one of the Union Army's youngest brigadier generals and, after returning to the Washington Territory, to conquer Mount Rainier.

One hundred and thirty-seven years later, as Washington celebrated the release of the state quarter on April 11, 2007, U.S. representative Jim McDermott took the podium in Seattle and, invoking the image of the endangered salmon that shares the quarter with Mount Rainier, recognized that, "as money, this beautiful Washington State quarter has a value of twenty-five cents. But its value will be priceless if this coin inspires us to save our wild salmon and stop global warming."

The same reckoning could be applied to the image of Mount Rainier and its subtle reminder of the brave men whose paths— literally and figuratively—crossed its glaciered slopes. If Washington's state quarter reminds us of such courage, it will indeed be priceless.

# 43

# IDAHO
## *"And Here We Have Idaho . . . "*

A peregrine falcon haughtily dominates Idaho's state quarter. Beneath its beak, an outline of the state is engraved, along with both the date, "1890" (the year Idaho entered the Union), and the state motto, "Esta Perpetua." Translated, that Latin phrase means "May it be forever," a far more majestic phrase than the state song chorus, "And here we have Idaho, winning her way to fame," another contender for the coin's design.

"May it be forever." The same could be said of the peregrine falcon, one of the fastest birds in the world. "The flight of this bird is of astonishing rapidity," John James Audubon once wrote. "It is

scarcely ever seen sailing, unless after being disappointed in its attempt to secure the prey which it has been pursuing, and even at
such times it merely rises with a broad spiral circuit . . . ."

But even with its speed, the falcon could not outdistance the perils of the modern age—particularly as the pesticide DDT and its
breakdown product, DDE, began to work their way into the bird's
food chain. As the toxic chemicals accumulated in the raptor's tis-
sues, it increasingly interfered with eggshell production. As a result,
female birds laid eggs with shells so thin that they either never
hatched or broke prematurely during incubation.

By the latter half of the twentieth century, the sentiment "may it
be forever" seemed an unlikely possibility as the falcon struggled to
survive in an increasingly hostile world. By the 1970s, the bird was
essentially extirpated in the eastern United States. Even in the
craggy vastness of the Rocky Mountains, its population plummeted
by two-thirds.

The falcon was not alone, of course, in its battle to survive in its
modern environment. But its prognosis, and that of so many of its
fellow species, seemed so grim that in 1973, Congress enacted the
Endangered Species Act (ESA). President Richard M. Nixon signed
the bill into law on December 28, 1973, at his vacation residence in
San Clemente, California.

"At a time when Americans are more concerned than ever with
conserving our natural resources," Nixon declared, "this legislation
provides the Federal Government with needed authority to protect
an irreplaceable part of our national heritage—threatened wildlife."
"Nothing," he added, "is more priceless and more worthy of preservation than the rich array of animal life with which our country has
been blessed. It is a many-faceted treasure, of value to scholars, scientists, and nature lovers alike, and it forms a vital part of the heritage
we all share as Americans."

By that point, the peregrine falcon was already listed as an endangered species pursuant to the earlier (and weaker) Endangered
Species Preservation Act of 1966 (along with such other iconic

species as the bald eagle, the whooping crane, the Sonoran prong-horn, the Florida manatee, the black-footed ferret, and the Eastern timber wolf). The falcon, as a migratory bird (after all, "peregrine" is derived from the Latin word for "wanderer"), also enjoyed some protection under the Migratory Bird Treaty Act. Finally, it was also the beneficiary—arguably, most directly—of such actions as the Environmental Protection Agency's ban of DDT in 1972.

It was 1973's Endangered Species Act, however, that publicly proclaimed it to be federal policy to preserve and protect America's endangered and threatened species. The act thus naturally became the public face of endangered species protection in the United States for the next three decades. Indeed, as the U.S. Supreme Court described it in the controversial *Tennessee Valley Authority v. Hill* case, it is "the most comprehensive legislation for the preservation of endangered species ever enacted by a nation."

Today, the ESA, as a general matter, attempts to achieve several goals. It outlines the procedures and criteria for listing (and delisting) a species (to include plants) as endangered; prevents any federal action from jeopardizing the continued existence of a listed species; bans the "taking," import, and export of an endangered species; and controls state and private landowners' actions that may result in the taking of a species.

The numbers of such species are considerable. In July 2007, 568 animal species (or distinct population segments of those species) and 746 plant species were listed as endangered or threatened in the United States. Hawaii leads the nation with 329, followed by California with 310, Alabama with 117, and Florida with 114.

So what animals and plants make up the ranks of the endangered or threatened? Some are likely familiar—such as the Florida panther, the Northern spotted owl, and the black-footed ferret. Others are likely not—such as Florida's Ochlockonee moccasinshell mussel, the Mississippi gopher frog, and Hawaii's Blackburn's sphinx moth.

Three animals—Oregon's coho salmon, Alaska's polar bear, and the "distinct population segment" of the gray wolf found in the northern Rocky Mountains—have been formally proposed for listing as threatened or endangered and may soon join the ranks. They will be listed if at least one of the following five criteria can be shown to exist: "the present or threatened destruction, modification, or curtailment of [a species'] habitat or range; over-utilization for commercial, recreational, scientific, or educational purposes; disease or predation; the inadequacy of existing regulatory mechanisms; or other natural or manmade factors affecting [the species'] continued existence."

But even as some species have been added to the list of endangered or threatened wildlife, others have been removed (or "delisted," in enviro-legal parlance) for one of three reasons: they are already extinct, they have recovered, or the "original data for classification [for their listing was] in error."

To date, nine species have had the misfortune to be delisted because of extinction: the Guam broadbill (or "chuguangguang," in the island's native tongue); the longjaw cisco and the blue pike (two species fished to extinction in the Great Lakes); the Amistad gambusia (a small fish wiped out when its only home, Texas's Goodenough Spring, was inundated by the Amistad Reservoir); the Mariana mallard (a large duck that once lived in the Pacific's Marianas Archipelago); Sampson's pearlymussel (a species of mussel once found in the Wabash and Ohio rivers); the Tecopa pupfish (shouldered out of existence in California by invasive foreign species); the Santa Barbara song sparrow (wiped out in a catastrophic fire on California's Santa Barbara Island); and the dusky seaside sparrow (doomed by habitat loss in Florida in the 1960s and 1970s).

Eighteen species (or population subsets of those species), however, have been delisted under far happier circumstances: They have been determined to have fully recovered to a point where the Endangered Species Act's protections are no longer required. For the sake of fairness, however, it should be noted that some observers have wondered if some of those species were not really endangered in the first place.

Regardless of such questions, the animal species found in the United States that have been deemed recovered and thus delisted are the American bald eagle; the Douglas County, Oregon, population of the Columbian white-tailed deer; the American alligator; the gray wolf; the Aleutian Canadian goose; the Arctic peregrine falcon; and the brown pelican populations found in Florida and Alabama. The delisted plant species are Robbins' cinquefoil, Eggert's sunflower, and Hoover's woolly-star. Overseas, delisted species include the Palau ground dove, the Palau fantail flycatcher, the Eastern gray kangaroo, the red kangaroo, the Western gray kangaroo, the Tinian monarch, the Palau owl, and the gray whale.

Closer to home, Idaho's American peregrine falcon joined the list of delisted species in 1999. By then, the U.S. Fish and Wildlife Service could tally 1,425 nesting pairs in the western United States, Alaska, and Canada, with additional pairs present in the eastern United States. By 2003, the service was able to count 3,005 pairs of falcons across the nation, providing compelling evidence that the falcon's recovery was flourishing.

The efforts of The Peregrine Fund's World Center for Birds of Prey, based in Boise, Idaho, have played an important part in such recovery operations through its captivity breeding and release program. Today, Idaho alone is home to thirty-four pairs of falcons, which is only a fraction of the approximately captive-bred 1,500 pairs that can now be found nationwide, thanks, in large part, to The Peregrine Fund's operations and efforts.

It was only appropriate, therefore, that in early June 2007, as the first Idaho state quarters began to appear in Boise's banks and cash registers, The Peregrine Fund released four new chicks at Camas Prairie. They joined seventeen other falcons that have been released at the site over the course of the past five years and, with any luck, will add to the falcon's ongoing recovery in the Rocky Mountains and elsewhere.

Esta Perpetua.

# 44

# WYOMING
## *All Things Being Equal . . .*

Surely no one needs an explanation of the iconic bucking bronco on
Wyoming's quarter. In fact, of the five final designs that culminated
from 3,200 narrative design concepts submitted to the Wyoming
Coinage Advisory Committee, four of them featured some version of
the bucking horse image. In addition to the winning design, the other
contenders were "Bucking Horse and Rider with State Outline";
"Bucking Horse and Rider with Teton Range"; "Bucking Horse and
Rider in Typical Wyoming Scene" (a ranch); and "Yellowstone National
Park—Old Faithful Geyser."

But the Equality State? Why does the quarter declare Wyoming to be the Equality State?

The answer is deceptively simple. But as often happens, the devil is in the details. Arguably, the roots of that answer can be found in the 1820s, when the so-called mountain men first visited Wyoming's towering mountain ranges and high plains in pursuit of fur. For such men, success or failure was a very personal calculus—a man rose or fell, succeeded or failed, lived or died by his skills and wits. In many ways, mountain men such as the Ireland-born Thomas Fitzpatrick and Jedediah Smith inculcated Wyoming with the idea of judging a man—or a woman—simply on his or her own merits. In the middle of the nineteenth century, tens of thousands of settlers traversed Wyoming en route to Oregon and California. The defiant independence of the region's Indians, however, encouraged most of the pioneers to hurry along to points west. It was not until 1867 that a gold rush sparked large-scale settlement, an influx supported by the arrival of the Union Pacific Railroad two years later.

Like the mountain men before them, those gold prospectors came to Wyoming to succeed or fail on their own merits—and to find both equal protection and equal treatment under the law as they sought their fortunes and built such boomtowns as South Pass City (eventually renamed Sweetwater), Miners Delight, and Atlantic City. The same could be said of the ranchers, cattlemen, and cowboys who followed. Equally important, these men had a vested interest in ensuring the continued growth of Wyoming's settlement, particularly in an age when so many other Western territories were competing for those same settlers.

Perhaps it should have come as little surprise, therefore, that when Wyoming became a territory in 1868, saloon keeper William H. Bright introduced a bill calling for women's suffrage in the territorial legislature the following year. Bright was, as fate would have it, not only a legislator but also the husband of a young wife who happened to be a devoted suffragette. He was also aware that legislatures in Washington, Nevada, and the Dakotas were considering similar bills—bills that, if passed, would be publicity coups for those population-hungry territories. Finally, and less admirably, he reasoned that if black suffrage (which he opposed) was irreversible, then he could not reconcile denying that same right to his wife in Sweetwater or his mother back home in Virginia.

Council Bill 70, "an act to grant to the women of Wyoming Territory the right of suffrage and to hold office," survived efforts to amend its language from "women" to "ladies" and to set the voting age for women at thirty. Passed by the legislature on December 10, 1869, it was signed into law by Governor John A. Campbell that same day. Campbell's signature made history: Wyoming officially became the first state or territory to give women the right to vote.

Within three months, the Wyoming Territory—and the nation—had its first female judge, Esther H. Morris, who was appointed by the governor to fill a justice of the peace seat in South Pass City vacated by James Stillman. When Stillman declined to surrender his docket to Morris, his refusal presented the new judge with the opportunity to preside over her first trial.

Two decades later, when Wyoming became a state in 1890, it was still the only state to allow women the right to vote, even at the risk, at the time, of jeopardizing its application for statehood. It was not until 1920 that the Nineteenth Amendment to the U.S. Constitution ensured that all (white) women in the United States enjoyed the same right. And even as the rest of the nation seemed to catch up with Wyoming's ideals, the state surged forward on that front once again—this time in the form of Nellie Tayloe Ross.

In 1924, Ross was Wyoming's first lady, married to William B. Ross. Two years earlier, her husband, a Democrat, had scored a remarkable political coup in heavily Republican Wyoming by being elected governor. His victory, which rested on a broad appeal to progressives of both parties, capped years of almost quixotic runs for political office.

Unfortunately, William Ross had little time to enjoy the laurels of his victory. On October 2, 1924, the governor died following complications from an appendectomy. The secretary of state, in his role as acting governor, called for a special election. The state's Democratic Party quickly turned to Nellie Ross and pressed her to run for her deceased husband's office to finish out the remaining two years of his term.

After initially refusing the request, Ross acquiesced and allowed her name to be put on the ballot, although she still refused to actively campaign. Her opponent, attorney Eugene J. Sullivan, felt no such compunctions and, for his part, campaigned vigorously against Ross.

Sullivan's efforts were to no avail. On November 4, 1924, Wyoming's voters handily elected Ross as their new governor. When she was inaugurated on January 5, 1925, she became the first female governor in the United States—beating out Texas's Miriam "Ma" Ferguson (who was elected on the same day as Ross) for the inaugural honors by a scant sixteen days.

During her term in office, Ross pursued her late husband's political and social agenda—cutting taxes, seeking government assistance for poor farmers, pursuing banking reform, and advocating the strengthening of Prohibition laws. She also campaigned for Wyoming to ratify an ultimately unsuccessful constitutional amendment that would have prohibited child labor.

Ross ran for reelection in 1926 but narrowly lost—a victim, in part, of increasing public pressure building against Prohibition and her continued hesitancy to campaign actively. Nevertheless, she remained active in politics. She campaigned for Al Smith in the 1928 presidential election and served as a vice chair of the Democratic National Committee.

In the presidential election of 1932, Ross campaigned actively for Franklin D. Roosevelt. In the wake of his inauguration, Roosevelt appointed Ross as director of the U.S. Mint—another female first for

Ross. She served for twenty years, making her the longest-serving director in the Mint's history, and only left office when the Republican Dwight D. Eisenhower claimed the White House in 1953.

Ross remained in Washington, D.C., to live out the remainder of her days, paying a final visit to Wyoming in 1972 at age ninety-six. She died five years later at the age of 101. "One of the great women in American history died yesterday in Washington, D.C.," the *Wyoming Eagle* declared.

Admirers bestowed similar accolades on South Pass City's Justice of the Peace Esther Morris, eventually calling her (rather hyperbolically) the "author of female suffrage." In 1954, they even lobbied successfully for her statue to be placed in the U.S. Capitol's National Statuary Hall, where she joined Shoshone Indian Chief Washakie as one of Wyoming's two representatives there.

In the end, however, whether it was Morris or Bright who was the driving force behind Wyoming's historic legislation is probably irrelevant. Their combined legacy is far more important and therefore rightly celebrated on the state quarter of Wyoming—the Equality State.

# 45

# UTAH
*Utah Makes a Good Point*

On Utah's state quarter, a sharp pike thrusts between two locomotives and drives home the point that, in 1869, the Union Pacific Railroad and the Central Pacific Railroad Company completed the transcontinental railroad at Utah's Promontory Point. And even though that particular spike and the rail that it once held fast have long since been torn up, the legacy of that same spike—and what it represented for the United States—is well worth recalling.

From some of the earliest days of America's western expansion, men dreamed of a transcontinental railroad—a railroad that, as the U.S. House of Representatives' Committee on Roads and Canals stated in

1850, would "cement the commercial, social, and political relations of the East and the West." As support for the idea of the transcontinental railroad grew, the relevant questions shifted from "why" and "if" to "where." The route of the railroad would bring commerce, settlement, industry, and enterprise to previously empty quarters of the nation. In the case of those lands deprived of the railroad's route, it would turn them into economic backwaters.

Not surprisingly, the debate between the possible routes quickly bogged down along sectional lines. Southern states wanted a southern route; the North preferred the northern routes. It was not until the Civil War removed the Southern voices from the calculus that a decision on a route was reached.

By then, the clamor for a transcontinental railroad had reached an all-time high. Such a conduit, supporters argued, would not only strengthen political bonds between California and the rest of the Union but, in a very real sense, would strengthen the military defense of the Pacific Coast against foreign powers as well. It would reduce the time and cost of transporting the mail and government supplies. And it would hasten the subjugation of hostile Indian tribes.

With the Railroad Act of 1862, Congress legislated such dreams into reality. It authorized the Union Pacific Railroad to build westward from the Missouri River to the California boundary or until it met the Central Pacific Railroad. President Lincoln later designated Omaha, Nebraska, as the project's eastern terminus. The act also empowered the Central Pacific to push east (from its terminus in Sacramento) and connect with the Union Pacific.

Equally important, the act provided the means of financing such a colossal endeavor. Pursuant to the act's provisions and supplemental legislation passed in 1864 and 1866, each railroad would enjoy a 200-foot right-of-way through the public domain and receive twenty sections of land for every mile of track it laid. Each mile of track completed would also earn the railroad company a bond subsidy of $16,000 a mile east of the Rockies and west of the Sierras, $32,000 a mile between the mountain ranges, and $48,000 a mile in the mountains. The act, as amended, even gave the railroad companies the right to raise further capital by issuing their own bonds.

The results of such incentives were what one historian called "financial buccaneering"—a series of corporate arrangements and schemes that would strike today's businessmen and regulators as unethical at best and illegal at worst. Nevertheless, in 1863, the nation's focus was not so much on the legal proprieties of the project's financing as on the monumental work at hand. That work began on January 8, 1863, when the Central Pacific broke ground in Sacramento. For its part, the Union Pacific began work in Omaha on December 2, 1863.

The Central Pacific sorely needed the benefit of its early start. Charles Crocker, the man tasked with overseeing the construction of the line, simply could not keep workers on the job. For every five workers he dispatched by train to the end of the line for construction work, three simply capitalized on the free train ride and pushed on west for Nevada, where the lure of silver mining beckoned. At a time when he needed 5,000 men, he could barely marshal 600.

In desperation, Crocker took the controversial step of recruiting Chinese immigrants. By 1865, he had 7,000 Chinese laboring on the railroad; by 1868, their numbers had grown to 11,000. If not for their labor, the Central Pacific would never have been able to push out of California.

Even with his new labor force, Crocker still faced challenges, in particular, the mountain fastness of the mighty Sierra Nevada range. For months, he and his crews used 500 kegs of black powder a day to blast their way through the foothills and into the mountains. The winters of 1866 to 1867 and 1867 to 1868, cursed with record snowfalls, exacerbated his difficulties. At times, the daily progress was literally measured in inches—and in human life. Approximately 1,200 Chinese workers lost their lives in Crocker's three-year battle against the Sierra Nevada.

In the East, work did not commence in earnest until the waning days of the Civil War. But when it did, it began with a vengeance. The Union Pacific deployed 10,000 workers in Nebraska and began surveying, grading, and laying track in Nebraska with almost military precision—largely thanks to the organizational and leadership skills of Granville Dodge, a former Union Army general. In fact, many of Dodge's workers were veterans themselves. Irish immigrants, Englishmen, Germans, Mexicans, and former slaves filled the ranks as well.

Living out of twenty-car work trains, the Union Pacific men rose at dawn each day, six days a week, and, mile by mile, advanced toward the setting sun at an average rate of three miles a day. Surveyors, ranging hundreds of miles ahead of the track under the protection of U.S. Cavalry escorts, staked out the route. Graders followed the surveyors, leveling the track bed. Then came the so-called iron men, manhandling the 700-pound rails into place and hammering them into place on the wooden railway ties—ten spikes to a rail, 400 rails to a mile.

Hard work inspired hard play, and, as the Union Pacific crews worked across the prairie, a parasitic horde of gamblers, saloon keepers, whiskey merchants, pimps, prostitutes, gunmen, and common criminals followed in their wake. The camps that sprung up to support such vice soon earned the nickname "hell on wheels."

By March 1869, the railroads had bested hostile Indians, unforgiving mountains, scorching deserts, and brutal winters and were racing across the Utah Territory. At this point, each company labored desperately to claim as much track—and government money and land—as possible, laying as much as ten miles of track a day. For a time, the competition was so heated that the two companies could not even agree on where their tracks would join.

Congress stepped in to resolve the dispute. It picked Utah's Promontory Point (or Summit, as it is often called) as the site where the tracks would join, fifty-six miles west of Ogden. The ceremonies marking the completion of the transcontinental railroad were originally planned for May 8, 1869, but unhappy Union Pacific workers blocked the train carrying company dignitaries and refused to let it pass until their back wages were paid. It was not until May 10, therefore, that the ceremony commenced.

It did so with a host of ceremonial gestures: The presentation of two golden spikes, one by David Hewes, a San Francisco construction magnate, and the other by the *San Francisco News Letter*; a silver spike offered as the Nevada Territory's contribution; and a spike of iron, silver, and gold provided by the Arizona Territory. The Pacific Union Express Company offered a silver-plated sledge; West Evans, the Central Pacific's tie contractor, provided a polished laurel tie.

After the ceremonial spikes were gently tapped into the tie (and quickly removed), a final, ordinary spike was readied to be hammered into place. A worker handed the sledge to Leland Stanford, president of the Central Pacific and namesake of Stanford University. He swung—and missed the spike, much to the delight of the hundreds of raucous railway workers crowding around.

Despite the miss, an eager telegraph operator signaled to the rest of the nation that the railway had been completed. Celebrations erupted from San Francisco, where Californians unveiled a banner that read, "California Annexes the United States," to Philadelphia, where citizens rang an already cracked Liberty Bell.

Back in Utah, however, the sledge was now in the hands of Thomas Durant—the abrasive, ambitious, and hard-driving president of the Union Pacific. He swung—and, like Stanford, missed the spike. Again, the workers roared with laughter.

Other executives and company officers finished driving the last spike home, and once the tie was securely in place, the Union Pacific's Engine No. 119 and the Central Pacific's Jupiter rolled forward and gingerly touched cowcatchers.

In the end, some 1,776 miles of track had been laid. The Union Pacific had claimed 1,085 miles; the Central Pacific the remainder. And for the first time, East was irrevocably linked to West.

Even though the stretch of track at Promontory Point was bypassed by a shortcut in 1903 (and torn up for scrap metal during World War II), the historical significance of Promontory Point in Utah's northern wilderness still resonated in the twenty-first century. In fact, it continued to sound so forcefully that when Utah selected a design for its state quarter in 2007, the image commemorating the completion of the transcontinental railroad edged out a beehive (the state symbol) and a gleeful snowboarder for a spot on the state's coin.

# 46

# OKLAHOMA
## *Two for the Price of One*

Forty-six quarters into the 50 State Quarters® Program and a state finally gave a nod to its Indian heritage. Even then, however, Oklahoma chose to do so in a rather indirect way with a depiction of the state wildflower, *Gaillardia pulchella*, better known as the Indian blanket. A swooping scissor-tailed flycatcher, the state bird, completes the scene.

The road to the Indian blanket's victory began in 2006, when Oklahoma solicited design concept submissions from its citizens. A review of hundreds of submissions led to the selection of ten semifinal design concepts. Those semifinalists boasted images that incorporated such themes as the state bird and wildflower, a gushing oil derrick, a windmill, a calumet (a traditional Indian "peace pipe"), the state outline, and, on at least half of the ten, a depiction of Ponca City, Oklahoma's *Pioneer Woman* statue.

Oklahomans selected five finalists that were submitted to the Treasury Department for review. The U.S. Mint converted the concepts into actual coin images and returned them to Oklahoma for a decision.

At that point, controversy struck. The young mother depicted in *Pioneer Woman* grasps her young son's hand in her left hand and, in her right, holds what most people assume to be a Bible. But sharp-eyed Oklahomans quickly recognized that the U.S. Mint's images of *Pioneer Woman* on four of the five finalist designs was sans book—Bible or otherwise. Many theorized that the book's absence was related to Mint-promulgated design policy that deemed "logos or depictions of specific . . . religious . . . organizations whose membership or ownership is not universal" as being "inappropriate design concepts."

In the end, the flap over *Pioneer Woman* and her book proved moot. In an online vote, 148,000 Oklahomans cast votes for their favorite design concept. Nearly half—76,643, to be precise—voted in favor of the flycatcher and the Indian blanket.

"Oklahomans have spoken and the results are clear," Governor Brad Henry concluded. "In the year of our glorious centennial, I felt it was important to give Oklahomans the final word on what will grace our commemorative quarter. Oklahoma has a rich heritage and diverse culture, and so it was a formidable challenge to distill everything that is Oklahoma down to a single design."

As Governor Henry's comments reflected, the year 2007 marked the centennial anniversary of Oklahoma's admission to the Union as its forty-sixth state in 1907. But back in 1907, and in the years that immediately preceded it, one did not need a state quarter design competition to provide a reminder of Oklahoma's diversity. Rather, the Sequoyah Constitutional Convention of 1905, which sought the admission of the new state of Sequoyah to the Union, underscored that same point quite handily.

The roots of the Sequoyah Convention can be found as far back as 1830, when Congress passed the Indian Removal Act. With that legislation providing the necessary authority, President Andrew Jackson aggressively pushed to relocate Indian tribes from their ancestral homes in the East to lands west of the Mississippi River. The immediate result was the "Trail of Tears"—the forced displacement and relocation of the Southeast's "Five Civilized Tribes" (the Cherokee, Choctaw, Creek, Chickasaw, and Seminole). Tribes such as the Osage and Quapaw, which were relocated to make room for the Five Civilized Tribes, shared in the hardships.

In the West, these tribes and others found a new home in the so-called Indian territory, a swath of unfamiliar land centered on modern-day Oklahoma. Sequoyah—the name of the Cherokee who invented the first Native American alphabet for his people—joined the Cherokee in their new home. Today, such cities and towns as Tulsa, Tahlequah, Ardmore, and Muskogee owe their existence to the Five Civilized Tribes and ancestors such as Sequoyah, who helped establish a pattern of settlement that in many ways mirrored the rest of America.

Like the rest of the United States, however, the Indian territory was not immune to the secessionist crisis that erupted in the middle of the nineteenth century. Some tribes sided with the Confederacy, furnishing the Confederacy with not only the Civil War's only Native American general officer, the Cherokee leader Stand Watie, but also a brigade of troops.

When the Civil War ended, the decision to support the Confederate States cost the Five Civilized Tribes dearly. In retribution, the U.S. government began settling Cheyenne, Arapaho, Kiowa, and Comanche in Indian territory, thereby cutting into the Five Civilized Tribes' land. Increasing settlement pressure from the

East reduced the Indian territory even further to the approximate perimeter of today's Oklahoma.

In 1890, when the Oklahoma Territory was organized, the Indian Territory gained a capital "T" but further shrank to merely the eastern half of the present-day state. Then, on April 15, 1897, the Cudahy Oil Company completed Nellie Johnstone No. 1, Oklahoma's first commercial oil well. Countless more would follow and, in the eyes of many historians, fueled the territory's drive toward statehood.

As momentum built toward statehood, delegates from the Indian Territory convened what would become known as the Sequoyah Constitutional Convention. In years past, the Indian Territory had broached the idea of—and even lobbied for—independent statehood for the territory, notably at a 1903 meeting in Eufaula. But in 1905, the Five Civilized Tribes came as close as they ever would to creating a new state.

At the time, the land that would one day become Oklahoma was firmly divided into two camps: the "single staters" and the "double staters." The latter included those representatives of the Chickasaw, Cherokee, Creek, Choctaw, and Seminole tribes who were determined to hold the federal government accountable for historical treaty promises that they would never be forced to become part of a state or territory without their consent. Notably, their ranks included many of the Indian Territory's white citizens as well.

On August 21, 1905, 167 delegates convened in Muskogee. Chief Pleasant Porter, of the Creek Nation, served as the convention's chairman; Charles N. Haskell, a prominent white citizen of the territory and a future governor of the state of Oklahoma, served as the vice chairman. Over the course of twenty-one legislative days, the convention worked to craft the framework of government for the prospective state.

The delegates faced a number of tasks and decisions: How many counties would there be? Where would the county seats be located?

How many jurors would be required to reach a verdict in a civil trial? Could citizens carry concealed weapons? Would Prohibition be the law of the land? How would the state government be organized? What would become the new state capital? And what would the new state be called? In the end, Fort Gibson was offered as the new state capital of a state that would be called Sequoyah (besting other offerings such as "Indianola" and "Tecumseh") and a proposed constitution was offered to the people of Indian Territory for ratification.

On November 7, 1905, 56,279 men in Indian Territory voted to ratify the Sequoyah constitution; 9,073 voted against it. Buoyed by its victory, the convention dispatched a delegation to Washington, D.C., to press for statehood for Sequoyah.

In the nation's capital, however, Sequoyah's delegation met with defeat.

Reflecting on the delegation's failure, Haskell later wrote:

We presented the constitution to Congress and our delegation urged statehood along the lines we proposed, but, as I feared, that body would not listen to our appeal. Congress flatly told the committee that it did not propose to make a separate state of Indian Territory. . . . They were invited by [Representative Joseph G.] Cannon to protest against joint statehood. They told him if Congress would not give them separate statehood they would be satisfied with single statehood. (Nesbitt 1936, 203)

Less than a year later, President Theodore Roosevelt signed enabling legislation that would make the Oklahoma Territory and the Indian Territory a single state. Oklahoma became the forty-sixth state on November 16, 1907, ironically taking its name from a pair of Choctaw Indian words meaning "red people."

Despite the failure of the Sequoyah Convention, Haskell took a philosophical view of the turn of events. The convention, he reflected, did more to prepare the Indians for statehood than any other thing done for them. They felt that an honest effort had been made to bring about statehood on the lines promised . . . . That Congress would not grant them this right was an obstacle that could not be overcome. I had pointed out to them in our first discussion of the subject the troubles that were in the way, but I felt that an honest effort should be made to carry out the agreement the government had entered into with the Five Civilized Tribes. When that effort had been made by some of the leading citizens of Indian Territory whose friendship they could not doubt they were willing to submit to the inevitable. (Nesbitt 1936, 195)

Today, thirty-nine federally recognized Indian tribes are headquartered in Oklahoma—more tribes than in any other state. Of Oklahoma's 3.25 million citizens, 250,000 are Indians. And but for an unsympathetic Congress in the winter of 1905, their ancestors might have been responsible for a program of fifty-one, rather than merely fifty, state quarters.

# 47

# NEW MEXICO
## *The Circle of Life*

As I write in the summer of 2007, New Mexico's state quarter has not yet been released. But when it is released in April 2008, it's just going to be a matter of time, isn't it? Just a matter of time, that is, before someone shrieks that New Mexico's coin features the sacred sun symbol of the Zia Pueblo. Thus, that person will argue, the quarter depicts the symbol of a "specific . . . religious . . . organization whose membership or ownership is not universal" in violation of U.S. Mint policy.

The Zia sun symbol may not be "universal," but as far as New Mexico is concerned, it certainly seems to have universal appeal. After all, the symbol has been found on the state flag since 1925. And when the seven-member New Mexico Coin Commission reviewed over 1,000 design submissions for the state's quarter, all four of the finalist designs prominently featured the Zia symbol, in a decision that reflected overwhelming popular preference.

"New Mexico's quarter design is simple, artistic and intriguing," declared Governor Bill Richardson when he announced the quarter's design on April 28, 2006. "It would be difficult to incorporate all the facets of our history and culture through any one image or a collage of images. The design is a creative, alluring symbol and a distinct representation of New Mexico."

If only one symbol could reflect and represent New Mexico's multifaceted culture and history, it would be difficult to find one more compelling than the Zia sun symbol. The symbol takes its name from New Mexico's Zia Pueblo, a settlement of Keres-speaking Indians situated atop a small mesa near the Jémez River in north-central New Mexico.

At one time, the Zia Pueblo was one of the largest of the state's Rio Grande pueblos, boasting eight plazas and 6,000 people. As of the 2000 census, however, the pueblo has decreased in size to a population of about 646 composed mostly of farmers and raisers of livestock living on their mesa in the foothills of the Nacimiento Mountains.

Some claim that the Zia Pueblo was inhabited as early as 1250 AD, which would date back to a time when Indians abandoned a larger swath of Pueblo sites across the greater Southwest. The cause for such relocation remains unknown; anthropologists have identified such potential factors as warfare, disease, the collapse of social integration, resource depletion, droughts, arroyo cutting and unpredictable special distributions of rainfall, and even witchcraft.

The descendants of the pueblo's first inhabitants have their own explanation for the migration. According to them, the Great Spirit told their ancestors that they must move to a place of spring rains and winter snows, safe from droughts, floods, and their enemies.

Listening, the Great Spirit's people migrated south into the bountiful country along the Rio Grande River, where their numbers soon grew. The people spread out, established separate villages, and even began to speak different languages.

Even then, however, the Great Spirit reminded them that if they were to continue to live in peace, they would have to remember to plant and tend their crops, to treat one another with dignity and respect, and to greet strangers with hospitality. They would have to remember to protect one another from their enemies, to remember and obey their laws and their leaders, and to honor their gods in prayer and ritual and dance. Most important, they would have to remember their shared experience as one people—and, in doing so, truly remain one people.

Regardless of the actual reasons for the massive migration, its results were far more ascertainable, specifically, the migration and consolidation of those populations into such locations as New Mexico's Rio Grande Valley.

Three centuries later, the Spanish arrived. Francisco Vasquez de Coronado explored New Mexico in 1541 in search of the fabled Seven Golden Cities of Cibola. Then, in 1598, Juan de Oñate founded the San Juan colony on the Rio Grande, the first permanent European settlement in the future state of New Mexico.

Spanish colonization introduced more effective farming implements to the Pueblo people and provided military protection from Navajo and Apache raiding parties. On the other hand, however, the Spanish severely restricted the Pueblo people's traditional religions and disrupted local economies by the imposition of the *encomienda* system—a system that essentially enslaved native peoples to the conquistadors to whom they were "entrusted." Nevertheless, for seven decades the Pueblo people lived in relatively peaceful servitude to their colonial overseers.

In the 1670s, however, drought and European-introduced diseases swept the region. The drought not only caused famine locally but also provoked increased attacks from neighboring tribes—attacks against which Spanish soldiers were unable to defend them. In response, the Pueblo people turned to their old religions, thereby provoking a wave of repression by the colony's Franciscan missionaries. The repression culminated in the events of 1675, when forty-seven Pueblo medicine men were arrested and accused of practicing witchcraft. Three were hanged, a fourth committed suicide, and the others were publicly whipped and sentenced to prison. Only a march on Santa Fe convinced the Spanish governor to release the imprisoned medicine men—and convinced the Pueblo people that the Spanish were not omnipotent.

Resentment simmered until 1680, when it erupted into open rebellion. In what became known as the Pueblo Revolt, the region's Indians ejected the Spanish from New Mexico. The survivors retreated to El Paso and soon began to plot to reconquer their former colony.

That effort began in earnest on August 10, 1690, when Domingo Jironza Petrís de Cruzate, the governor of the exiled colonists, led a force of eighty Spaniards and 120 Pueblo allies out of El Paso and north toward Santa Fe. Two and a half weeks later, Jironza's force reached Zia Pueblo.

Forming a battle line, the returning exiles and their Pueblo auxiliaries stormed the mesa. In the fierce and bloody battle that followed, 600 Zia Pueblo lost their lives. Many others were taken captive, including a warrior named Bartolomé de Ojeda. Suffering two wounds he believed to be fatal, Ojeda, who had been baptized into the Catholic Church in the years before the 1680 uprising, called for a Franciscan friar to hear his confession and administer the last rites.

Meanwhile, Jironza realized that he had won a Pyrrhic victory. Over half of his Spanish officers and troops—the backbone of his expedition—were wounded. Rather than press on with this reconquest, he decided to withdraw to El Paso. He took Ojeda, who seemed to have miraculously survived his wounds, with him.

In El Paso, Ojeda not only provided key intelligence about the fragmenting Pueblo alliance but also revealed gory details regarding the deaths of a number of Franciscans in the 1680 revolt. His testimony helped to inflame the Spanish colonists' thirst to reclaim their lost colony. In August 1692, a four-month campaign of reconquest began. That October, even the remnants of Ojeda's home pueblo of Zia acquiesced to Spanish rule, with Ojeda eventually becoming the governor and principal captain of both the Zia and Santa Ana pueblos. Historians have recognized that, but for the cooperation of Pueblo leaders such as Ojeda, New Mexico might never have returned to Spanish control.

In the years to come, control of New Mexico passed from Spain to Mexico and finally to the United States. By 1912, New Mexico became the forty-seventh state; by 1925, the state legislature had realized that a new flag was needed to replace the crowded banner that had ushered in statehood. And, once again, the Zia Pueblo played a key role in New Mexico's history.

In Santa Fe, Dr. Harry Mera, a physician and anthropologist at the Museum of Anthropology, noticed a pot displayed in the museum, one crafted by an anonymous Zia potter of the late 1800s. The pot featured a circle of white ringed in red, from which three rays emanated in each of the four prime directions. In the center were two triangular eyes and a rectangular mouth in black. Suitably inspired, Mera stylized a red ring with four rays and offered it as New Mexico's state symbol—the same symbol that appears on its modern-day flag.

Mera may not have realized it at the time, but the symbolism that underlay the Zia design further underscored the wisdom of his choice. The four rays reflect the significance of the number four, as illustrated in the four directions of the compass, the four seasons of the year, the four times of the day (sunrise, noon, evening, and night), and in life's four divisions (childhood, youth, adulthood, and old age). Furthermore, the Zia believe that humans have four sacred obligations: to develop a strong body, a clear mind, a pure spirit, and a devotion to others' welfare. For its part, the circle represents the circle of life, without beginning and without end.

That same circularity can be observed in the Zia sun symbol itself. As New Mexico's state quarter reminds us, it is a symbol that traces its roots to the thirteenth century but finds expression through its universal message on the coinage of the twenty-first century.

# ARIZONA
## *The Grand Design*

If you plan a visit to Arizona's Grand Canyon, do not let the state quarter mislead you. Despite the imagery depicted on its reverse, you will not find an iconic saguaro cactus in the canyon—the towering saguaros grow farther south, in Arizona's Sonoran Desert. It is a discrepancy that attracted no small amount of debate and discussion when Arizona contemplated a design for its addition to the 50 State Quarters® Program.

So consider yourself forewarned. And regardless of what else you know about the Grand Canyon, rest assured that it is probably more than John Wesley Powell knew in 1869, when he boldly decided to undertake an exploration of its forbidding wilderness.

To say "boldly" is not mere hyperbole. The Grand Canyon is a massive 277-mile long rift carved in the Colorado Plateau, spanning as much as eighteen miles in width and reaching depths of over one mile in places. Owing to its overwhelming size and grandiose vistas, the Grand Canyon presents an awesome spectacle—from its uppermost peaks to the rolling rapids of the Colorado River running through its depths.

In September 1540, members of a Spanish patrol led by García López de Cárdenas and guided by Hopi Indians were the first Europeans to visit the canyon. Despite several days of trying, the Spaniards were unable to reach the canyon's floor. Even three centuries later, the canyon continued to defy exploration, such as when two steamboat expeditions only forced their way as far into the canyon as Black Canyon in 1857.

In 1869, however, the canyon met its match in the form of a wiry, bearded, one-armed army officer and naturalist named John Wesley Powell.

In his youth, Powell had cobbled together an academic career distinguished primarily by oft-interrupted studies at Illinois College, Wheaton College, and Oberlin College. Nevertheless, he displayed an abiding interest in natural sciences and demonstrated a remarkable adventurous streak evident in such endeavors as a four-month hike across Wisconsin and a rowboat trip down the Mississippi River from St. Anthony, Minnesota, to the Gulf of Mexico.

With the outbreak of the Civil War, Powell volunteered and soon rose through the ranks to command an artillery battery, only to be shot through the wrist at the Battle of Shiloh. The resulting amputation cost him most of his right arm. Nevertheless, he returned to duty and saw hard fighting at Vicksburg, Atlanta, and Nashville, and found occasional diversions collecting fossils and unearthing Indian artifacts. He ended the war with the rank of major, an honorary degree from Illinois Wesleyan University, and a proven ability to lead men.

After the war, Powell became a professor of geology at Illinois Wesleyan and also helped found the Illinois Museum of Natural History. Field study beckoned, however, and he soon began a series of explorations of the American West. The first came in 1867, when he led a scientific expedition to Colorado's Rocky Mountains. The following year, he did the same, this time joining the first group of climbers to summit Longs Peak—the mountain featured on Colorado's state quarter.

By now, Powell's mind was fired with the idea of another expedition—to fully explore the Grand Canyon by running a boat down the Colorado River. During 1868–1869 he planned his expedition while wintering with the Ute Indians (where he earned the Indian name *Ka-pu-rats*, or "Arm Off"). As spring came, Powell traveled to Chicago and procured four specially designed boats—three larger, water-tight vessels, twenty-one feet in length and made of oak, and a smaller, more maneuverable boat constructed of pine and christened the *Emma Dean* after Powell's wife.

Able to take advantage of the recently completed Union Pacific Railroad, Powell transported his boats to Green River, Wyoming, where he joined what one historian described as a "ragtag collection of adventure seekers, unemployed veterans, and assorted nobodies" assembled for the impending adventure. The attitude of Frank Goodman, who recounted his story several decades later, may have been close to universal. "Having nothing particular to do at the time," his interviewer recounted, "as trapping is best from November to April on account summer pelts are inferior to winter furs, he joined up with Mr. Powell."

The magnitude of Powell's impending endeavor was rivaled only by the modest scale of his organization and financing. The railroads had provided free transportation, the U.S. government authorized him to draw rations from U.S. Army posts en route, and several academic institutions, including the Smithsonian Institution, contributed several hundred dollars. But for the most part, Powell financed the expedition with $2,000 of his own money.

On May 24, 1869, Powell and his nine companions launched their descent of the canyon from the Green River trestle and began a daring voyage into the abyss of the unknown. Americans would not see its likes again until a century later, when the United States dispatched the Apollo mission to the moon. This time, the vehicles of discovery bore the names *Emma Dean*, *Maid of the Cañon*, *Kitty Clyde's Sister*, and *No Name*.

According to Goodman, "the trip started out fine—a joy ride through new country and a jolly good time." Red Canyon, at the Green River's Ashley Falls, presented their first challenge. Powell lost some of his supplies running those rapids but pressed on. A few days later, worse trouble struck. In Lodore Canyon, the expedition lost the *No Name*, nearly a ton of cargo, all three of the important barometers, and, in Goodman's case, practically all of his clothes. At this point, the expedition was scarcely three weeks old.

By the time the remnants of the flotilla reached the calmer waters and could collect itself, it was clear that Powell now had too many men and not enough boats or provisions. At this point, according to Goodman's chronicler, the trapper "figured he would just as soon take his chances with the Indians as in the river—did not care much now where the river went to." Wearing only a set of red flannel underwear and carrying his extra pair of shoes with him, Goodman hiked out of the canyon. Ten days later, he reached safety at a newly established Indian agency among the Ute Indians.

Meanwhile, Powell continued down the river, passing through Glen Canyon. "Past these towering monuments, past these mounded billows of orange sandstone, past these oak set glens, past these fern decked alcoves, past these mural curves, we glide hour after hour, stopping now and then, as our attention is diverted by some new wonder." Today, however, one must rely on Powell's description— the whole region was flooded when the Glen Canyon Dam was built.

Powell's sense of wonder only heightened as he entered the Grand Canyon. But even the canyon's grand spectacle began to dim as one bone-jarring rapid led to another and the men's supplies dwindled with each passing day. Finally, on August 29, William H. Dunn, Oramel Howland, and Howland's brother Seneca had had enough of the interminable canyon. They decided to try their luck climbing for safety to the canyon's rim rather than face a particularly daunting section of rapids in their path.

"Some tears are shed," Powell wrote. "It is rather a solemn parting; each party thinks the other is taking the dangerous course." For his part, Powell believed that the end of the canyon was surely within reach. But he could not dissuade Dunn and the Howland brothers, and they left the expedition at what became known as Separation Canyon.

In the end, the three men's decision cost them their lives. They were never seen again. Some say they died at the hands of Paiute Indians who mistook them for miners who had earlier killed an Indian woman. Others surmised they met their fate at the hands of white outlaws.

In a cruel twist of fate, Powell's men emerged from the canyon only a day later—with a scant five days of supplies left. On August 30, after an expedition that had spanned ninety-nine days, covered nearly 1,000 miles, and bested almost 500 rapids, they reached the mouth of the Virgin River, where they encountered a small group of Mormon settlers fishing.

Acclaimed as a national hero for his daring descent, Powell retraced his route in 1871 to 1872 in an expedition with much better funding. In 1881, he became the second director of the U.S. Geological Survey. Powell also served as the director of the Smithsonian Institution's Bureau of Ethnology until his death in 1902. By then, the Grand Canyon was already under federal protection; it would become a national park in 1919.

Some estimate that by 2010, as many as 7.5 million men, women, and children will be coming from around the world to marvel at the

Grand Canyon. No wonder that, in 2007, Arizonans decided that it would share the canyon—and the saguaro cactus—with those who had not yet made the trip. Other finalist designs included a version of the Grand Canyon scene by itself; a cactus-desert landscape; John Wesley Powell running the Colorado River; and a pair of World War II Navajo code talkers.

It was the combined Grand Canyon–Saguaro cactus design, however, that proved to be the clear favorite in an online poll conducted by Governor Janet Napolitano's office, and that was tabbed to appear on the state quarter. And even though the Powell image trailed a distant fifth in the voting, it is hard to think of the Grand Canyon without imagining what it must have been like for the one-armed major and his motley crew of adventurers to have conquered its hidden depths.

# 49

# ALASKA
## *Call of the Wild*

Many state quarters celebrate the triumph of technology and the conquest of frontiers—for example, the settlement of Jamestown, the building of the transcontinental railroad, the Wright brothers' first flight, and the exploration of space. Alaska, on the other hand, chose to remind America of the untamed wilderness that first brought conquistadors, explorers, and settlers to North America's shores. And nothing provides a better reminder than the grizzly bear.

Just ask Michael Mungoven.

In May 2006, Mungoven was running along a wooded path near his North Fork, Alaska, home with his two dogs. As he passed a thick clump of black spruce, a violent thrashing of branches signaled that he and his dogs were not alone on this particular Sunday morning. A split second later, a male grizzly bear burst through the spruce a scant foot away.

"He was on all fours but had his shoulders up big and his head was about a foot over my head," Mungoven recalled. "He was saying, 'This is how big I am. How about you?'"

Mungoven fell backward and, for a moment, tried to scramble back up. The bear, however, had other ideas.

"He didn't want me to get up so he bit me on the left butt cheek, the left side of my chest, under my arm on the left side, and then on the left side of my head and neck," Mungoven remembered. "Split my neck wide open, took most of my left ear off and split my scalp open from the temple to behind the ear."

"That's when I figured out that things weren't quite going as well as they could be," he added. "I dropped (not that I ever got further up than about waist high) and curled up on my left side. He was behind me and I heard him bounce in, two big tremors and bam, he bit me hard on the right shoulder. Then he skipped around in front of me and I saw him looking down the trail for my dogs."

"He went around my feet and then started to go back into the brush, but I saw a gleam in his eye and he spun around like a ballerina and darted in for one last bite, got me on the right butt. 'Son of a gun, I said, you didn't need to do that.' Then he turned and I saw his butt slip back into the brush."

Bleeding heavily, Mungoven began stumbling the 1,000 yards back to his house. A hundred yards down the trail, he found his two dogs waiting for him.

"They were at the road, waiting for me to come out of the woods," Mungoven later told a newspaper reporter. "They were just sitting there, like, 'OK, when you're done playing with the bear, we'll be right here waiting for you.'"

Mungoven's wife, Lisa, was less sanguine when he stumbled through the front door, his left ear dangling from his scalp. Wasting no time, she piled him into their truck and sped him the eighteen miles to Homer and the nearest hospital.

"It's not the first time I've walked in the door and said, 'Honey, we need to go to the emergency room,'" Mungoven reflected. "I don't really think she was expecting a bear attack, though."

Once at the hospital, eleven hours of surgery followed as a surgeon worked to repair bites on the left side of his head, his left shoulder, and both buttocks. Although the bites had come close to his spine and to arteries in his neck and leg, the bear's attack, incredibly, did not break any bones, sever any nerves, or hit any major arteries.

Mungoven spent three days in the hospital, eventually concluding that he had surprised the bear shortly after it had killed a moose calf.

"I got real lucky, but I saw in that bear's eyes that he didn't mean me any particular harm, he was just being a bear," Mungoven said. "Now the next day he did show up in our driveway, which was a little eerie. I figure he thought I would be laying in a pile somewhere up the trail and he was looking to collect me after he finished his moose. Glad I disappointed him."

"You'll have to ask the bear for his version; it's probably different," Mungoven added.

Meanwhile, local authorities expressed little interest in hunting down the angry bear.

"We're not going into the pucker brush chasing a bear that's already mauled one person," the head of the local Alaska State Trooper detachment told the *Homer Tribune*.

In Alaska, it is not surprising that in such cases, discretion proves to be the better part of valor. Too often, bear attacks in Alaska's backcountry have proven fatal.

In the summer of 2005, for example, a couple was killed by a bear in their tent in Alaska's Arctic National Wildlife Refuge in June. Two years earlier, another couple met a similar fate in Katmai National Park. And in the summer of 2000, another camper's partially consumed body was found at the unfortunately named Run Amuk campground in Hyder, Alaska.

But before visions of bears "run amok" cause any travel plans to Alaska to be canceled, recognize that anywhere between thirty and 120 people die annually in the United States from bee and wasp stings. Deer seem to be far more dangerous: They claim about 150 lives each year in the United States, mainly in collisions with cars.

Lethal statistics aside, the grizzly—also called the brown bear—remains a powerful symbol in the state known as the "Last Frontier." A fully grown male can reach 900 pounds, stand nine feet in height, smell prey as far as a mile away, and charge across the ground as fast as a galloping horse. With 30,000 bears ranging throughout Alaska, the state is home to 98 percent of the country's grizzly population. At some points along Alaska's southeastern coast, there is approximately one bear per square mile.

Perhaps it was not surprising, therefore, that the mighty grizzly bested a sled dog team, a polar bear, and a miner panning for gold as Governor Sarah Palin's design choice for Alaska's state quarter.

"I think nothing could be more Alaskan," Palin told a crowd gathered in Anchorage on April 23, 2007. "I like to think this is a mama grizzly doing what she does best: Taking care of her young."

Palin based her decision on input received from the Alaska Commemorative Coin Commission, which reportedly received more than 30,000 votes and comments on the final four designs.

When questioned at the time as to final vote tallies, a government spokesperson could only speak in general terms. "I know it was really close between the grizzly and the musher," the spokesperson said. "The polar bear was third and the gold panner was way down low, probably fewer than 10 percent."

Mark Vinsel, executive director of United Fishermen of Alaska and an artist himself, headed the commission. He emphasized the challenge the state faced in choosing an iconic emblem. In all, the commission received 851 suggestions of possible designs before the four finalists were selected.

"Alaska has more beautiful emblems or elements than we could put on the coin," Vinsel said. "The brown bear is probably the animal that covers the most of our real estate here. The salmon represents our pristine environment and natural resources."

For his part, Mungoven could not agree more. Bearing no grudge—pardon the pun—against the bear that attacked him, he even voted in favor of the bear design.

"I am no bear expert," Mungoven admits. "I spend much of my field work time in bear country [working for the U.S. Department of Agriculture's National Resource and Conservation Service], and to be honest I try to avoid them. Alaska is a difficult and complex place to live. It's hard to get anywhere, and when you do, it's usually buggy, boggy, or brushy. Doing anything other than staying in your kitchen in this state generally requires a fairly determined effort. You are usually on your own with a thin connection to continued security."

"The trade-offs," Mungoven continues, "are the landscapes, the colors, the diversity, the long twilights in spring and fall and the occasional gatherings of wildlife that seem implausible—in general, just the extreme nature of it all."

"The bear is a difficult animal to see and a complex animal to live and work around," he adds. "Despite the bucolic views from places like the McNeil River, bears can be remarkably dangerous. They also are stunningly agile and move with a fluidity that is mesmerizing. They are tension, strength, and appropriateness all wrapped up in one focused package. That beauty, remoteness, and danger are what I think overlay both bears and this state."

If the Alaska state quarter is any indication, thousands of Alaskans think the same way.

# 50

# HAWAII
## *All the King's Men*

Better late than never. After forty-nine states and forty-nine quarters, a state finally decided to depict a Native American (or a native Hawaiian, to be precise) on one of the 50 State Quarters® Program coins. The native Hawaiian in question is King Kamehameha I, also known as Kamehameha the Great. His may not be a household name in the United States, but then again, neither was Caesar Rodney, forty-nine quarters and nine years ago when he graced Delaware's quarter.

For its part, Hawaii elected to impose an image of Kamehameha alongside a map of the islands. The state motto *"Ua mau ke ea o ka aina i ka pono,"* or "the life of the land is perpetuated in righteous-ness," appears on the lower left side of the coin.

Somewhat ironically—after all, he was a king—Kamehameha owed his appearance to a public online poll through which 26,000 Hawaiians weighed in with their opinions. In his initial foray into the vagaries of modern democracy, the king bested such alternate de-signs as one that had him sharing the limelight with Diamond Head, one that featured a hula dancer instead of the king, and another that depicted a surfer.

"I am honored to be able to submit a design that emphasizes our proud history, unique geography, diversity, and host culture," Gover-nor Linda Lingle said in an unveiling ceremony. "I think it says a lot about us, that recognition, again, so that's what's important. It's who we feel we are as a people, not what visitors might feel about us."

According to legend, Kamehameha was born on the "big island" of Hawaii at the time when Halley's comet swept past the earth in 1758. As the comet's journey left a trail of light across the Pacific night sky, the island's *kahunas* prophesied that a child would be born who would be the "slayer of kings." Suitably alarmed, King Alapai ordered the baby killed.

Alapai, however, was too late—the worried parents spirited their baby son away, hid him in a cave, and arranged for him to be raised in secret by an otherwise childless couple. They christened the child Paiea, or "hard-shelled crab." Later, as he grew to manhood, Paiea would take the name Kamehameha, meaning "the very lonely one" or "the one set apart."

Alapai eventually learned that Kamehameha survived and, per-haps regretting his earlier unsuccessful foray into infanticide, invited Kamehameha to join him in the royal court. Kamehameha later rose to serve as a trusted aide to his uncle, King Kalaniopuu, and, again according to legend, underscored his promising destiny by pushing over Hilo's great Naha Stone in a feat of superhuman strength.

Chroniclers remembered him as a tall, strong, fearless warrior who, in the words of one historian, traveled "in an aura of violence."

When Kalaniopuu died in 1782, his kingdom was divided between Kamehameha and Kalaniopuu's son, Kiwalao. It was a divide along secular and temporal lines; Kiwalao inherited most of the island, while Kamehameha was entrusted with the care of the Hawaiian war god, Ku. By dividing power in that manner, the stage for political strife seemed set.

Such strife was not long in coming. Local district chiefs, dissatisfied with Kiwalao's rule, began agitating for revolt. They found a ready ear in Kamehameha, and by that summer, a full-fledged civil war raged across the big island of Hawaii. In July of that year, the two opposing armies took up position in the hostile terrain of Mokuohai, a dry, scrubby field of broken lava rock along Keealakekua Bay. For seven days, the two factions skirmished inconclusively.

But on the eighth day, Kiwalao's men caught Keeaumoku, one of Kamehameha's generals, along with a small consort of bodyguards that had gotten too far ahead of the rest of Kamehameha's forces. Keeaumoku's men were overwhelmed and the general himself was wounded.

Arriving on the scene, Kiwalao knelt over Keeaumoku's inert body to strip him of his ceremonial necklace. At that moment, however, Keeaumoku rallied and clutched Kiwalao in a deathly grip. He held him fast until friendly troops arrived on the scene, scattered Kiwalao's own bodyguards, and stabbed the king to death. His followers, hearing of their leader's demise, panicked. They fled in canoes or trudged upland into the high country and safety, leaving Kamehameha in possession of a broad swath of the island of Hawaii.

Over the next few years, battles and conflicts with other chiefs ebbed and flowed. Meanwhile, in 1789, Kamehameha found two unlikely instruments of further conquest stranded on Hawaii's shores—a pair of British sailors, John Young and Isaac Davis.

Through a combination of reward and coercion, Kamehameha groomed the two foreigners into trusted lieutenants.

In return, Young and Davis not only aided in Kamehameha's relations with the increasing numbers of American and European sailing vessels visiting Hawaii but also trained his soldiers in the use of Western musketry and cannons. To finance his growing arsenal, Kamehameha began capitalizing on the hungry world market for Hawaii's sandalwood, a high-quality wood that also produces oil in its heartwood and roots that is used in perfume, soap, and medicinal products. The king began imposing port duties on visiting ships as well, further adding to his coffers.

In 1790, Kamehameha invaded Maui, scoring an initial victory so great that slain enemy soldiers dammed a stream with their bodies. But in Kamehameha's absence from the island of Hawaii during his campaign on Maui, a new enemy, his cousin Keoua, launched his own attacks against Kamehameha's villages.

After Kamehameha's return to Hawaii, the armies of the two cousins fought a pair of pitched battles. In the course of one of Keoua's maneuvers across the island, however, a massive volcanic blast of steam killed a number of his soldiers. For the intensely superstitious Hawaiians, the incident indicated Keoua's fall from favor with the gods. Perhaps Keoua thought that himself.

Keoua eventually surrendered to Kamehameha in 1791. According to one account, he was sacrificed on the altar of Ku, the war god. Keoua's demise left Kamehameha in undisputed control of the island of Hawaii. Other rivals threatened him, however—notably Kahekili, the king of Maui who also ruled Oahu and several other islands.

Like Kamehameha, Kahekili had enlisted Western sailors and mercenaries into his army and, with their support, battled his rival Kamehameha into an inter-island stalemate. Kahekili's death fragmented Kamehameha's opposition, however, and, as armadas of Western-style warships and Hawaiian war canoes ferried Kamehameha's ever-increasing armies among the islands to do battle, the ascendancy of "the slayer of kings" seemed increasingly inevitable. A series of dramatic battles ensued, notably the bloody Battle of Nuuanu on Oahu, which climaxed with hundreds of defeated enemy soldiers either jumping or being pushed off a cliff to their mangled death below.

By 1795, Kamehameha had conquered all of the islands by force of arms except Kauai and Niihau. Even those islands came under his control in 1810. Kamehameha could then boast that for the first time in recorded history, the Hawaiian islands were unified under one ruler. Kamehameha succeeded in establishing a line of kings and queens that managed to preserve the islands' independence for nearly a century until the United States annexed them in 1898.

During his own reign, Kamehameha wisely relied on a series of governors to rule the various islands, providing them some degree of autonomy. And although he continued to enforce the harsh *kapu*, or taboo, system of laws and punishment, he outlawed human sacrifice. Kamehameha was particularly known for his so-called law of the splintered paddle, a code of laws intended to protect noncombatants during time of war.

Kamehameha died on May 8, 1819, and in ancient Hawaiian tradition, his remains were buried at a secret location. He still stands, however, in gold-leafed splendor in front of the Hawaii State Supreme Court building. Another statue of the king can be found in the U.S. Capitol's National Statuary Hall, and, of course, on Hawaii's state quarter.

# ACKNOWLEDGMENTS

First, thank you to my lovely wife, Elizabeth. With her patience and tolerance, she always pays the greatest price for these random writing projects of mine.

Another thank-you goes to John Brackin, who graciously pointed me to his editor, Bob Pigeon, at Da Capo Press. And, of course, thank you to Bob, who fell for this hare-brained scheme of mine—a book about $12.50 worth of change—and his colleagues, Ashley St. Thomas, Trent Knoss, Annie Lenth, Michele Wynn, Julia Hall, Lissa Warren, Jonathan Crowe, and Kevin Hanover.

Thank you, my cadre of volunteer editors and proofreaders (in other words, anyone who made the fatal mistake of expressing the slightest modicum of interest in any of my chapters): Leslie Allen; Beverly Bashor; Keisha Beckham; Steven Burns; Henry Drake; Gail and Katherine Klyce; Kristin Larremore; Elizabeth McCrae; Kate McBride; Shannon Miller; Melissa Robertson; and Charles Youngson. I'm sure I forgot someone—my sincere apologies to whomever you are.

Thank you to the people across the country who were kind enough to respond to random requests for interviews and information, people such as Congressman Mike Castle of Delaware and his gracious staffer Meredith Sullivan; David Biagini; Bart Burnell; Daniel Carr; Captain Paul DeGaeta, skipper of the *Victory Chimes;* Heather Doughty; Dr. Curtis Freese, of the World Wildlife Fund; David Ganz, a former member of the Federal Commemorative Coin Advisory Committee; Lucy Gnazzo, a former member of Pennsylvania's Commemorative Coin Commission; Patrick Heller, the owner of Liberty Coin Service in Lansing, Michigan, and a former member of Michigan's gubernatorial coin commission; Paul Jackson; Andy Jones; Rick Marsh, president of the Vermont Maple Sugar Makers Association; Lennis Moore; Mike Mungoven; Meg Nicolo, of the American Prairie Foundation; Eddy Seger; Catheryn Shaw, former Miss Georgia Peach; Debbie Tinker, the executive director of Georgia's Dade County Chamber of Commerce; and Louis Waddell, a historian with the State of Pennsylvania. Again, I'm sure I missed someone—if so, my apologies.

And finally, thank you to the great staff of the City of Birmingham's Linn-Henley Research Library—one of the Southeast's great treasures and one of the most outstanding public libraries in our country.

# SELECTED BIBLIOGRAPHY
# AND RECOMMENDED READING

## GENERAL

Citizens Coinage Advisory Committee Web site, at http://www.ccac.gov.

"Fifty State Commemorative Quarters Program," at http://www.quarterdesigns.com.

Hagenbaugh, Barbara. "State Quarter Program Gets New Push to Include D.C., U.S. Territories." *USA Today,* January 11, 2007.

Milner, Clyde A., ed. *The Oxford History of the American West.* New York: Oxford, 1994.

Public Broadcasting Service. *The West,* at http://www.pbs.org/weta/thewest/program.

United States Mint. "The United States Mint 50 States Quarter Program," at http://www .usmint.gov/mint_programs/index.cfm?action=50_state quarters_program.

United States Commission of Fine Arts Web site, at http://www.cfa.gov.

Wilson, Charles Reagan, et al., eds. *The New Encyclopedia of Southern Culture.* Chapel Hill: The University of North Carolina Press, 2007.

Worden, Leon. "'Canada 125' and the U.S. 50-State Quarters." *COINage Magazine,* November 2005.

_____. "50-State Quarters: Credit Where Credit Is Due." *COINage Magazine*, December 2005.

_____. "50-State Quarters: Quarter-ly Art." *COINage Magazine,* December 2005.

## ALABAMA

"Helen Keller," Federal Bureau of Investigation Freedom of Information Act File (copy in possession of author).
"Helen Keller, 87, Dies." *New York Times*, June 2, 1968.
Herrman, Dorothy. *Helen Keller: A Life*. New York: Alfred A. Knopf, 1998.
Office of the Governor. "Ceremonial Launch of Alabama's Quarter Featuring Helen Keller, Ivy Green Estate, Tuscumbia." March 13, 2003.
Schuur, Diane, with David Jackson. "Helen Keller." *Time*, June 14, 1999.


## ALASKA

Alaska Department of Fish and Game's Division of Wildlife Conservation. "Alaska's Bears," at http://www.wildlife.alaska.gov/index.cfm?adfg=bears.main.
DeMarban, Alex. "Anchor Point Jogger Survives Mauling by Grizzly." *Anchorage Daily News*, May 31, 2006.
Lee, Jeannette J. "Alaska Quarter Chosen." *Anchorage Daily News*, April 23, 2007.
Mungoven, Mike. E-mail correspondence with author, October 10, 2007.


## ARIZONA

Dolnick, Edward. *Down the Great Unknown: John Wesley Powell's 1869 Journey of Discovery and Tragedy Through the Grand Canyon*. New York: Harper Perennial, 2002.
Fischer, Howard. "Arizonans Vote Canyon-Saguaro Design for New State Quarter." *Sierra Vista Herald*, May 1, 2007.
Grand Canyon National Park Web site, at http://www.nps.gov/grca.
The Powell Museum, at http://www.powellmuseum.org.
Steinlfacher-Kemp, Bill. "John Wesley Powell: How a One-Armed Naturalist Became the Nation's Greatest Explorer." *Illinois Heritage*, Fall 2001.


## ARKANSAS

Cockburn, Andrew. "71958: Finders Keepers." *National Geographic*, March 2002.
Crater of Diamonds State Park. "History of the Crater of Diamonds State Park," at http://www.craterofdiamondsstatepark.com.
"Crater of Diamonds State Park." *The Encyclopedia of Arkansas History and Culture*, at http://encyclopediaofarkansas.net/encyclopedia/entry-detail.aspx?entryID=11.
"Diamond Mining." *The Encyclopedia of Arkansas History and Culture*, at http://encyclopediaofarkansas.net/encyclopedia/entry-detail.aspx?entryID=2146.
"Huckabee Unveils the Design for the Arkansas State Quarter." *Arkansas Outdoors Weekly*, October 9, 2002.

MSNBC. "Arkansas Man Discovers 2.37-Carat Diamond—Visitor to Mineral-Rich Park Names Stone After His Wife." January 1, 2007, at http://www.msnbc.msn.com/id/16427207/?GT1=8921.


## CALIFORNIA

Biagini, David. E-mail correspondence with author, June 28, 2007.
Fox, Stephen. *John Muir and His Legacy: The American Conservation Movement.* Boston: Little, Brown, 1981.
"John Muir Exhibit," at http://www.sierraclub.org/john_muir_exhibit.
"John Muir, Aged Naturalist, Dies." *New York Times,* December 25, 1914.
Muir, John. *Nature Writings: The Story of My Boyhood and Youth, My First Summer in the Sierra, the Mountains of California, Stickeen, [and] Selected Essays.* New York: Penguin Books USA, 1997.
Office of the Governor. "Governor Schwarzenegger's Remarks at the Release of the 2005 California State Quarter," at http://gov.ca.gov/index.php?/speech/2392.
Turner, Frederick. *John Muir: Rediscovering America.* New York: Da Capo, 2000.
Yosemite National Park Web site, at http://www.nps.gov/yose.


## COLORADO

"Artist Says New Colorado Quarter Depicts Longs Peak." *Summit Daily News,* May 24, 2006.
"Camp Hale," at http://www.mscd.edu/~history/camphale.
Dunham, Mikel. *Buddha's Warriors: The Story of the CIA-Backed Tibetan Freedom Fighters, the Chinese Invasion, and the Ultimate Fall of Tibet.* New York: J. P. Tarcher, 2004.
McCarthy, Roger E. *Tears of the Lotus: Accounts of Tibetan Resistance to the Chinese Invasion, 1950–1962.* North Carolina: McFarland and Company, 1997.
Reid, T. R. "Military to Idle NORAD Compound: Operations Will Move to Nearby Base, but Cold War Bunker to Stand Ready." *Washington Post,* July 29, 2006.


## CONNECTICUT

Campbell, Susan. "Tall Tree, Tall Tales: The Legendary 'Chunks of Chartah.'" *Hartford Courant,* August 10, 2007.
Goucher, W. H. *Wadsworth, or the Charter Oak.* Hartford, CT: Goucher, 1904.
Hollister, G. H. *A History of Connecticut: From the First Settlement of the Colony.* Hartford, CT: Case, Tiffany and Company, 1857.


## DELAWARE

Architect of the Capitol. "Caesar Rodney," at http://www.aoc.gov/cc/art/nsh/rodney.cfm.
McCullough, David. *1776.* New York: Simon and Schuster, 2006.

Ryden, George H. *Letters to and from Caesar Rodney.* New York: Da Capo Press, 1970.
Scott, Jane. *A Gentleman As Well As a Whig: Caesar Rodney and the American Revolution.* Newark: University of Delaware Press, 2000.
Seger, Eddy. Phone interview with author, April 30, 2005.


FLORIDA


*Houston Chronicle.* "January 28, 1986: The Challenger Disaster," at http://www
.chron.com/content/interactive/special/challenger/index.html.
National Aeronautics and Space Administration. "Challenger STS 51-L Accident," at
http://www.hq.nasa.gov/office/pao/History/sts511.html.
National Aeronautics and Space Administration. "Remembering Columbia STS-107,"
at http://history.nasa.gov/columbia/index.html.
National Aeronautics and Space Administration's Johnson Space Flight Center. "Astronaut
Biographies," at http://www.jsc.nasa.gov/Bios/index.html.
Reagan, Ronald. "Eulogy Remarks—Challenger Memorial Service," at http://www.chron
.com/content/interactive/special/challenger/docs/eulogy.html.


GEORGIA


*The New Georgia Encyclopedia.* "Peaches," at http://www.georgiaencyclopedia
.org/nge/Article.jsp?id=h–962.
*The New Georgia Encyclopedia.* "Raphael Moses," at http://www.georgiaencyclopedia
.org/nge/Article.jsp?id=h–2908.
Peach County, Georgia. "The Georgia Peach Industry," at http://www.peachcounty
.net/peaches.cfm.
Shaw, Catheryn. Phone interview with author, January 29, 2007.
Tinker, Deborah. E-mail correspondence with author, June 12, 2007.


HAWAII


Architect of the Capitol. "King Kamehameha I," at http://www.aoc.gov/cc/art/nsh/
kamehameha.cfm.
Bingham, Hiram. *A Residence of Twenty-One Years in the Sandwich Islands.* Hartford:
Hezekiah Huntington, 1849.
Greene, Linda W. *A Cultural History of Three Traditional Hawaiian Sites on the
West Coast of Hawai'i Island.* Denver: National Park Service, 1993.
Tregaskis, Richard. *The Warrior King: Hawaii's Kamehameha the Great.* New York:
Macmillan, 1973.


IDAHO


Ballard, Amy. "Into the Wild: Peregrine Falcons Released on Camas Prairie." *Times-
News,* June 13, 2007.

Bean, Michael J. *The Evolution of National Wildlife Law.* New York: Praeger, 1983.
"General Statistics for Endangered Species" (July 5, 2007), at http://ecos.fws.gov/
    tess_public/SummaryStatistics.do.
"History and Evolution of the Endangered Species Act of 1973, Including Its Relationship
    to CITES," at http://www.fws.gov/endangered/esasum.html.
Stafford, Robert T., in letter of transmittal included in "A Legislative History of the En-
    dangered Species Act of 1973," as amended in 1976, 1977, 1978, 1979, and 1980
    (Washington, D.C.: U.S. Government Printing Office, 1982), III.


## ILLINOIS

Goodwin, Doris Kearns. *Team of Rivals: The Political Genius of Abraham Lincoln.*
    New York: Simon and Schuster, 2005.
Lincoln, Abraham. *The Collected Works of Abraham Lincoln.* Piscataway, NJ: Rutgers
    University Press, 1990.
Lincoln Home National Historic Site Web site, at http://www.nps.gov/liho/index.htm.
*The Lincoln Legal Papers Curriculum: Understanding Illinois Social History
    through Documents from The Law Practice of Abraham Lincoln, 1836–1861,* at
    http://www.papersofabrahamlincoln.org/LLP_Curriculum_Online.htm.


## INDIANA

Davidson, Donald, and Rick Schaffer. *Autocourse Official Illustrated History of the
    Indianapolis 500.* Silverstone, United Kingdom: Crash Media Group, 2006.
The Indy 500 Web site, at http://www.indy500.com.
Taylor, Rich. *Indy: Seventy-Five Years of Racing's Greatest Spectacle.* New York: St.
    Martin's Press, 1991.


## IOWA

"Going Back to Iowa: The World of Grant Wood," at http://xroads.virginia.edu/
    ~MA98/haven/wood/home.html.
"Grant Wood," at http://www.crma.org/collection/wood/wood.htm.
"The Launch of the Iowa Quarter," at http://www.iowaquarter.com.
McDonald, Julie Jensen. *Grant Wood and Little Sister Nan: Essays and Remembrances.*
    Iowa City, IA: Penfield Press, 2000.
Roberts, Brady M. *Grant Wood: An American Master Revealed.* San Francisco:
    Pomegranate Art Books, 1995.
"Vilsack-Pederson Administration Unveils Commemorative Medals Honoring Veterans, Re-
    leased on November 11, 2003," at http://www.iowa-roa.org/ia/pages/press/VetMedals.html.


## KANSAS

Armes, George A. *Ups and Downs of an Army Officer.* Washington, D.C.: 1900.

Holley, Joe. "Oldest Buffalo Soldier Dies at 111." *Washington Post*, September 13, 2005.

Leckie, William H. *The Buffalo Soldiers: A Narrative of the Black Cavalry in the West*. Norman: University of Oklahoma Press, 2003.

Rodenbough, Theophilus R., ed. *The Army of the United States: Historical Sketches of Staff and Line*. New York: Maynard, Merrill, and Co., 1896.


KENTUCKY


Churchill Downs Web site, at http://www.churchilldowns.com.

Drager, Marvin. *The Most Glorious Crown: The Story of America's Triple Crown Thoroughbreds from Sir Barton to Affirmed*. Chicago: Triumph Books, 2005.

DuBow, Shane. "High Stakes in the Bluegrass." *National Geographic*, May 2003.

Keeneland Web site, at http://www.keeneland.com/default.aspx.


LOUISIANA


Audubon, John J. *The Birds of America, Vol. 7*. New York: J. J. Audubon, 1844.

U.S. Fish and Wildlife Service. "Brown Pelican," at http://www.fws.gov/endangered/i/b/sab2s.html.


MAINE


DeGaeta, Paul. Telephone interview with author, July 3, 2007.

Fish, John Perry. *Unfinished Voyages: A Chronology of Shipwrecks—Maritime Disasters in the Northeast United States from 1606 to 1956*. Orleans, MA: Lower Cape Publishers, 1989.

"Marcus A. Hanna," at http://www.uscg.mil/hq/g-a/awl/bclass/wlm/Marcus.htm.

"Pemaquid Point Light," at http://lighthouse.cc/pemaquid.

"Victory Chimes: America's Windjammer," at http://www.victorychimes.com.


MARYLAND


Archives of Maryland Online. "Muster Rolls and Other Records of Service of Maryland Troops in the American Revolution," at http://www.msa.md.gov/megafile/msa/speccol/sc2900/sc2908/000001/000018/html/index.html.

Fischer, David H. *Washington's Crossing*. New York: Oxford University Press, 2003.

McCullough, David. *1776*. New York: Simon and Schuster, 2006.

"Two-Bit Identity Crisis." *Washington Post*, March 14, 2000.

Wright, Robert K. *The Continental Army*. Washington, D.C.: Center for Military History, 1983.

## MASSACHUSETTS

Fischer, David H. *Paul Revere's Ride*. New York: Oxford University Press, 1995.
Tourtellot, Arthur B. *Lexington and Concord: The Beginning of the War of the American Revolution*. New York: W. W. Norton, 2000.

## MICHIGAN

Bourrie, Mark. *Many a Midnight Ship: True Stories of Great Lakes Shipwrecks*. Ann Arbor, MI: University of Michigan Press, 2005.
Brown, David G. *White Hurricane: A Great Lakes November Gale and America's Greatest Maritime Disaster*. Camden, ME: International Marine, 2004.
Ratigan, William. *Great Lakes Shipwrecks and Survivals*. Grand Rapids, MI: William B. Eerdman's Publishing Company, 1960.

## MINNESOTA

Gardner, William C., et al. "Economic Impact and Social Benefits Study of Coldwater Angling in Minnesota" (report prepared for the Minnesota Department of Natural Resources), June 2002.
Newman, Peter C. *Empire of the Bay: The Company of Adventurers That Seized a Continent*. New York: Penguin, 2000.
Podruchny, Carolyn. *Making the Voyageur World: Travelers and Traders in the North American Fur Trade*. Lincoln: University of Nebraska Press, 2006.
"Voyageurs National Park: Special History—the Environment and the Fur Trade Experience in Voyageurs National Park, 1730–1870," at http://www.nps.gov/archive/voya/history/futr/intro.htm.
Voyageurs National Park Web site, at http://www.nps.gov/voya.

## MISSISSIPPI

*Confederate Military History, Vol. 9: Mississippi*. Wilmington, NC: Broadfoot Publishing Co., 1987.
Howell, H. Gray, Jr. *Griffith's/Barksdale's/Humphrey's Mississippi Brigade in the Army of Northern Virginia: A Muster Listing*. Carrollton, MS: Pioneer Publishing, 2004.
"A Parole List of the Confederate States of America's Army of Northern Virginia," reproduced in the *Southern Historical Papers*, Vol. 15 (1887).

## MISSOURI

Ambrose, Stephen E. *Undaunted Courage*. New York: Touchstone, 1997.
Jefferson National Expansion Memorial Web site, at http://www.nps.gov/jeff/historyculture/index.htm.

Jones, Landon Y. *The Essential Lewis and Clark*. New York: Ecco Press, 2000.
"Missouri History: Why Is Missouri Called the Show-Me State?" at http://www.sos.mo
 .gov/archives/history/slogan.asp.


## MONTANA

American Prairie Foundation. "Bison Released on Montana Plains—New Prairie Wildlife Re-
 serve Is Home to Conservation Herd of Bison," November 17, 2005, at http://worldwildlife
 .org/news/displayPR.cfm?prID=220.
"Bison Restoration," at http://www.americanprairie.org.
"Conservationists Creating Bison Preserve." *USA Today*, November 13, 2005.
Freese, Curt. E-mail correspondence with author, October 25, 2007.
Harrington, John. "Montana Quarter Takes the Spotlight." *Helena Independent Record*,
 January 30, 2007.
McKee, Jennifer. "New State Quarter Unveiled." *Helena Independent Record*, June 30,
 2006.
Puckett, Karl. "Serengeti of Montana? Ambitious Reserve Takes Shape South of Malta."
 *Great Falls Tribune*, July 1, 2007.
Wind Cave National Park Web site, at http://www.nps.gov/wica/index.htm.


## NEBRASKA

Mitchell, John G. "The Way West." *National Geographic*, September 2000.
Nebraska State Historical Society. "More About Chimney Rock National Historic Site," at
 http://www.nebraskahistory.org/sites/rock/moreinfo.htm.
"Nebraska's Popular Chimney Rock Eroding." *USA Today*, July 16, 2006.
"The Oregon Trail," at http://www.isu.edu/%7Etrinmich/Oregontrail.html.
Western Trails: An Online Journey, at http://www.cdpheritage.org/exhibit/westernTrails/
 index.cfm


## NEVADA

Downer, Craig C. "Velma Bronn Johnston, a.k.a. Wild Horse Annie," at http://www
 .unr.edu/wrc/nwhp/bios/women/Johnston.htm.
National Mustang Association Web site, at http://www.nmautah.org/wild.htm.
Wild Horse Organized Assistance Web site, at http://www.wildhorseorganizedassistance.org.


## NEW HAMPSHIRE

New Hampshire Division of Parks and Recreation. Old Man of the Mountain Historic Site,
 at http://www.franconianotchstatepark.com/oldman.html.
*Wooley v. Maynard*, 430 U.S. 705 (1977).

## NEW JERSEY

Fischer, David H. *Washington's Crossing*. New York: Oxford University Press, 2003.
Wood, W. J. *Battles of the Revolutionary War*. New York: Da Capo Press, 2003.


## NEW MEXICO

Fallaw, Joshua. "The Zia Pueblo and the New Mexico State Flag," at http://www.associate
    content.com/article/18198/the_zia_pueblo_and_the_new_mexico_state.html.
Garcia, Daniel V. "N.M. State Quarter Unveiled." *Daily Lobo*, April 26, 2007.
New Mexico Office of the State Historian. "1200–1500 Pueblo Villages on the Rio
    Grande," at http://www.newmexicohistory.org/filedetails_docs.php?fileID=1422.
New Mexico Office of the State Historian. "The Zia Sun Symbol," at http://www.new
    mexicohistory.org/filedetails_docs.php?fileID=21249.
"New Mexico State Quarter Project," at http://www.governor.state.nm.us/nmquarter.php.
Salzmann, Joy A. *Native Americans of the Southwest*. Boulder: Westview Press, 1997.


## NEW YORK

Lazarus, Emma. *Selected Poems*. New York: The Library of America, 2005.
Moreno, Barry. *The Statue of Liberty Encyclopedia*. New York: New Line Books,
    2005.
Statue of Liberty National Monument Web site, at http://www.nps.gov/stli/index.htm.


## NORTH CAROLINA

Crouch, Tom D. *The Bishop's Boys: A Life of Wilbur and Orville Wright*. New York:
    W. W. Norton, 1989.
_____. *First Flight: The Wright Brothers and the Invention of the Airplane*. Wash-
    ington, D.C.: General Printing Office, 2002.
Kelly, Fred C., ed. *Miracle at Kitty Hawk: The Letters of Orville and Wilbur Wright*.
    New York: Da Capo Press, 2002.
Robinson, Peter. "Why the Wright Brothers Came to Kitty Hawk." at http://www.nc-climate
    .ncsu.edu/flight/.
Wright Brothers Aeroplane Company Web site, at http://www.first-to-fly.com.


## NORTH DAKOTA

Hornaday, William T. *The Extermination of the American Bison*. Washington, D.C.:
    Smithsonian Institution Press, 2002.
Lott, Dale F. *American Bison: A Natural History*. Berkeley: University of California
    Press, 2002.

## OHIO

"John Herschel Glenn, Jr.," at http://www.jsc.nasa.gov/Bios/htmlbios/glenn-j.html.

"Neil A. Armstrong," at http://www.jsc.nasa.gov/Bios/htmlbios/armstrong-na.html.

Newcott, William R. "John Glenn: Man with a Mission." *National Geographic*, June 1999.

Pyle, Rod. *Destination Moon: The Apollo Missions in the Astronauts' Own Words*. New York: Collins, 2005.

Sparrow, Giles. *Spaceflight: The Complete Story from Sputnik to Shuttle—and Beyond*. New York: DK Publishing, 2007.


## OKLAHOMA

Maxwell, Amos. "The Sequoyah Convention, Parts I and II." *Chronicles of Oklahoma*, Vol. 28, Nos. 2 and 3 (1950): 161–192, 299–340.

Mullin, Jeff. "Quarter Design Shortchanges Oklahoma." *Enid Eagle*, May 23, 2007.

Nesbitt, Paul. "Governor Haskell Tells of Two Conventions." *Chronicles of Oklahoma*, Vol. 14, No. 2 (1936): 189–217.

Office of the Governor. "Gov. Henry Announces Design of State Commemorative Quarter," at http://www.ok.gov/governor/display_article.php?article_id=927&article_type =1&print=true.

"Pioneer Woman Not to Appear on State Quarter With or Without Book." *Tulsa World*, April 30, 2007.

"Why Is the Pioneer Woman's Bible Not on the Quarter?" *Tulsa World*, April 26, 2007.


## OREGON

"Crater Lake National Park: Park History,"at http://www.nps.gov/archive/crla/crlacr.htm.

Crater Lake National Park Web site, at http://www.nps.gov/crla.

Haines, Aubrey L. *Yellowstone National Park: Its Exploration and Establishment*. Washington, D.C.: National Park Service, 1974.

Office of the Governor. "Governor Kulongoski Announces Oregon Commemorative Quarter Design," at http://www.oregon.gov/Gov/quarter.shtml#drafts.

Unrau, Harlan D. "Crater Lake National Park Administrative History," at http://www .nps.gov/archive/crla/adhi/adhi.htm.

"The Yellowstone Expedition." *New York Times*, September 18, 1871.


## PENNSYLVANIA

Ferling, John E. *Adams vs. Jefferson: The Tumultuous Election of 1800*. New York: Oxford University Press, 2004.

Gnazzo, Lucy. Phone interview with author, June 7, 2007.

McCullough, David. *John Adams*. New York: Simon and Schuster, 2001.

Pennsylvania Capitol Preservation Committee. "History," at http://cpc.state.pa.us/main/ cpcweb/history/index.html.

Rosenfeld, Richard N. *American Aurora*. New York: St. Martin's Griffin, 1998.
Waddell, Louis. E-mail correspondence with author, July 18, 2005.


## RHODE ISLAND

"America's Cup History," at http://www.sportsline.com/sailing/americascup/history.
America's Cup Web site, at http://www.americascup.com/en.
Herreshoff Marine Museum Web site, at http://00002vw.previewcoxhosting.com/Tops/
     index.htm.
Thompson, Tim. *The Story of the America's Cup: 1851–2000*. Los Angeles: Warwick, 2000.


## SOUTH CAROLINA

Fort Moultrie Web site, at http://www.nps.gov/fosu/historyculture/fort_moultrie.htm.
Fortescue, John W. *The War of Independence: The British Army in North America,
     1775–1783*. Mechanicsburg, PA: Stackpole Books, 2001.
Kaufmann, H. W. *Fortress America: The Forts That Defended America, 1600 to the
     Present*. New York: Da Capo Press, 2004.
South Carolina Historical Society. "Carolina Day," at http://www.southcarolinahistoricalsociety
     .org/wire/RevWar/CarolinaDay/bdesc.html.
United States Department of Agriculture. "Sabal Palmetto," at http://plants.usda.gov/
     java/profile?symbol=SAPA.
Ward, Harry M. "Moultrie, William," at http://www.anb.org/articles/01/01–00640.html;
     *American National Biography Online* (February 2000).
Wood, W. J. *Battles of the Revolutionary War*. New York: Da Capo Press, 2003.


## SOUTH DAKOTA

Daly, Dan. "U.S. Mint Director to Unveil S.D. Quarter." *Rapid City Journal*, November
     11, 2006.
Mount Rushmore National Memorial Web site, at http://www.nps.gov/moru.
Smith, Rex A. *The Carving of Mount Rushmore*. New York: Abbeville Press, 1985.
Taliaferro, John. *Great White Fathers: The Story of the Obsessive Quest to Create
     Mount Rushmore*. New York: PublicAffairs, 2002.


## TENNESSEE

"The Carter Family: Will the Circle Be Unbroken?" Public Broadcasting System, at
     http://www.pbs.org/wgbh/amex/carterfamily.
Kosser, Michael. *How Nashville Became Music City U.S.A.: Fifty Years of Music
     Row*. Milwaukee: Hal Leonard, 2006.
McKee, Margaret. *Beale Black and Blue: Life and Music on Black America's Main
     Street*. Baton Rouge: Louisiana State University Press, 1981.

"Music," *The Tennessee Encyclopedia of History and Culture*, at http://tennesseeencyclopedia.net/showcat.php?cat=Music&dcat=Music.

## TEXAS

Dobie, J. Frank. *Up the Trail from Texas*. New York: Random House, 1955.
*Handbook of Texas Online*, at http://www.tsha.utexas.edu/handbook/online.
Worchester, Donald E. *The Chisholm Trail: High Road of the Cattle Kingdom*. Lincoln: University of Nebraska Press, 1980.

## UTAH

Ambrose, Stephen E. *Nothing Like It in the World: The Men Who Built the Transcontinental Railroad*. New York: Simon and Schuster, 2000.
Public Broadcasting System. "The West. Episode 5: The Grandest Enterprise Under God," at http://www.pbs.org/weta/thewest/program/episodes/five.
Utley, Robert M., and Francis A. Ketterson, Jr. *Golden Spike: National Historic Site, Utah*. Washington, D.C.: National Park Service, 1969.

## VERMONT

Belluck, Pam. "Warming Trends: Warm Winters Upset Rhythms of Maple Sugar." *New York Times*, March 3, 2007.
Marsh, Rick. E-mail correspondence with author, June 13, 2007.
"Vermont Maple Sugar Makers' Association and Vermont Maple Foundation," at http://www.vermontmaple.org.

## VIRGINIA

Historic Jamestowne Web site, at http://www.nps.gov/jame/index.html.
Hoobler, Dorothy. *Captain John Smith: Jamestown and the Birth of the American Dream*. Hoboken, NJ: Thomas Wiley and Sons, 2006.
Price, David. *Love and Hate in Jamestown: John Smith, Pocahontas, and the Heart of a New Nation*. New York: Knopf, 2003.
Woolley, Benjamin. *Savage Kingdom: The True Story of Jamestown, 1607, and the Settlement of America*. New York: HarperCollins, 2007.

## WASHINGTON

Green, Sara Jean. "Washington Quarter Makes Debut." *Seattle Times*, April 12, 2007.
Jones, Tricia. "State of Change." *Columbia*, May 21, 2007.
Meeker, Ezra. *The Tragedy of Leschi*. Everett, WA: The Printers, 1980.

*The Online Encyclopedia of Washington State History,* at http://www.historylink .org/This_week/index.cfm.

Remarks of Representative Jim McDermott at Washington State Quarter Unveiling, at http://www.house.gov/mcdermott/sp070411.shtml.


## WEST VIRGINIA

"Bridge Day," at http://www.officialbridgeday.com.

Keenan, Steve. "Bridge Day BASE Jump Accident Report Released." *Register-Herald,* April 10, 2007.

"New River Gorge Bridge," at http://www.nps.gov/neri/planyourvisit/nrgbridge.htm.

*Outside Magazine Online.* "Legendary BASE Jumper Dies at West Virginia Bridge Day Event" (October 24, 2006), at http://outside.away.com/outside/news/20061024_1.html.


## WISCONSIN

"Cheese." In "Cheesemaking in Wisconsin," *Dictionary of Wisconsin History,* at http://www.wisconsinhistory.org.

Heller, Patrick. E-mail correspondence with author, July 16, 2007.

"Wisconsin Commemorative Quarter," at http://www.wdfi.org/newsroom/wi_quarter.


## WYOMING

Massie, Michael A. "Reform Is Where You Find It," at http://wyoarchives.state.wy.us/articles/ massie/page1.htm.

"Wyoming Unveils Quarter This Fall." *Jackson Hole Star Tribune,* June 13, 2007.

# INDEX

Adams, John, 2, 8, 9, 10
Alabama, 127–132
Alapai, King, 296
Alaska, 289–293
Aldrin, Edwin "Buzz," 100, 101
Ambrose, Stephen, 144
American Prairie Foundation (APF), 244–245
American Revolution, 13–18, 31–42, 44–47, 52
America's Cup, 73–77, 78
Anderson, Michael P./family, 160–161
Andros, Sir Edmund, 27–29
*Apollo I* disaster, 100
Arizona, 283–288
Arkansas, 145–150
Armes, George, 201–202
Armstrong, Neil, 98, 100–101
Ashbury, James, 75
Astor, John Jacob, 191

Audubon, John James, 104–105, 253–254
*Aurora*, Philadelphia newspaper, 8–9, 10, 11
Auto racing, 110–113

Bailey, Sarah, 182
Baldacci, John, 137–138
Banner, John C., 146
Baring, Walter S., 213–214
Barnes, Roy, 23
Barr, Charlie, 76
Barrett, James, 34
Bartholdi, Frederic-Auguste, 62, 63
Bartram, William, 20
BASE jumping, 207–209
Basham, Wesley Oley, 147
Basler, Kathy, 149
Batchelder, Ernest, 171
Bayard, James A., 10

Bears/attacks, 289–293
Behm, Kim, 170
Bell, Alexander Graham, 128
Bell, John, 125
Berckmans, Prosper J. A., 21–22
Biagini, David, 182, 183
Black, William M., 153
Bloor, Mother Ella Reeve, 130
Blues music, 91, 95–96
Boone, Daniel, 89
Borglum, Gutzon/Lincoln, 236–239, 240
Brackett, Richard N., 146
Breckinridge, John, 125
Bright, William H., 260–261, 263
Bronn, Joseph, 211–212
Brown, Benjamin, 203
Brown, David M., 161
Brucellosis, 243–244, 245
Buckley, Len, 224
Buffalo/bison, 230–233, 243–245
Buffalo Soldiers, 200–203
Burke, Garrett, 182, 183
Burr, Aaron, 9–10
Burros and horses/protection, 212–215
Bush, Jeb, 162
Butler, Ralph, 157

Cadwalader, John, 15
California, 181–186
Campbell, John A., 261 ·
Campbell, Lord William, 47
Carr, Daniel, 66, 77
Carson, Kit, 220
Carter Family (musicians), 93, 94
Case, J. I., 177
Cass, Lewis, 35
Castroneves, Helio, 113
Catesby, Mark, 230
Cattle drives, 164–167
Cellucci, Paul, 36
Chaffee, Roger, 100
*Challenger* mission/disaster, 158–160
Challis, Bill, 235
Chanute, Octave, 68
Charbonneau, Toussaint, 142
Charles II, King, 26

*Charles S. Price* (freighter), 153, 154–156
"Charter Oak," Connecticut, 25, 26, 28, 29–30
Chawla, Kalpana "K. C."/family, 161
Cheese industry, 178–179
Chimney Rock ("Elk Penis"), Nebraska, 217–218, 219–220, 221, 222
Chisholm, Jesse, 166
Chisholm Trail, 164, 166–167
Churchill, John/Henry, 87
Civil War, 115–120, 248, 251, 273, 284
Clagett, William H., 195, 196
Clark, Laurel Blair Salton/family, 161
Clark, M. Lewis, 87–88
Clark, William, 140, 140–144, 200
Cleveland, Grover, 63
Clinton, Hillary, 148
Clinton, Sir Henry, 44, 45
Cody, James, 182
Cody, William F. "Buffalo Bill," 232–233
Coleman, Edmond T., 250–251
Collins, Darrel, 69
Collins, Michael, 100–101
Colorado, 223–228
Colter, John, 141
*Columbia* mission/disaster, 158, 160–162
Commonwealth, Pennsylvania, 7–8, 12
Connecticut, 25–30
Conover, C. T., 247
Coolidge, Calvin, 237
Cornwallis, Lord, 40–41
Coronado, Francisco Vasquez de, 279
Corps of Discovery, 140–144
Corum, Bill, 88
Country music, 92–95
Crater Lake/National Park, 194, 196–198
Crocker, Charles, 267
Currie, Nancy, 102
Cuthbert, Alexander, 75

Dairy industry, 177–178
Dalai Lama, 225

Daniels, John, 70
Davis, Gray, 181, 182
Davis, Isaac (British sailor), 297–298
Davis, Isaac (minuteman), 32, 34, 36
Davis, Jefferson, 89
Dawes, William, 33
DDT/effects, 106, 254, 255
Dean, Howard, 79–80
Debs, Eugene, 130
DeGaeta, Paul, 137, 138
Delaware, 1–6
Diamonds/diamond mining, Arkansas,
    146–150
Doane, Gustavus C., 195
Dodge, Granville, 268
Douglas, Stephen, 124, 125
Doyle, Jim, 176
Drouillard, George, 142
Duane, William, 8–9
Dulles, Allen, 226
Duluth, Sieur, 188
Dunham, Issac, 135
Dunlap, Gary, 148–149
Dunn, William H., 287
Duno, Milka, 112
Durant, Thomas, 269
Dutton, Clarence E., 196

Easley, Michael F., 71
Eiffel, Alexandre-Gustave, 62–63
Einstein, Albert, 130
Emerson, Ralph Waldo, 31, 32, 185
Endangered/extinct species, 106–107,
    254–257
Endangered Species (Preservation) Act,
    106, 254–255
Environmental Protection Agency,
    U.S., 106, 255
Ethanol, 179
Ewing, James, 14–15
Eyck, Jan van, 172
Falcon, peregrine, 253–255, 257
Featherston, Winfield S., 116–117
Ferguson, Miriam "Ma," 262
Ferrell, Jim, 30
50 States Commemorative Coin
    Program Act/restrictions, 97

Files, Richard "Kip," 138
Fiser, John C., 117, 118, 119
Fish and Wildlife Service, U.S., 106,
    107, 257
Fisher, Carl, 111
Fisher, Sarah, 112
Fishing, Minnesota, 187–188, 192
Fittipaldi, Emerson, 112
Fitzpatrick, Thomas, 260
Flight
    "First Flight"/Wright brothers,
        67–71
    space flight/program, 97, 98, 99–102,
        157, 158–162
Florida, 157–162
Floyd, Sergeant, 142
Flynn, Elizabeth Gurley, 130
Fore, Henrietta Holsman, 162
Fortescue, Sir John, 47
Foster, Stephen C., 85, 89
Foster, Mike, Jr., 107, 108
Franchitti, Dario, 113
Francis, Daniel, 191
Franklin, Aretha, 96
French, Daniel Chester, 32, 35–36
Fur trade/industry, 188–192

Gagarin, Yuri, 99
Gage, Margaret, 33
Gage, Sir Thomas, 32, 33, 35
George III, King, 32
Georgia, 19–24
Gilmore, James, III, 59, 60
Gist, Mordecai, 38–39, 40, 41
Glendening, Parris, 37, 38
Glenn, John, 98–99
Glover, John, 15
Gnazzo, Lucy, 11, 12
Gone with the Wind (Mitchell), 131
Goodman, Frank, 285, 286
Goodnight, Charles, 165
Grand Canyon, 283–284, 285–288
Grand Ole Opry, 91, 93–94
Granholm, Jennifer M., 156
Grant, Ulysses S., 196
Grattan, Emma, 171
Greaney, John, 226, 227

Great Lakes, 151–156
Greene, Nathaniel, 41
Grissom, Virgil "Gus," 99, 100
Guthrie, Janet, 112

Handy, W. C., 95
Hanna, Marcus, 135–136
Harroun, Ray, 111–112
Haskell, Charles N., 274, 275–276
Hawaii, 295–299
Hayden, Ferdinand V., 195
Hayes, Isaac, 96
Hedges, Cornelius, 195
Helen Keller's Journal (Keller), 131
Heller, Patrick, 156
Hennepin, Father, 188
Henry, Brad, 272
Herreshoff, Nathanael Greene, 75–76, 77
Hillman, John W., 193–194
Hodges, Jim, 48
Holden, Bob, 144
Holder, W. D., 117
Hoover, Herbert, 130
Hornish, Sam, Jr., 113
Horse racing, 86–88
Horses and burros/protection, 212–215
House Committee on Un-American Activities, 129, 130
Howland, Oramel/Seneca, 287
Huckabee, Mike, 149, 150
Huddleston, John W., 146–147
Hudson Bay Company, 189, 190, 191
Hunt, James B., 71
Husband, Rick Douglas/family, 160
Huston, Joseph Miller, 8

Iacocca, Lee, 65
Idaho, 253–257
Illinois, 121–126
Independence vote (America), 3–4, 11
Indiana, 109–113
Indians
  buffalo and, 230, 231
  Buffalo Soldiers and, 200–203
  Jamestown, Virginia and, 57, 58–59
  of Minnesota, 190, 191, 192

Oklahoma and, 272–276
Washington territory war/effects, 248–250, 251
Industrial Workers of the World (IWW), 130–131
Indy 500/Indianapolis Motor Speedway, 110–113
Iowa, 169–174

Jacks, Ariston, 149
Jackson, Paul, 144
James II, King, 26–27, 28, 58
Jamestown, Virginia, 55–59, 60
Jarvis, Anna, 205
Jarvis, Gregory B./family, 159–160
Jasper, William, 46, 47
Jazz music, 107
Jefferson, Thomas, 9–10, 140–141, 239
Jironza, Domingo, 280
Johnson, Lyndon, 127–128
Johnson, Thomas, 41
Johnston, Charlie, 212
Johnston, Velma, 211–215
Jones, W. Andy, 29–30

Kahn, Stan, 148
Kalaniopuu, King, 296–297
Kamehameha I, King, 295, 296–299
Kansas, 199–203
Kautz, August Valentine, 248–250, 251
Keenan, Chris, 154–155
Keller, Helen, 127–132, 154
Kelly, Gene, 130
Kennedy, John F., 99–100
Kentucky, 85–90
Kentucky Derby/Churchill Downs, 87–88
"Keystone State" theories, 8–11
King, B. B., 95–96
Kiwalao, 297
Klippel, Henry, 193–194
Krawczewicz, Bill, 37, 38
Kulongoski, Ted, 197–198

Langford, Nathaniel P., 195
Lazarus, Emma, 64–65
LeConte, Joseph, 196

Lee, Charles, 45
Lee, Robert E., 118, 119, 237
Leete, Andrew, 27–28
L'Enfant, Pierre Charles, 11
Leschi, Nisqually chief, 248–250, 251
Leutze, Emanuel, 13, 17–18, 169
Lewis, Meriwether, 140–144, 200
Lewis, Oliver, 88
Lighthouses Act (1789), 135
Lincoln, Abraham, 89, 121, 122–125,
    126, 236, 239, 248, 266
Lincoln Memorial, 35–36
Linenger, Jerry, 156
Lingle, Linda, 296
Linnehan, Richard, 102
Lipton, Sir Thomas, 75, 76–77
López, García, 284
Louie, Jon, 182
Louisiana, 103–108
Louisiana Purchase, 107–108, 140–141
Loving, Oliver, 165
Lyles, John M., 116
Lynyrd Skynyrd, 20

MacKenzie, Alexander, 140
Magnol, Pierre, 116
Magnolias, 116, 120
Maine, 133–138
Maple sugar/syrup, 79–83
Marion, Francis ("Swamp Fox"), 45
Marr, Clarence, 136
Marsh, Rick, 80
Marshall, John, 16
Maryland, 37–42
Massachusetts, 31–36
Matthews, Mark, 200, 203
Maynard, George, 53
McAuliffe, Sandra Christa
    Corrigan/family, 160
McCallum, Scott, 176
McCarthy, Roger, 226–227
McCool, William C. "Willie"/family,
    160
McCormick, Cyrus, 177
McCoy, Joseph G., 165–166
McCullough, David, 9, 16
McDermott, Jim, 251–252

McKean, Thomas, 3, 4, 10
McKeeby, Byron H., 170
McMullen, Fayette, 250
McNair, Ronald E./family, 159
Meagher, Thomas Francis, 195
Meeker, Ezra, 249
Meyer, Louis, 112
Michigan, 151–156
Michikinikwa (Chief Little Turtle), 110
Millar, Austin/Howard, 147
Miller, Daniel, 163
Miller, Zell, 23
Minnesota, 187–192
Mississippi, 115–120
Missouri, 139–144
Mitchell, Margaret, 131
Monroe, James, 16, 17
Montana, 241–245
Moore, Johnny, 70
Moore, Lennis, 170
Morgan, J. P., 75
Mormon Trail, 221
Morris, Esther H., 261, 263
Morton, John, 11
Moses, A. Benton, 249, 250
Moses, Raphael, 21
Motejl, Catherine, 173
Moultrie, William, 44–45, 46–47
Muir, John, 181, 182, 183, 184–186,
    209
Mungoven, Michael, 289–291, 293
Musgrove, Ronnie, 120
"My Old Kentucky Home" (Foster), 85,
    89

Napolitano, Janet, 288
National parks' history, 194–197, 203
Nebraska, 217–222
Nelson, Robert, 21
Nevada, 211–215
"New Colossus, The" (Lazarus), 64–65
New Hampshire, 49–53
New Jersey, 13–18
New Mexico, 277–282
New River/Gorge Bridge, 205–209
New York, 61–66
Newport, Christopher, 57, 59

Nielsen, Niels F. F., Jr./family, 51
Nixon, Richard M., 101, 254
NORAD, 225
Norbeck, Peter, 237
North Carolina, 67–71
North Dakota, 229–233
Noyon, Jacques de, 188

O'Bannon, Judy/Frank, 109, 110, 113
Ohio, 97–102
Ojeda, Bartolomé de, 280–281
O'Keefe, Sean, 162
Oklahoma, 271–276
"Old Man of the Mountain," New
    Hampshire, 49–52, 53
Õnate, Juan de, 279
Onizuka Ellison S./family, 159
Oregon, 193–198
Oregon Trail, 218–221
O'Sullivan, Florence, 44
Owens, Frances/Bill, 223, 224

Palin, Sarah, 292
Palmetto tree, 43–44, 45, 46, 47, 48
Papenfuse, Edward C., 38
Parker, Dorothy, 130
Parker, John, 33
Parker, Sir Peter, 44, 45, 47
Pataki, George, 66
Patrick, Danica, 112
Patton, Judi/Paul E., 88–89
Pawlenty, Tim, 192
Peach industry/history, Georgia, 19–24
Peer, Ralph, 92–93, 95
Pelican, brown, 103–107
Pelkey, Michael, 208–209
Pemaquid Point/lighthouse, Maine, 57,
    134–138
Pennsylvania, 7–12
Perrot, Nicholas, 188
Perry, Rick, 168
Perry, Roland Hinton, 8
Pesticides/effects, 106, 254, 255
Pinckney, Charles Cotesworth, 9
Pioneer Woman statue, 272
Piper, Edward, 164
Pitcairn, John, 33

Pleasant Porter, Chief, 274
Polk, James, 124
Popham, George, 57
Powell, John Wesley, 283, 284–287,
    288
Prescott, Samuel, 33
Presidential $1 Coin Program, 126
Presley, Elvis, 96
Price, David, 55–56, 58
Pueblo people/Revolt, 278–282
Pulitzer, Joseph, 62

Railroad (transcontinental), 265–270
Rainer, Mount/National Park, 196,
    247–248, 250–251, 252
Raleigh, Sir Walter, 134
Rall, Johann, 16
Ramon, Ilan/family, 161–162
Read, George, 3
Reliance (yacht), 73–74, 76–77
Resnik, Judith, 159
Revere, Paul, 33
Reyburn, Samuel W., 147
Rhode Island, 73–78
Rice, Buddy, 113
Richardson, Bill, 278
Ridge, Tom, 11, 12
Riley, Bob, 132
Roberts, Guy, 50
Robeson, Paul, 130
Robinson, Doane, 236, 237
Rockefeller, John, 75
Rockwell, Charles, 178
Rodney, Caesar, 1–5, 6, 295
Rogers, Tom, 38
Rolfe, John, 58
Roosevelt, Franklin D., 262–263
Roosevelt, Theodore, 185, 239, 275
Ross, Nellie Tayloe/William B., 261–263
Rowan, John, 89
Rumph, Samuel H., 21, 22
Rushmore, Charles E., 235, 240
Rushmore, Mount/National Memorial,
    235–240
Russell, Charles M., 242, 245
Rutledge, John, 45
Ryan, George, 125–126

Sacajawea, 142, 143
Schloeman, Linnie, 173
Schubert, Brian/daughter, 208–209
Schwarzenegger, Arnold/Maria, 182–183, 186
Schweitzer, Brian/family, 242
Scobee, Francis R. "Dick"/family, 158
Scott, Dortha, 149
Seaman, Newfoundland dog, 141, 142
Seger, Eddy, 1, 5, 6
Sequoyah (Cherokee Indian), 92
Sequoyah Convention (1905), 272–276
Shaheen, Jeanne, 51–52
Shannon, George, 141
Shaw, Catheryn, 23–24
Shepard, Alan, 99
Sheridan, Philip, 231, 236
Siegelman, Don, 131, 132
Sierra Club, 181, 185
Skaggs, Ricky, 96
Skeeters, Isaac G., 193–194
Slavery, 124, 131, 279
Smallwood, William, 17, 39, 40, 41
Smith, Al, 262
Smith, Francis, 32–33, 34–35
Smith, Jedediah, 260
Smith, J. I., 178
Smith, John, 56, 57–58
Smith, Michael J./family, 159
Smith, Milton, 153, 156
Socialism and Helen Keller, 127, 129–131, 132
Soul music, 96
South Carolina, 43–48
South Dakota, 235–240
Space flight/program, 97, 98, 99–102, 157, 158–162
St. James, Lyn, 112
Stand Watie, Cherokee leader, 273
Stanford, Leland, 269
Stanley, Nathaniel, 28
Stark, John, 52
Starr, Kevin, 182–183
Statue of Liberty, 61–66
Steel, William Gladstone, 196–197
Stepp, George, 148

Stevens, Hazard/Isaac, 250–251
Stifft, Charles S., 146
Stillman, James, 261
Stirling, William, 39, 40–41
Stookey, Shawn, 92
Strawn, Shirley, 148, 150
Stuart, Marty, 96
Sullivan, Anne, 128
Sullivan, Eugene J., 262
Sullivan brothers, 170
Sumter, Thomas, 45
Sundquist, Don, 91

Talcott, John, 28
Tate, William J. "Bill"/Addie, 67–69, 70
Tennessee, 91–96
Texas, 163–168
Thomson, William, 45, 46
Thoroughbred horses, 85, 86–88, 90
Tibet and Colorado, 225–228
Tinker, Deborah, 23
Titov, Gherman, 99
Todd, Mary, 123
"Trail of Tears," 273
Treat, Robert, 27
Twain, Mark, 29, 127

Utah, 265–270

Van Trump, Philemon, 250–251
Vandiver, Willard D., 139
Varennes, Pierre Gaultier de, 189
Vermont, 79–83
Verrazzano, Giovanni da, 73
Vickers, Charles, 247
Villa, Pancho, 203
Vilsack, Thomas J., 169–170
Vinsel, Mark, 293
Virginia, 55–60
"Voyageurs," 189–192

Waddell, Louis, 8, 10–11
Wadsworth, Joseph, 28, 29, 30
Wahpowety, 248
Washakie, Shoshone Indian Chief, 263
Washburn, Henry, 195

Washington, 247–252
Washington, George, 13–18, 38, 39, 41,
  45, 239
*Washington Crossing the Delaware*
  (Leutze), 13, 17–18, 169
Waterstradt, Rose, 173
Weaver, Donna, 97
Webster, Daniel, 50
West Virginia, 205–209
Wheeler, O. W., 166
White, Edward, 100
Whitman, Marcus, 218
Williams, Roger, 77
Williamson, Ansel, 88
Williamson, William, 237
Wilson, Ruby, 96
Wilson, Woodrow, 197
Wind Cave National Park, South
  Dakota, 243–244
Wingfield, Edward-Maria, 56, 57
Winthrop, John, 133
Wisconsin, 175–180

Wise, Bob, 205
Women's suffrage, 92, 131, 260–261,
  263
Wood, Grant DeVolsen/family, 169,
  170–174
World Wildlife Fund (WWF), 244,
  245
Wright, Orville/Wilbur, 67–70,
  98
Wyllys, Samuel/Ruth, 26, 28
Wyoming, 259–263

Yacht racing, 73–77, 78
Yellowstone/National Park, 195–196
York, slave of William Clark, 141, 142,
  200
Yosemite/National Park, 182, 196, 208,
  209
Young, Brigham, 221
Young, John, 297–298

Zia sun symbol/Pueblo, 277–282